Among the Berti of Northern Darfur (Sudan), as among many Muslim societies, the formal religious practices are predominantly the concern of men, while local, unorthodox customary rituals are performed mainly by women. It is usual to dismiss such local, popular practices as pre-Islamic survivals, but Professor Holy shows that the customary rituals constitute an integral part of the religious system of the Berti. Carefully analysing the symbolic statements made in Berti rituals, Professor Holy demonstrates that the distinction between the two classes of rituals is an expression of the gender relationships characteristic of the society. He also examines the social distribution of knowledge about Islam, and explains the role of the religious schools in sustaining religious ideas.

The work is not only an ethnographic study of ritual, belief and gender in an African society. It also makes a significant contribution to current anthropological discussion of the interpretation and meaning of rituals and symbols.

Cambridge Studies in Social and Cultural Anthropology

Editors: Jack Goody, Stephen Gudeman, Michael Herzfeld, Jonathan Parry

78

Religion and custom in a Muslim society

A list of books in the series will be found at the end of the volume.

RELIGION AND CUSTOM
IN A MUSLIM SOCIETY

The Berti of Sudan

LADISLAV HOLY

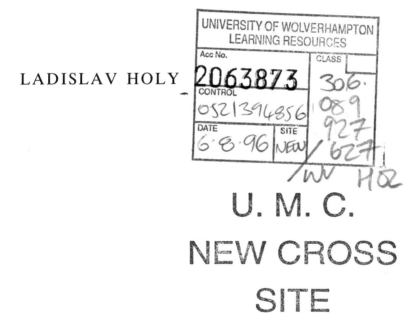
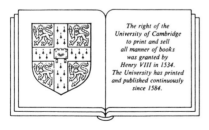

The right of the
University of Cambridge
to print and sell
all manner of books
was granted by
Henry VIII in 1534.
The University has printed
and published continuously
since 1584.

CAMBRIDGE UNIVERSITY PRESS
Cambridge
New York   Port Chester
Melbourne   Sydney

Published by the Press Syndicate of the University of Cambridge
The Pitt Building, Trumpington Street, Cambridge CB2 1RP
40 West 20th Street, New York, NY 10011-4211, USA
10 Stamford Road, Oakleigh, Melbourne 3166, Australia

First published 1991

Printed in Great Britain at the University Press, Cambridge

British Library cataloguing in publication data

Holy, Ladislav, 1933–
 Religion and custom in a Muslim society: the Berti of
 Sudan. – (Cambridge studies in social and cultural
 anthropology: 78)
 1. Sudan. North Darfur. Berti. Cultural processes
 I. Title
 306.089927627

Library of Congress cataloguing in publication data

Holy, Ladislav.
 Religion and custom in a Muslim society: the Berti of Sudan/
 Ladislav Holy.
 p. cm. (Cambridge studies in social and cultural
 anthropology: 78)
 Includes bibliographical references and index.
 ISBN 0-521-39485-6
 1. Berti (African people) 2. Sudan–Social life and customs.
 3. Muslims–Sudan. I. Title. II. Series.
 DT155.2.B47H65 1991
 305.896′50624–dc20   90-20417
                                                          CIP

ISBN 0 521 39485 6

Contents

Illustrations

Preface and acknowledgements

The material for this book was collected between 1961, when I started my intermittent fieldwork among the Berti, and 1986, when I was in the field for the last time. I visited the Berti area on six occasions and my stays there stretched from three to nine months. I spent in total a little over three years in the field. Most of the time, I lived in the village of Dūda, three kilometres south of the market and well at Madu, in the northern part of the Berti area along the track connecting Melit and Malha. My wife and I had our own household there in 1965 and then again in the late 1970s and early 1980s, before the village was temporarily abandoned during the drought in the mid 1980s. Its inhabitants lost virtually all their donkeys and, being unable to transport water to the village, camped in the vicinity of the well in Madu where we joined them in 1986. In 1980, we spent two months in the village of Watkani, about six kilometres south of Melit and, in 1986, we lived for three months in Am Ja ʿāl, about ten kilometres east of the market and wells in Sayah.

My field trips to Darfur were sponsored by the Czechoslovak Academy of Sciences, the International African Institute, the Queen's University of Belfast, the Carnegie Trust and the Social Science Research Council. I am very grateful for the generosity of these bodies. In the Sudan my work would have been impossible without the continual hospitality and help I was given. I should like to express my appreciation of the hospitality and assistance received from the members of staff of the Department of Anthropology at Khartoum University. Furthermore, I wish to acknowledge the invaluable help provided by the Governors of Darfur, and later the Governors of Northern Darfur Province, and their staff. Special thanks are due to Abdullahi Osman el-Tom, a Berti whom I supervised as a doctoral student in Social Anthropology, and who was with me in the field in 1978 and 1980 living as a member of our household while pursuing his own research into the role of Berti religious leaders. My discussions with him helped me to understand many aspects of Berti religiosity.

I cannot name all the Berti who so willingly helped me, allowed me to join in their activities and responded with remarkable patience to my enquiries. I wish, nevertheless, to express my special thanks to Ādam Abbakar and his wife Fātna who were my hosts in Dūda and over the years became my and my wife's close friends. Our own household in Dūda was adjacent to theirs and, apart from being an invaluable source of information, they provided constant and unselfish help in coping with the practical aspects of life in a Berti village.

My thinking and writing have been profoundly influenced by invaluable comments on the earlier drafts of the manuscript made by Kay Milton, Richard Werbner, Richard Fardon, Paul Baxter and Roy Dilley. Special thanks are due to my wife Alice who accompanied me on all my trips to Darfur from 1965 and who shared with me the joys and frustrations of the fieldwork and gave me immeasurable support during the writing of this book. She died a few days before I completed the final revision of the manuscript and I gratefully dedicate this book to her memory.

Material contained in Chapter 2 was first published in *Reason and Morality* (ASA Monographs 24, ed. J. Overing, 1985) and some of the material contained in Chapters 3 and 6 was first published in *Man* (N.S.) 18 (1983) and 23 (1988). I gratefully acknowledge the permission of the Association of Social Anthropologists and the Royal Anthropological Institute to use it in this book.

The Berti speak a dialect of Arabic which resembles the Arabic spoken by other Darfur peoples but is quite distinct from the standard spoken Arabic as well as from the colloquial Arabic spoken in the riverain Sudan. Berti Arabic does not differentiate gender and has done away with a number of Arabic phonemes, particularly thā, dhāl, the aspirated ḥ, and the emphatic ṣ, ḍ, ṭ and ẓ. The standard Arabic qāf is pronounced like the English g in 'go'. I follow the standard system of the transliteration of Arabic. But with the exception of a few words of classical Arabic, to preserve the flavour of Berti speech, I transliterate from the dialect rather than from the classical or standard Arabic words with which the dialect is connected. The long vowels, none of which is diphthongised, are indicated as ā, ē, ī, ō and ū. I have kept familiar words in their standardised English usage: for example, Darfur, El Fasher, Koran, Sufism.

Republic of the Sudan

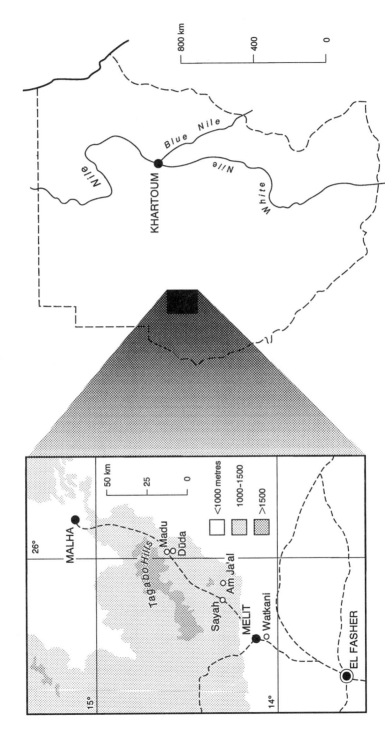

KHARTOUM

Blue Nile

Nile

White Nile

Nile

800 km

400

0

26°

MALHA

Tagabo Hills

Madu
Duda

Am Ja'al

Sayah

MELIT

Watkani

15°

14°

EL FASHER

50 km

25

0

<1000 metres

1000–1500

>1500

The Berti area, Northern Darfur

Introduction

Muslim societies encompass widely diverse economic, political and social structures and relations. In spite of their diversity, their members share the basic core beliefs and practices which Islam sets forth in the 'five pillars'. They enjoin the believers to bear witness to the oneness of God, to perform the five daily prayers, to fast during the month of Ramadan, to pay annual alms and, if possible, to go on the pilgrimage to Mecca at least once. These fundamental elements of belief and practice endow Islam with its essential unity, for they are agreed upon by all Muslims as norms which they, with varying degrees of success, seek to fulfil. The degree of emphasis put on each one of them is, nevertheless, highly variable throughout Muslim communities, societies and traditions. Beyond these minimal and formal requirements, diversity reigns. In addition to the core beliefs and a number of common Islamic symbols, there are numerous ideological and practical accretions present in all Muslim societies which account for the actual diversity of Islam. Muslim societies thus differ not only in their political, economic and social-structural arrangements but also in their ritual practices and religious institutions. Orientalists and anthropologists have for long struggled with the problem of how best to conceptualise and account for the observable diversity of religious belief and practice in various Muslim societies and communities.

Students of Islam and the processes of Islamisation – both Muslims and non-Muslims alike – have always conceptualised this diversity in terms of a dichotomy between belief and ritual practice expressed in religious texts and exegetical comments of recognised religious scholars and actual belief and practice of specific Muslim communities. This dichotomy was first conceptualised in historical terms and the actual beliefs and practices which deviated from the texts and their authoritative interpretations were seen as a mixture of Islamic elements and the local lore surviving from the pre-Islamic times. This historical view was gradually replaced by the conceptualisation of the same dichotomy in terms of the distinction between the Great and Little traditions formulated by Robert Redfield (1956) which had at least the advantage that it did not make unwarranted assumptions about the historical origin of various beliefs and practices. It too, however, had its disadvantages. Many scholars found the distinction between the two broadly defined traditions too vague in the absence of institutional religious organisation in Islam which could unambiguously define its Great tradition and suggested other ways of conceptualising the observable diversity in Islamic belief and practice. Thus one type of Islam, variously described as true, pristine or pure faith and orthodox opinion and classified as scriptural, normative, orthodox, formal or official Islam was contrasted with popular, alternative, folk, local, rural or informal Islam, Islamic heterodoxy, aberrant practice, superstitious accretions or rural folk religion (Ahmed 1976: 88; Waardenburg 1978, 1979; Gellner 1981; Graham 1983: 61–2; Stewart 1985; Kielstra 1985; Denny 1985). All these terms, and a host of others which have been used to express the same basic dichotomy, do not obviate the difficulties and drawbacks which the conceptualisation of the diversity of Islam in dichotomous terms entails.

The first of these difficulties is that many forms of Islam only uncomfortably straddle the conceptual boundary between its two basic types. For example the Shi'ites cannot simply be seen as representing a kind of popular Islam when they themselves claim to represent true Islam and deny that the Sunnis do so. Similarly Sufism – at least in the form it attained through the influence of al-Ghazzālī – cannot simply be classified as popular Islam when the Sufis themselves claim that they represent a more profound Islam than the *'ulamā* in their emphasis on Islam's inner aspects and the importance of religious experience (Waardenburg 1978: 323).

These two examples should suffice to illustrate that to conceptualise the variety of Islamic belief and practice in terms of the Great tradition of a world religion and the Little tradition of local, regional and village culture is both simplistic and unilluminating. The reason is that it is as much the Great as the Little tradition which is problematic (cf. Rahman 1985: 195–7). The Great tradition is not simply something that has been agreed among scholars but always something that has been agreed among some specific scholars in a specific place and at a specific time (cf. Eickelman 1981a: 12). In consequence, one could probably better speak of various Great traditions than simply the Great tradition.

Even if the Great tradition is as problematic as the Little one, the latter is, nevertheless, always defined negatively. Its very existence is generated in a discourse which reflects the unequal distribution of knowledge and power. It is a discourse in which only the knowledgeable and powerful have a voice and are in a position to formulate the dichotomy by opposing what they believe and practise to what the others believe and practise. Those who are denied the knowledge and power are not in a position to participate actively in the discourse. The conceptualisation of the dichotomy is then not only elitist (cf. Stirrat 1984: 206) but also inevitably arbitrary. The Little tradition is thus constituted as passive, non-autonomous and above all non-sovereign, not only with regard to the Great tradition but also with regard to itself. As it is the Great tradition that defines and the Little one that is defined, the former becomes inevitably the source of knowledge about the latter. The relationship between the two is thus radically a matter of power. The Little tradition, being passive, only accepts from the Great tradition.

This conceptualisation of the relationship between the two traditions is the function of the 'orientalist search for an ahistorical Islamic "essence"' (Eickelman 1981a: 1; 1981b: 203). It becomes, however, dubious, when we consider the historical development of Islam: 'There was a time when Sufism was unheard of in Islam. Then there was a time when Sufism arose and was generally opposed by the 'Ulamā'. Then Sufism multiplied into various types and engulfed the entire body-social of Islam. Lastly, we witness a time when the attempt has been to reform and reinterpret Sufism, and it may well be in the process of transformation' (Rahman 1985: 195).

Whatever justification there may exist for conceptualising Islam in dichotomous terms, the manner of the construction of the dichotomy has important consequences for the way in which research into the diversity of belief and ritual practice within Islam is conducted. In practice, research is often limited almost exclusively to noting what a specific community or society has accepted from the Great tradition, as it is formulated in standard religious texts, and how its members deviate from it (Eickelman 1981b: 202). R. Tapper commented on this widespread practice in his observation that many ethnographers of Middle Eastern societies are simply 'content to record that their subjects are Muslims and note ways in which their customs differ from Islamic prescriptions' (1984: 217). Even if many anthropologists have gone much further than that in their studies of Islam as actually practised in specific settings, they have mostly concentrated on particular elements of Islamic Little tradition such as saints, shrines and spirits (e.g. Geertz 1968; Gellner 1969; Gilsenan 1973, 1982; Crapanzano 1973; Eickelman

1976).[1] The result of such research is to eradicate the plurality of differences among Muslims in the interest of one difference, that of setting the Great tradition off from everything else. It results in the formulation of evaluative judgements of religious processes which are not always sociologically adequate. Turner suggests that the relationship between scholarly religion and its popular manifestations may be understood

> as an interaction between social groups interpreting their practices by reference to common formulae. Popular religion is not historically merely a vulgarisation of the Islamic mysticism of Ibn Al-Arabi and Al-Ghazzali since intellectualised mysticism and popular religion have always stood side-by-side oriented to different clientele with different social and religious interests. This is not to ignore the fact that the general societal status of popular religion has been fundamentally transformed by decolonisation, puritan reformism and national ideology . . . [I]t is more accurate to regard popular and official religion as a form of differentiation and specialisation of religious services relevant to different lay markets than to treat 'mass religiosity' as the contaminated offspring of pure religious consciousness. (B. Turner 1985: 56)

Although the various terms which have been used to express the basic dichotomy in Islamic belief and practice are ostensibly employed as descriptive and classificatory devices, they are, nevertheless, always evaluative. A belief or practice is orthodox or unorthodox, scriptural or popular, or whatever, not of itself but only from a specific point of view which is always a view of those who are at home with texts and, in consequence, tend to see Islam from above. Anthropologists are at home in villages and, in consequence, tend to see Islam from below (Gellner 1981: 99). This is, of course, the reason why they have never been happy with orientalists' habitual perception of the dichotomy, because their experience has taught them that a point of view is never the only one, and because it is part of their accepted wisdom that to arbitrate on true and correct points of view may be appropriate for theologians but not for students of religion as a cultural system.

The diversity of religious beliefs and practices in various Muslim societies has, however, been a problem not only for the students of Islam but for the Muslim community itself. In spite of the fact that Islam does not recognise any institutional religious authority or organisation entrusted with defining the 'official' religious view, the relationship between 'official' and 'popular' religion has not disappeared but has rather become more subtle and intricate. The problem of a basic

---

[1] These studies do not, of course, exhaust the anthropological interest in Islam as practised and understood in specific settings. For the assessment of other major trends in the study of Islam in local contexts see Eickelman 1981.

dichotomy within Islam is perceived by the Muslim community as a fundamental one of juridical and theological nature. Ahmed, who looks at the diversity of Muslim beliefs and practices from within Islam itself, rejects the view of those who have concluded that there is not one Islam but various islams (El-Zein 1974: 172; 1977: 231, 242–4; Mortimer 1982), and sees the diversity of Islam in terms of a universal and unchanging ideal with a varied and changing interpretation throughout the Muslim world (Ahmed 1988: 4–5). Waardenburg applies the term 'normative' Islam to this 'absolute religious ideal' which continues 'to exist largely beyond the daily needs and ideals of the lived religion' (1978: 331). According to him, this concept 'can be used without prejudice for all Muslim groups who appeal to Islam as their norm for individual and social life' (Ibid.: 329). 'The normative Islam is what Muhammad as a prophet and leader of the community instituted as Islamic religion, especially through the revelation he brought (the Koran) and the example he gave in words and deeds (the *Sunna*)' (ibid.: 327).

The normative Islam constitutes and has always constituted the valid Islam of the religious scholars who have specialised knowledge of revelation and religion (ibid.: 333). It is precisely this fact which enables Ahmed to say that 'it is true that in the thought of Muslim scholars and in their texts there is clarity, and a broad consensus regarding the ideal, it is also true that the way Muslims order their lives is sometimes far from the ideal' (Ahmed 1988: 5).

The classification of the observable beliefs and practices in terms of ideal norms and a deviation from them is of course again evaluative, and as such is of particular use to those who have a practical interest in the beliefs and practices in the sense that they want to do something about them. It need not only be the proselytisers who want to disseminate the ideal. It may also be theologians who want to condemn or justify an existing practice. To do that, they have to evaluate it by placing it on an agreed-upon classificatory scale, one end of which is defined by the norm and the other one by complete disregard of that norm. Normative Islam has been invoked for practical purposes throughout Islamic history in numerous waves of purification which have been an integral part of the Islamic tradition from its very beginning. For example, Ibn Taimīya (A.D. 1263–1328) invoked it to condemn and suppress 'popular' practices among Muslims in his time (Waardenburg 1978: 317). It was invoked in a similar way by various reformers of Islam in the last century, as well as by the present-day fundamentalist movements which call for a return to the true Islam of the Koran and *sunna* – the sayings and actions of the Prophet and his companions.

For the student of religion who does not want to change, condemn or justify existing beliefs and practices but to understand what they mean to those to whom they belong, there is little point in classifying them according to how closely or remotely they approximate the ideal. If what the people believe and practise is the only ideal they themselves know, then in terms of their knowledge of the world it is also the only reality. If we then compare their beliefs and practices with an ideal known only to the analyst but not to them, we compare something that exists and is real with something that does not exist and is unreal in the world we are trying to understand. Surely that amounts to committing a categorical mistake. This point should be borne in mind. When I occasionally compare Berti belief and practice with 'normative' Islam, I am making a comparison which the Berti themselves cannot make.

Even if the evaluative connotations of the various terms used to express the basic dichotomy in Islam are disregarded, and even if they are taken in their purely descriptive sense, another uneasiness about them remains. It stems from the fact that they are still habitually used to classify systems of belief and ritual practice of whole communities or societies as if these systems were undifferentiated monolithic wholes – a view which is again blatantly contradicted by the experience of anthropological fieldwork. Recent anthropological studies of Islam as it is practised in specific local settings indicate that there are opposing conceptions of Islam in almost every studied locale. Eickelman refers to them as universalistic conceptions which are explicit and more general in their implications, and particularistic conceptions which are largely implicit and tied to particular social contexts (Eickelman 1981b: 203; cf. also El-Zein 1977: 242–3). Given this situation, the concepts of 'norm' or 'orthodoxy' cannot so easily be swept under the carpet for they are indispensable to the understanding of the lived religion or 'practised' Islam (Waardenburg 1978: 322). They need, however, to be seen as concepts which have their place within any particular form of Islam as it is practised and lived in any particular community or society, rather than concepts which can be applied to Islam as a whole and then used to judge and evaluate its particular forms and expressions.

In the villages in which anthropologists are at home, people are often illiterate and their adherence to the Muslim faith and their belonging to the wider community of Islam is proclaimed through other symbols of the divine word than the Book. In his discussion of Islam as it is lived and practised by the Berbers of the central High Atlas, Gellner points out that the word, when incarnated, becomes flesh (1981: 117) and the physical or spiritual succession from the Prophet or early Muslim holy men becomes a more important form of legitimation than either the book, which is beyond the reach of the illiterate, or the wider Islamic consensus formulated in the urban centres, from which they are cut off by a hostile relationship. In the eyes of the more learned urban folk this is of course heretical and sinful. What is the view from below? Gellner mentions two views. On the one hand he says that the tribesmen

know how they are seen and they do not repudiate the judgement. At the same time, they do not in any way desire to opt out of the wider community of Islam. Their attitude really is that of Saint Augustine: Lord, make me pure, but not yet. They recognise standards of purity in terms of which their own tribal society fails, yet at the same time wish to remain as they are, indefinitely. They are quite aware of the conflict and contradiction, yet at the same time the contradiction is not articulated clearly or stressed. (Gellner, 1981: 117)

On the other hand he says that the holy lineages

must serve tribal, non-urban ends, but they must also link the tribes with a wider and urban-oriented ideal of Islam. They serve both local and tribal needs and universal Islamic identification. They hamper the diffusion of good and proper Islam, in a way, by giving the tribesman [sic] an excuse for pretending that they are *already* good Muslims, and that they already possess the institutional framework of faith; and yet at the same time, they keep the door open for the propagation of 'purer' Islam by endorsing it in the course of those very practices in which they deviate from it. (Gellner 1981: 130; cf. also Gellner 1969: 298–9.)

One of course cannot consider one's beliefs and practices as heretical and sinful and at the same time consider oneself a good Muslim. But this does not mean that Gellner is wrong in at least one of his characterisations of the Berbers' own views. These two views can easily co-exist in the same community or society, reflecting the varying awareness of its particular members of the alternative to their belief and practice. Such variation has probably been present throughout Islam's history and has been generated through pilgrimages to Mecca as well as through local and regional pilgrimages at which people from different cultures and social settings meet and which function as important channels for the flow of information across cultural and social boundaries (Gilsenan 1973: 17). Migrants, traders and itinerant scholars also disseminated similar information (Ahmed 1976: 85). The awareness of alternatives to local belief and practice has of course increased recently. Nowadays hardly any community is effectively cut off from the wider society of which it is a part. Not only is it linked with the wider society or state through economic and political ties, but it is also linked to its beliefs and ritual practices. The awareness of them is facilitated by the spread of the radio and formal school education which disseminate the views of those who have the power to interpret authoritatively the Islamic faith and who see themselves as guardians of the orthodoxy, at least as it is defined by the educated elite of each particular state who control the means of communication.

Different members may hold different views about the purity or deviance of beliefs and practices current in their society. This suggests again that the image of the co-existence of Great and Little traditions in Islam, or of normative Islam and the deviations from it, is too simplistic and results from looking at the situation from above, from within the Great tradition or from the 'normative' pole of the dichotomy. Seen from above, a particular society or community may be cut off or differ from the wider Islamic consensus and hence be seen as aberrant or deviant. Nevertheless, it may have itself a high degree of its own normative consensus through which it defines itself as orthodox. Or, more likely, the same differentiation between orthodoxy and deviance may be expressed within it. What may be seen as orthodox by some within the community may be seen as aberrant and deviant by others. Instead of thinking in terms of basic polarities between the Great tradition or 'normative' Islam and beliefs and practices which deviate from it, a more appropriate image is that of nesting segments of belief and practice. At each 'level of segmentation' what is and what is not proper Islam may be disputed. Gaddafy has restricted the legitimacy of Islamic belief and practice to the Koran alone and denied the authority of the *sunna*, for human interpretation is heavily involved in these orally transmitted traditions. This view presumably constitutes the Islamic orthodoxy in Libya. Yet a theological commission in Saudi Arabia, under the chairmanship of the *qāḍī* of Medina, found his views guilty of apostasy (Gellner 1981: 62).

Similar disagreements pervade all 'levels of segmentation' from the widest Muslim community, where the split between Sunni and Shi'a Muslims is their most obvious manifestation, down to any particular Muslim group or society. The point is that 'orthodoxy' and 'deviance', the 'true belief' and 'superstition', are not simply descriptive and evaluative labels which can be nonproblematically appended by the analyst to particular views and practices. They are concepts which belong to the actors themselves and, like their other concepts, are part of the discourse which we call their culture.

This book is an anthropological study of the 'practical religion' of the Berti people of the Northern Darfur Province of the Republic of the Sudan. As such, it is a description of the discourse about belief and ritual practice in which the Berti are engaged and in which the questions about what is a true belief and what is an erroneous one, and what is an appropriate ritual and what is a superstitious act, are contested issues.

It has already been mentioned that in rural societies as well as among certain strata of urban population there is a shift of legitimation from the Book or the abstract consensus to legitimation grounded in physical or spiritual success from the Prophet or his successors and early Muslim holy men. In the wider Sudanese society, to which the Berti are linked through economic and political ties, this kind of legitimation is all pervasive and Sufi orders or brotherhoods are a characteristic feature of the Sudanese Islam (Trimingham 1949: 195–241; Daly 1985). The Khatmiyya order and the Ansar, the spiritual descendants of the supporters of the Mahdi, form the basis of the two most important political parties in the Sudan (Warburg 1985; Al-Shahi 1987), and the religious leaders who come from the established families associated with the Khatmiyya and the Mahdist movement have always played an important role in Sudanese politics (Voll 1972). Unlike most northern Sudanese, the Berti villagers do not follow any particular Sufi orders and, in fact, many of them are unaware of their existence. Only a few Berti belong to the Tijāniyya brotherhood which has spread in Darfur since the 1950s (O'Fahey 1980: 178, n. 31). Until now the brotherhood has remained restricted to towns and large market centres, recruiting its members mostly from among merchants, who are much more directly integrated to the wider Sudanese society than the predominantly illiterate villagers. Thus, among the Berti, as elsewhere in the Middle East, the Tijāniyya order is associated with the wealthy and the politically powerful (on Tijāniyya see Abun-Nasr 1965, and on Tijāniyya in the Sudan Trimingham 1949: 236–9).

Although the religious leaders (*fugarā*, sg. *fakī*) perform important rituals on behalf of the community, they do not have an importance in Berti society parallel to that of the shaikhs of the various Sufi orders, or the *igurramen*, saints and marabouts of North Africa. They achieve their status solely by virtue of their learning and not by virtue of their descent. They do not possess or control divine grace (*baraka*), are not guardians of saintly shrines and are not seen as being any closer to God than the members of the community whom they serve. They have to have the knowledge of the Koran to be recognised as *fugarā* but that in itself does not lend them a special closeness to God. It can merely facilitate it if it is used as an instrument of devotion for, in the Berti view, closeness to God is achieved solely through piety. This, in principle is accessible to anybody who 'fears God' and follows the prescriptions and obeys the prohibitions which were revealed by God to his Prophet.

Many orientalists (Gibb and Brown 1957; Gibb 1969) and Muslim jurist-theologians (cf. Waardenburg 1978: 317) have seen the emergence and spread of Sufism as a move from the pure, scriptural Islam towards popular religion characterised by its syncretic mixture of Islamic beliefs and practices with various local beliefs, practices and customs. On this view, the Berti Islam – at least as far as its professed beliefs go – could be seen as closer to the 'scriptural' end of the spectrum, which insists on the equality of believers and does not recognise any intermediaries between them and God, than to the hierarchical nature of Sufism. It would also appear to go against the ecstatic nature of Sufism in its insistence on the Book as the ultimate legitimation of particular beliefs and practices. The overall picture is, however, not that simple. For a start, there is no agreement among all Berti on what exactly the Book is. For those with school education and some *fugarā*, the Book is the Koran. For the illiterate villagers and some *fugarā* anything that is written constitutes the Book. On this view, practices described in various astrological books and manuals on the 'magical' uses of Koranic verses are as orthodox as the beliefs and practices of strictly Koranic origin.

My discussion of the Berti discourse about what is and what is not proper Islam concentrates on practices and their underlying beliefs which the Berti classify as *'awāid* (sg. *'āda*, custom) and which they conceptually distinguish from practices classified as *dīn* (religion). The vitality and dynamism of Islam lies in part in its receptivity to local custom and its ability to incorporate diverse customary practices. This ability of Islam to adapt itself to local traditions can be traced back to its very origin. Although Islam brought about a radical change in Arab society, it did not outlaw all the pre-Islamic customs but, on the contrary, incorporated many of them into its own system of law. This adaptability to local custom became even more significant when Islam spread gradually into areas with cultures radically different from that in which it originated. The Islamic scholars and jurists understood the important role of custom in the local application of Islamic law (*sharīʿa*), and local custon (*'āda* or *'urf*) was recognised as an ancillary source of *sharīʿa* provided it was currently and commonly practised by the Muslim community and did not contradict the explicit provisions of the Koran and *sunna* (Al-Awa 1973). Not only have practices that did not manifestly contradict the basic tenets of Islamic belief often been tolerated or even redefined and sanctioned during the process of Islamisation, but also the survival of customary practices which clearly contradict Islamic law, notably those concerning marriage or inheritance, is a well-known feature of many overtly Muslim societies. The Berti concept of *'āda* is, however, different from the customary law which persists in Muslim societies alongside Islamic law proper. The Berti refer to their 'customary law' and other customs which distinguish them from non-Berti as '*sunna* Berti' (Berti tradition) whereas '*āda* designates various ritual practices which are not seen as originating in the Koran or *hadīth* but which, nevertheless, most Berti do not see as being in conflict with the rituals understood as properly Islamic.

I start the discussion by describing the beliefs and practices which the Berti classify as religion (*dīn*) and which constitute the local Islamic orthodoxy (Chapter 1). As in many other Muslim societies, the religious rituals are predominantly the concern of men, whereas the customary rituals ('*awāid*) are more distinctly the concern of women. These two classes of rituals thus express certain views about men and women and are indicative of the relations between them. Before describing the customary rituals and the cosmological beliefs which underlie them, I describe in Chapter 2 the models of gender relations which the Berti men and women formulate both verbally and in symbolic form. The notions about the relations between the sexes which these models embody are also expressed in the customary rituals. These rituals employ only very few verbal formulae and there are no myths explicitly linked to them; most of them are performed in complete silence which is frequently seen as a precondition of their efficacy. They are carried through symbolic action and their understanding requires an understanding of the meanings of the symbols which they employ. In Chapter 3, I look at the rituals as instrumental acts aimed at achieving specific goals and describe the symbols which they employ to achieve their envisaged ends. In Chapter 4, I consider the cosmological constructs in which the rituals are grounded and describe the symbols through which they are expressed. These constructs embody a basic dichotomy between the world of humans, who are the only creatures who know God, and the non-human world of creatures and objects, which exist without any awareness of God. It is the same dichotomy which the Berti also see expressed in Islam as they understand it. This congruence is discussed in Chapter 5 in which I look in detail at the way in which the Berti picture the overall relationship between their custom and their religion. For the most part, the customary rituals accompany situations which are not subject to any ritual elaboration in Islam. However, because they co-exist easily with the dominant religious ideology, they also accompany the life-cycle rituals (Chapter 6), which the Berti classify as religious events, and which very often are subject to greater elaboration and appear to have greater importance than the religious rituals themselves. This is particularly so in case of circumcision (Chapter 7). Although most customary rituals are not seen as contradicting or challenging the dominant Islamic ideology, not all of them are seen in this light, and in Chapter 8 I discuss rituals which the pious Berti consider to be practices from which good Muslims should abstain because they express superstitious beliefs. In spite of being branded by the pious as non-Islamic superstitions, they have a vitality which many other customary rituals lack. To understand why this is the case, we have to pay attention not only to the knowledge about the world from which both religious and customary rituals spring and which they express, but also to the social distribution of this knowledge. This I do in the concluding chapter, where I discuss the knowledge held by the illiterate villagers, of the *fugarā* and of the Berti with at least some school education and describe how the social distribution of knowledge among these three main categories affects the persistence and change of Berti customs as well as the persistence and change of beliefs and practices which the Berti see as constituting their Islamic religion.

1

The Berti and Islam

According to their own tradition, the original homeland of the Berti is the Tagabo Hills region in Northern Darfur Province of the Republic of the Sudan. Until quite recently, the Berti spoke their own language and the linguistic material which I collected among them in 1961 was analysed by Petracek (1975; 1978), who classified it as one of the Central Sahara language group and closest to Zaghawa. This linguistic evidence would indicate that their original migration into their present territory was from the northwest, but if such a migration indeed occurred, it must have been a very early one. Probably the first historical reference to the Berti is in 'the description of the world' compiled by Giovanni Lorenzo d'Anania, which was first published in 1573 in Naples and revised and expanded in two subsequent editions in 1575 and 1582. The third chapter of this work is concerned with the description of Africa (Lange 1972: 299–301) and towards its end d'Anania describes the city of Vri which can be identified as Uri – nowadays a ruined hill-top palace in Northern Darfur (Arkell 1946; Balfour-Paul 1955: 11) which might have been the capital of the early Tunjur state (O'Fahey and Spaulding 1974: 111). D'Anania also enumerates the peoples subject to the rule of Vri's 'emperor' Nina: Aule, Zurla, Sagava, Memmi, Musulat, Morga, Saccae and Dagio (Lange 1972: 342–5). Although Aule and Zurla remain obscure, all the other names can be identified as those of the present-day Darfur peoples: Zaghawa (Sagava), Mimi (Memmi), Masalit (Musulat) and Daju (Dagio). D'Anania's Morga seem to be the Birged who, according to Macmichael, call themselves Murgi (1922, vol. 1: 78). The Berti, who still knew at least some of their old language in 1961, mentioned that they originally called themselves Siga and that Berti was a name by which they were known by others.[1] Taking into consideration

---

[1] Macmichael, whose data on Darfur tribes were collected in the 1910s, mentions that the Berti were known as Kurmu to the Fur, as Sulgu to the Birged and as Bayti to the Meidob. They called themselves Sigáto (Macmichael 1922. vol. 1: 64).

that d'Anania seems consistently to substitute 'a' for 'i', for example in his rendering of Masalit as Musulat or Murgi as Morga, Saccae is most probably his corruption of Siga. If this interpretation is correct, it would indicate that the Berti have been established in Darfur at least since the middle of the sixteenth century.

An estimated 30,000 Berti now inhabit their original area round Melit, their traditional centre, situated about 55 km northeast of El Fasher, the capital of the Northern Darfur province. I did my fieldwork only in that area and I am unable to say to what extent my description would be true of other Berti areas.

One such area lies around Um Keddada and Taweisha in eastern Darfur. The Berti migrated there during the second half of the eighteenth century as part of a wide-scale population movement out of northern into eastern Darfur, presumably triggered by a prolonged drought. In this century, many Berti from northern Darfur settled around Taweisha during the years 1914–18 and the Berti settlement of the Taweisha area was further facilitated by the drilling of boreholes there in the late 1950s and 1960s. As a result of this gradual out-migration, probably more Berti live now in eastern Darfur than in their original homeland. A number of Berti, intermingled with the Fur, also live around and partly in El Fasher, and small Berti colonies dating back to the Mahdist period exist elsewhere in the Sudan, particularly in Gedaref and near Um Ruwaba in Kordofan. More recently a number of Berti have settled in Gezira.

The Berti area of Northern Darfur is an upland plateau lying from 700 to 1,000m above sea level with isolated sandstone and basalt hills rising above it and culminating in the sandstone and volcanic mountains of the Tagabo Hills chain, which reaches an altitude of 1,500m. Apart from the hills, the area consists of stable old sand dunes. The vegetation of the open grassland of the dry savannah is determined by the scant precipitation which averages 300mm a year and falls during the three-month rainy season starting at the beginning of July.

Economy and social structure
Nowadays the Berti speak their own dialect of Arabic and, unlike most of their neighbours, they are fully sedentary in small villages – clusters of individual homesteads – often consisting of less than 100 people. The core of each village is formed by men who are members of the same patrilineage and are usually genealogically close. Most married couples reside virilocally, but the incidence of uxorilocal residence is high (21.8 per cent). If husband and wife are of different lineages, an uxorilocal marriage is the starting point of the growth of a new lineage within the

village, which eventually leads to fission of the village along lineage lines. The fission of villages is a perpetual process which is usually triggered, in the larger villages, by disputes over land or, more generally, by disputes about which *shēkh* to follow.

Individual homesteads in the village consist of a circular or nearly square yard enclosed by a millet straw fence about six feet high. In this enclosure are one to three conical roofed houses of millet straw and grass and approximately the same number of flat-roofed, rectangular shelters of the same material.

Each homestead is inhabited by an individual family or by what remains of such a family after divorce or death. The composition of the homestead is affected by the fact that a couple do not establish their own homestead immediately after they marry and start to cohabit as husband and wife. First the husband must complete the transfer of bridewealth to his wife's parents, and the latter must agree to their daughter's establishing her own independent household. It is their duty to furnish it with the money received as bridewealth. This generally takes several years to pay, and the average time between the wedding and setting up house is four years. During this time, both husband and wife live with their natal families and the husband regularly visits his wife in her natal home. One or more children are born to most couples before they establish their own homestead, and a typical Berti household at the time of its inception consists of a married couple and their children. Later it grows to include the elementary families of the parents and those of their daughter or daughters. In the final stage, after the married children have left, the homestead is typically inhabited by an elderly married couple or a widow living on her own. Only rarely does the elderly widowed father of a husband or wife live with the couple, and even more rarely do some other kin reside permanently with them.

Boys usually marry between the ages of 20 and 24, girls between 18 and 22. The Berti express a strong preference for marriage between closely related kin. A marriage between the children of two brothers is considered the best, followed by a marriage between the children of a brother and a sister or between the children of two sisters. If no close cousin is available, a marriage within the lineage is usually sought, and a considerable preference is also expressed for marriages within the same village or cluster of villages. Intermarriage between the Berti and neighbouring tribes rarely occurs. A girl's marriage and a boy's first marriage are always arranged by the parents, and the boy's father is responsible for the payment of bridewealth.

Some men, as they grow older, take additional wives according to their own wishes, the bridewealth being their own responsibility. But the polygyny rate is not high; only 20 per cent of all married men have two, or occasionally, three wives. The co-wives do not share the same homestead and the husband circulates between the homesteads of his wives which, as a rule, are built in different villages.

Each homestead, irrespective of its composition, constitutes a household and a basic unit of production. The Berti have a mixed economy, the main element of which is hoe cultivation practised on rain-fed fields. The most important crop is millet; other cultivated plants are sorghum, okra, sesame, water melons, roselle, cucumbers, pumpkins and occasionally tomatoes.

Pastoralism constitutes the second component of the Berti economy. Cattle and goats are kept in the villages in the rainy season and in cattle camps near a well in the dry season. Camels and sheep are on pasture outside the village throughout the year. Donkeys, camels and, less frequently, horses are used for riding and transport.

The third component of the economy has been traditionally the collecting of wild-growing gum arabic, which was the only real cash crop. Most of the gum-yielding trees died in the severe droughts of the early 1970s and early 1980s; this, together with the drop in price of gum arabic on international markets, has drastically reduced its production, which is no longer seen as profitable.

Berti are not self-sufficient in their production; they depend heavily on the local markets, and cash plays an important role. It is needed for payments of bridewealth, damages and government taxes as well as to secure an immediate material existence. Berti have to buy many products which form the basis of daily nutrition, such as red peppers, dried tomatoes, oil, salt, sugar and tea as well as a variety of manufactured goods. As gum arabic has never alone been sufficient to produce the necessary cash, the surplus of all cultivated crops is marketed. Cattle merchants visit the Berti every year to buy sheep and cattle, and goats are regularly marketed locally. In recent years, an increasing number of young Berti men have been leaving for Libya to work as labour migrants for several years in order to increase the cash supply.

If a household is short of labour due to the absence of some of its members, illness or a woman's pregnancy, it mobilises a work party of kin and neighbours who are provided with a supply of millet beer. Rich households regularly employ poor Berti or Meidob for weeding their fields or herding their animals (Holy 1987).

The traditional political system of the Berti was centralised and pyramidal with the paramount chief occupying the apex. Subordinate to him were the *omdas* standing at the head of *omodiyas* – lower level political subdivisions. The office of paramount chief was abolished by the Sudanese government in the late 1960s, and the Berti are now administered through the hierarchy of village, divisional and regional councils within the provincial council of Northern Darfur. The system of *omodiyas* has been maintained and, for the Berti, the *omdas* still represent important authorities wielding a certain amount of judicial power. Subordinated to each *omda* are individual *shēkhs*, whose own following range widely from a few to several hundred men. Most *shēkhs* are 'masters' of lineage territories responsible for the collection of *'ushūr* (tithe), part of which is given to the *omda*, but some *shēkhs* have no authority in the distribution of land because they do not live in their own lineage territory.

The main duty of the *shēkh* is to collect the annual animal tax from his followers. He also accompanies his followers to the local court and settles minor disputes in informal moots together with village elders – all married men who have their own homesteads. A certain political role is played by lineages, which are responsible for the payment of blood money in case of homicide, injury or damage inflicted by a member of one lineage on the property of another.[2]

Islamisation of Darfur

The Islamisation of the Berti was part of the gradual penetration of Islam into the Darfur sultanate in which the crucial internal commitment to Islam came from the rulers, and the new religion spread gradually from the ruling institution outwards and downwards (O'Fahey 1980: 122).

It is impossible to say with any certainty when the Berti area fell under the sultan's control, but it is most likely that it was fully incorporated into the Darfur sultanate in the mid-eighteenth century and remained a part of it until the end of the sultanate in 1916. The Darfur sultanate was the heir of earlier, pre-Islamic state formations, the existence of which is suggested by numerous prehistoric sites scattered throughout Darfur. As hardly any of them have so far been excavated, the history of state formation in Darfur before the seventeenth century can be surmised only on the basis of local traditions. According to them, the first rulers in Darfur were the Daju whose state centred upon the area south and southeast of Jebel Marra, and in the sixteenth and the first half of the seventeenth century was superseded by the Tunjur state, the centre of which lay to the north of Jebel Marra.

According to existing traditions, the founder of Darfur sultanate was Sulaymān, a Fur of the Keira clan, from whom all the subsequent

---

[2] For a more detailed description of the Berti social structure see Holy 1974.

sultans traced their descent. According to O'Fahey's interpretation of the early historical traditions of the Fur, the Keira kingdom in Jebel Marra might originally have been a tributary state of the Tunjur empire, and the ruling family of the Keira clan probably took over the Tunjur position in Darfur after the Tunjur rule collapsed. Sulaymān's rule may be dated with some confidence to the mid-seventeenth century. He initiated the expansion of the Fur state beyond Jebel Marra and, by subjugating other tribes to his rule, he created the multi-ethnic sultanate which existed until the conquest of Darfur by the British in 1916 (O'Fahey and Spaulding 1974: 107–86; O'Fahey 1980: 8–13).

Oral traditions credit Sulaymān with the introduction of Islam, with building mosques for his subjects and with encouraging Islamic practices (Nachtigal 1971: 278–9; O'Fahey 1974: 123; 1979: 193). During his reign, however, the Islamisation of the sultanate did not progress beyond the 'quarantine' stage (Fisher 1973: 31) when the faith was represented by the immigrant holy men employed to provide religious services at the court (O'Fahey 1980: 10). The Islamisation of the sultanate entered into the 'mixing stage' (Fisher 1973: 31), and Islam probably came to be established as a state religion of Darfur only during the eighteenth century, and possibly only towards the end of it, when sultan 'Abd al-Raḥmān established the permanent capital in El Fasher. Prior to his accession, 'Abd al-Raḥmān himself lived for many years as a holy man (O'Fahey 1979: 193; 1980: 11). But, even at his time, Islam at the court was still far removed from the belief and practice propagated by the holy men. For example, 'Abd al-Raḥmān's attempt to ban the drinking of millet beer in 1795 was not very successful and beer continued to be brewed by the women in his palace (Browne 1806: 201).

It was probably only during the nineteenth century that the gradual Islamisation reached its 'reform' stage (Fisher 1973: 31) at least in the very heart of the sultanate. Sultan Muḥammad al-Ḥusayn, who reigned in the middle of the century, was described as a pious Muslim who actively encouraged visits by foreign scholars (Nachtigal 1971: 313–15) and other sultans too projected a consciously Muslim image:

They built numerous mosques, sought the prayers of their holy men in time of peril, consulted with their *qāḍīs* [judges] on points of law, made a formal procession each Friday from the palace to the mosque, and sent a *maḥmal* [a symbolic cover for the Ka'ba] to Mecca. When the state was under threat, the sultans not only turned to the [holy men] for spiritual aid, but made use of their learning in defence of the state . . . The sultans had succeeded by the mid-nineteenth century in presenting their African kingdom, in its external dealings at least, as a remote but acceptable member of *dar al-islam*. (O'Fahey 1980: 125–6)

The slow and gradual Islamisation of the sultanate was the result of the missionary activities of immigrant holy men. O'Fahey gathered some documentary evidence which suggests that probably 'the earliest wave of immigrants were from the west, beginning perhaps as early as the sixteenth century when Dār Fūr was still ruled by the Tunjur, and . . . only in the eighteenth century did Dār Fūr become a missionary field for holy men from the Nile Valley' (O'Fahey 1980: 117) where Islam had been established since the fifteenth century. Other holy men arrived from Egypt by the 'forty days road' (ibid.: 118), which was an important trade route connecting Darfur with Asyut. The holy men were attracted to Darfur probably not only by missionary zeal but also by trading opportunities. Whatever might have been their motives, they were positively induced by the sultans who encouraged them to settle by building mosques for them and by granting them lands, rights and tax immunities (ibid.: 55–62, 115–26; O'Fahey and Spaulding 1974: 164–71).

As the activities of the immigrant holy men were made possible through the support and countenance of the sultans, the pattern of the Islamisation of Darfur can be seen as the result of the existence of a centralised state. Given the important role which the sultans and the central political institutions played in spreading Islam, it is plausible to surmise that the heartlands of the sultanate were Islamised earlier and more thoroughly than the outlying areas (O'Fahey 1979: 202). There is no documentary evidence about the actual process of Islamisation of the Berti. However, as Islam seems to have become fully established in the capital of Darfur sultanate only during the eighteenth century, it is probable that not until much later did it become a meaningful spiritual force in the remote Berti villages. This surmise is supported by some circumstantial evidence.

It is usually assumed that Islamisation and Arabisation are two aspects of the same process (O'Fahey 1979: 202; 1980: 122; Kapteijns 1985: 14) and they seem indeed to have gone hand in hand in the centre of the sultanate: although Fur remained the spoken language even at the court of the last sultan, 'Alī Dīnār, Arabic had become 'the language of the chancery' by about 1700 (O'Fahey 1979: 191; 1980: 14). If Islamisation and Arabicisation also went hand in hand among the Berti, we can assume with some degree of plausibility that their conversion to Islam is of a comparatively recent date. In 1961, I met people who remembered a few words of the old language and two old men who still spoke it between themselves. It is thus quite probable that the original Berti language was still widely spoken in the last century, or even during the first decades of the present one. According to Macmichael, the Berti certainly spoke their own language in the second decade of this century (Macmichael 1922, vol. 1: 66, 118). Nowadays, the Berti are incredulous when told that they have not spoken Arabic from the dawn of time, and the name Siga, by which they were originally known, carries for them no connotations. But certain phonetic sounds (for example ŋ), which are not of Arabic origin, survive in their speech and certain words of their language are definitely not of Arabic origin (for example ŋaŋa – a small baby, *baghu* – millet beer, known in Sudanese Arabic as *merīsa*, and particularly names of various household implements like *dulaŋ* – a clay pot for beer, *tokolai* – a small gourd vessel, *gongobai* – a walking stick, etc.). Their Arabic does not differentiate gender and has done away with a number of Arabic phonemes. This all indicates that the language change – and also the penetration of Islam which most likely went with it – must have been both rapid and comparatively recent.

The fact that individual holy men were the distinctive agents of the Islamisation of Darfur accounts for the differences that exist between the Islam in Darfur and that in the rest of the Sudan. Whereas in the riverain Sudan, *ṭarīqas* or Sufi brotherhoods have always been the main form of practised Islam, there is virtually no reference to *ṭarīqas* in Darfur before the end of the last century and even nowadays they are still less significant in Darfur than further east (O'Fahey 1979: 203; 1980: 120, 122). Islam, as it is practised among the Berti, shares many features of the Islamic practice common throughout Darfur. On the other hand, in some of its aspects, Islam in Darfur and among the Berti is linked with the practices common throughout the whole of northern Sudan. For example, like all Muslims in the Sudan, the Berti follow the Maliki school which places utmost importance on the *ḥadīth* – the reported sayings of the Prophet, his companions and other pious scholars of early Islam – as the source of Islamic law. However, only those Berti villagers who have attended school and have had some formal religious education may be aware of different interpretations of Islamic law and of the existing differences in worship. For the majority of the Berti there is just one Islam – that which they themselves profess.

In the different cultural and social settings in which it now exists, Islam has remained a vital force and retained its significance because of its capacity to be reinterpreted in a variety of ways according to the local conditions. In this respect, Berti Islam is no exception. They too have imposed their own interpretation not only on its basic doctrinal structure but also on the practices which it prescribes, permits or forbids. In the process, they have created their own version of it that deviates from the 'normative Islam' but locally constitutes an orthodoxy. All the Berti subscribe to it and any heresy from it is for them unthinkable.

The 'five pillars' of Islam

With the exception of the smallest hamlets, each Berti village has its own mosque (*masīd*) – a simple shelter built in the open space in the middle of the village and consisting of a flat millet-straw roof supported by several stakes and surrounded by a low fence of thorny branches. Here communal sacrifices are performed periodically, children are taught the Koran and men meet to discuss village affairs, to entertain guests, or simply to chat during their leisure time or to do some work, like spinning cotton thread, sewing garments or sewing and repairing leather bags. Females never enter the mosque except when young girls join to learn the Koran. Repairs to the mosque and to the thorn fence which surrounds it are done collectively by all the men from the village who are summoned to perform this task by the '*agīd al-hilla*, the man in charge of organising all communal economic, political and ritual activities of the village community. His position, like all positions of authority in Berti society, is hereditary in the patrilineal line but subject to the approval of village elders.

The pious among the Berti, apart from some illiterate villagers and some women, are aware of the 'five pillars' of Islam: the profession of the Islamic creed (*shahāda*) that there is only one God and Mohamed is his messenger, and the duty to pray, to give alms, to fast and to make the pilgrimage to Mecca if one can afford it. The Berti are distinctly lax

Figure 1 Men eat a sacrificial meal in the village mosque

about the five daily prayers. Only the local religious leaders – *fugarā*
(sg. *fakī*) – and a few older men in each village pray regularly five
times a day. Most men perform their daily prayers only during the
month of Ramadan, a very few may pray at least on Friday at noon
during the rest of the year. The Friday prayers are not held in
individual villages, as they must be attended by at least thirteen
worshippers, a number which even a village with a population of three
or four hundred cannot usually muster. They are held in mosques in
market centres, which resemble the ordinary village mosques, and are
attended by the merchants who live there and people from neighbouring villages who come to the market, which is also held on Fridays.
These people are mostly *fugarā* and the occasional old man or, more
rarely, a woman, from each village. The prayer is led by one of the
fugarā, who himself lives in the market centre. The communal prayer
at the end of Ramadan is the only prayer during the year in which
most women participate. Unlike individual prayers, the collective
prayers for rain, at death or during Muslim festivals are performed
enthusiastically by virtually all adult males.

This emphasis on collective rather than individual rituals is also
manifest during Ramadan, which is the only time of intense religious
activity for all Berti. All men fast but women are much more lax in this
duty and quite a few of them have a drink of water or a quick mouthful
of cold millet gruel when they cannot be seen by others, despite the fact
that breaking the fast is believed to bring misfortune on the whole
community. After a meal before sunrise, most men from the village pray
together in the mosque and the older men in particular also pray there
together during the day.

The Berti observe the payment of religious dues (*zaka*) and alms
(*sadaga*) for they bring *ajr* – a reward from God for a good deed – which
will be counted against the bad deeds on the Day of Judgement and
decide a person's final destination in either heaven or hell. After the
grain has been threshed, one tenth of it is put aside as *'ushūr* (tithe) or
karāma. Two-fifths of *'ushūr* go to the *shēkh* who has the right over the
cultivated land (see Holy 1974: 94–105) and three-fifths are distributed
as *zaka*. Part of it is given to the village *fakī* as a reward for his services
and part is distributed to the old or otherwise incapacitated people in
the village who are not able to cultivate land. The *shēkh* himself
distributes about a third or two-fifths of the *'ushūr* he collected to the
needy people in his village. Another due which is seen as a religious
duty which brings *ajr* is paid after Ramadan by each household head on
behalf of all household members. It amounts to slightly over five pounds
of millet per member of the household. It can be paid either in kind or in

cash and it is again distributed between the *shēkh*, the village *fakī* and the old people in the village.

Even though pilgrims to Mecca increase their status in the eyes of the community and are always addressed by the honorific title *Haj* (pilgrim; a female is addressed as *Hajja*), few Berti men have been on a pilgrimage and a woman who has been to Mecca is exceptional. Even those who can easily afford the cost of the pilgrimage are ready to claim the distance to Mecca as an excuse.

Koranic schools

A great number of Islamic prescriptions form part of the knowledge of the illiterate villagers. However the transmission of the whole vast corpus of religious knowledge is severely restricted by the nature of Islam as a 'religion of the book' and, in consequence, a great deal of this knowledge is the exclusive possession of the local religious leaders – *fugarā*. These leaders on the whole constitute about two per cent of the total population. Most of them are local men but some are Fur or Zaghawa who have married Berti women and settled in their villages. Until some three decades ago, before the spread of school education in the rural areas of Darfur, they were the only men in most Berti villages with at least some knowledge of reading and writing. The *fugarā* are graduates of the Koranic schools in which children are taught to memorise at least some verses or whole suras of the Koran and learn some of the fundamentals of Islamic belief, law and practice – most importantly, how to pray and how to perform the ablutions before prayer. The teaching is done by a *fakī* and the school (*khalwa*) is attended by both boys and girls ranging in age from about five to the late teens. The pupils meet every night, except Thursdays, either in the village mosque or in a shelter in the *fakī*'s own homestead. The Berti claim that there were more Koranic schools in the past than there are nowadays and they see the gradually increasing number of elementary schools in rural areas as the main reason for the alleged decline in popularity of the Koranic schools. It is not impossible that most of the larger villages had a Koranic school at some time in the past. Koranic schools tend to wax and wane rather rapidly in line with the changing population of particular villages and the enthusiasm of particular *fugarā* for teaching, and they have most likely done so in the past as well. Chanting the Koran is seen as a worthy religious practice which protects the whole village. A village without fire (i.e. the fire lit in the Koranic school) is said to be 'dark' and haunted by the devil. But only about twelve per cent of villages currently have Koranic schools and only about ten per cent of children attend them. Most of these schools cater exclusively for the children from the village. Classes are held only in the evenings, and no reading or writing is taught. Only a very few large villages have Koranic schools attended by pupils from outside the village who live and work for several years as members of the *fakī*'s own household while learning the Koran from him. In this type of school, three sessions are held during a day: before dawn, in the afternoon and in the evening after sunset. Reading and writing are an important part of instruction. The pupils learn these skills first by writing individual letters of the alphabet and later by copying Koranic verses and suras on a wooden slate (*lōh*) with a sharpened millet stalk used as a pen. A paste of soot and gum arabic is used as ink. Reading and writing are not seen as having any intrinsic value as such. Value is placed only on the memorisation of the Koran, and reading and writing are merely means which facilitate the achievement of this goal.[3]

The resulting literacy is a restricted one (Goody 1968a: 11–20) both in that it has penetrated only a small section of the population and in that it is used almost exclusively in the religious context (Goody 1973: 41). Graduates of Koranic schools, including the *fugarā*, are usually reluctant to use writing in their secular life. When lists of men who have contributed financially to feasts and sacrifices, or lists of items in a bride's trousseau are to be compiled, the task is usually undertaken by those who have been to school or by merchants who are used to writing lists and letters as part of their business. Only when none of them is around will a *fakī* agree to write the list. Although *fugarā* may read out letters sent to illiterate villagers by their relatives, most of them are reluctant to write such letters themselves and the job is again usually done by a merchant or somebody who has been to school.

The length of time spent in a Koranic school varies greatly. Some boys and most girls attend for only a few months and sometimes for only a few weeks, others attend for a few years. Those whose aim is to memorise the whole Koran and to become *fugarā* attend Koranic schools for several years, often moving from a lesser *fakī* to a well-known one. There is, however, no exegesis of the Koranic text even in prestigious Koranic schools run by well-known *fugarā*. The word of God which is written down in the Koran is seen as truly mysterious and beyond the full comprehension of any individual; it has to be preserved in precisely the same perfect form in which it was revealed to the Prophet. In line with this attitude is also the view that God's word is much more effective when it is fully committed to memory in exactly the same form in which it was revealed; reading it from the written text is

[3] For a more detailed description of Berti Koranic schools see Osman el-Tom 1982.

only a poor substitute for this ultimate achievement. In consequence, a good *fakī* is a man who is able to recite the Koran rather than a man who is able to discuss and explain it. To have memorised the whole Koran, or at least its most important and most frequently recited suras (like, for example, the *Yā Sīn sura*) is a necessary condition for being recognised as a *fakī*. But a *fakī* also needs other knowledge than the knowledge of the Koran, and he acquires it by apprenticing himself to a well-known *fakī* after he has spent several years in a Koranic school.

Not all *fugarā* enjoy the same reputation. Those who have served their apprenticeship for only a few years are hardly ever held in great esteem. A good *fakī*'s apprenticeship may last more than ten years during which time he may move several times from one teacher to another or even attend one of the famous Koranic schools in the Fur region of Darfur where the knowledge of the 'magical power' of the Koran is taught, or as the Berti themselves say, where the *fakī* learns the 'secrets' of the Koran. These 'secrets' consist in knowing which verses have the power to cure certain diseases, which bring about rain, repel locusts, etc. The belief in the 'magical' efficacy of Koranic verses deriving from the fact that they come from God, as well as the belief in the protective power rendered by the sheer physical presence of the Koran, is widespread throughout the Muslim world (cf. Nasr 1972: 51). The teacher often reveals his knowledge of the 'secrets' of the Koran to only a few of his favourite students.

The *fakī* usually ends his apprenticeship by staging a large sacrifice in his own village attended by people from many neighbouring villages. During the sacrifice it is announced how many times he recited the whole Koran from memory or, as the Berti express it, 'how many times he memorised the Koran'. The general feeling is that it should be done at least three times before a man can be considered to be a really good *fakī*.

Nowadays, many *fugarā* buy from the market not only various books on Islamic theology and science, but also books on astrology, divination or the interpretation of dreams from which they are able to learn more 'secrets'.[4] The *fakī*'s learning thus does not terminate with the end of his apprenticeship but continues virtually throughout his whole life in line with the prophetic instruction to 'seek knowledge from the womb to the grave' which is known to, and readily quoted by, virtually every *fakī*. Most *fugarā* keep a small library which consists of a few printed books and an *umbatri* ('that which mentions everything'). *Umbatri* is a collection of handwritten papers which form a loose-leaf book held

---

[4] For the list of such books in circulation among the Berti *fugarā* see Osman el-Tom 1983.

together by a string and carried around wrapped in a piece of cloth. The papers contain extracts which the *fakī* copied from printed books, from the handwritten books of other *fugarā* and which he has inherited from his father or some other close kinsman who was a *fakī* himself. The extracts contain descriptions of religious rituals, different methods of divination, descriptions of the precise content and form of various amulets, the use of various Koranic formulae for curing diseases, protecting crops from birds and locusts, bringing on rain and for numerous other benevolent as well as malevolent purposes. Any time the *fakī* comes across a 'secret' which he does not know, he copies it into his ever-growing *umbatri*.

The village *fakī*

In every village there is at least one *fakī* who is referred to as *fakī al-hilla* (the village *fakī*) and who is responsible for the welfare of its inhabitants and for the conduct of public religious rituals. He is usually chosen by village elders from among the various *fugarā* who reside in the village, but if none of them is considered to be sufficiently qualified, a *fakī* from outside may be invited to occupy the position, which is held for life. The village *fakī* leads the public prayers performed during the two main annual religious festivals: *'īd al-fatur*, on the first day following the fasting month of Ramadan, and *'īd al-dahīya*, the commemoration of Ibrahim's offer to sacrifice his son on the tenth day of the twelfth lunar

Figure 2 Communal prayer on *'īd al-fatur*

month. Although the former one is referred to as ʿīd al-saghayir (minor festival) and the latter as ʿīd al-kabīr (great festival) throughout the Arab world, for the Berti ʿīd al-fatur is the main religious holiday of the whole year. The celebration of both festivals is very similar. People wash themselves and put on their best clothes, sprinkle themselves with perfume and women anoint themselves with oil. A communal prayer is held in the morning on a site east of the village which has been cleared of grass. Older men sit in a row facing east towards Mecca with the younger men sitting behind them in one or two rows; a gap is left between the men and the women, who sit behind the men, again in parallel rows. The *fakī* who leads the prayer stands in front of the worshippers. The prayer is fairly similar to the daily prayer and follows the form which has been standardised throughout the Maliki Muslim world. When the prayer is over, people shake hands wishing one another blessed ʿīd and uttering other standardised phrases which express the wish for future well-being and health, for God's forgiveness of sins, for his blessing of the dead, for his accepting the fast and for people's forgiveness of one another. Men then assemble in the village mosque while women return to their houses to prepare food. A bull is usually sacrificed and, as well as the meat, several dishes of millet gruel and relish are brought to the mosque where they are consumed by the men as *karāma* (offering to God). Women assemble in or behind one of the homesteads for their separate *karāma*. In the afternoon, men and women move around in separate small groups to visit all the homesteads in the village and to wish their inhabitants well.

The village *fakī* also officiates at weddings and funerals and advises on the division of inheritance which, however, rarely proceeds according to Koranic injunctions and more often than not totally excludes daughters (see Holy 1974: 39–40, 43–4). Prayers for rain and for chasing away birds are other services which he provides for the community. The villagers themselves see these prayers as his main and most important duty.

In the Berti view, only God can send or withhold rain but he uses this power either as a reward for people being kind and polite to one another or as a punishment for their selfish or immoral behaviour. The recent drought is often seen as God's punishment for theft, robbery and for people's selfishness, stinginess, greediness and their disregard for the needs of the old. Many Berti claim that these bad deeds and qualities have been on the increase in recent years as people have become more and more oriented towards the acquisition of wealth at the expense of their less fortunate neighbours, and that the recent drought was the consequence of this.

The village *fakī* can either perform his prayers for rain on his own or the men from the village can perform them collectively. Both types of prayers are called *du 'a* as is, in fact, any prayer the purpose of which is to induce God to grant a specific favour.

When performing his prayer, the *fakī* stays secluded in his house or, in some villages, in a special hut called *khalwa* (privacy or seclusion) which is built specifically for this purpose in the centre of the village near the mosque. Throughout his seclusion he must be alone, speaking to nobody. The *fakī* performs his rain prayers every year. If the rainy season starts on time, he goes into seclusion immediately after the onset of the first rains to ensure their uninterrupted continuation and he usually stays secluded for a week. If the rains are late, he goes into seclusion to hasten their arrival and he may stay secluded for two or three weeks until the rain eventually arrives. If the first rains are followed by a period of prolonged drought and the millet starts showing signs of withering, the *fakī* is put under pressure to resume his prayers. A good *fakī* who 'fears God' does not sleep in his hut for longer than necessary and he devotes all his time to repeating specific Koranic verses. Among them is the very first verse of the Koran which the Berti considers to 'open the doors of the worlds' and numerous other verses which contain the words 'water', 'rain' or 'clouds'. The *fugarā* thus ascribe their own meaning to the Koranic text which derives from their consideration of the Koran in terms of the reality as understood by the Berti; at the same time, it relates to this reality through being pragmatically manipulated for various specific purposes (Osman el-Tom 1985: 428–9; 1987: 243). 'Sympathetic' thought, which underlies many other religious practices, is clearly the basis of this manipulation. An alternative to the continuous recitation of various Koranic verses is the recitation of the word *istikhfār*, which can be translated as 'plea' or 'asking for forgiveness' and which implies the belief that God will forgive the sins of the community, or the word *mughītu*, which is one of God's ninety-nine names. It means 'delivering help or relief' and it is seen as appropriate also because it derives from the same root as one of the words for rain (*ghēth*). The name of the angel Michael may also be recited, as he is believed to have been entrusted by God to send rain.

The *fugarā* regard seclusion as a dangerous undertaking, as the names of God which they recite are extremely powerful, or 'hot', as the Berti say, and may impair the strength of those who recite them repeatedly. They also repel devils (*shayātīn*) and malevolent spirits (*junūn*, sg. *jinn*) who become angry because of the suffering which the names of God cause them and may avenge themselves on a *fakī*. But, on the whole, the rain prayer is less dangerous than the uttering of the 'hot' names of God or 'hot' Koranic verses to cure madness, which is believed to result from the *shētān* (devil) grasping a person. The *shētān* may avenge himself on any member of a *fakī*'s family; virtually all cases of mental disorder among a *fakī*'s kin are believed to be the result of his use of 'hot' names of God and Koranic verses.

The *fakī*'s seclusion is often accompanied by a public *du 'a* performed by all the men from the village. It is organised by *'agīd al-hilla* and he, together with the elders, has the right to penalise any man who fails to participate without a valid excuse.

The *du 'a* may be performed in the village mosque in which the men assemble every morning after sunset for about an hour. But it is more usual to hold it during the day at the rainy-season waterhole. The men count the hundred beads of the rosary and at each bead recite either the first two opening verses of the Koran, which every man knows even if he has not been to a Koranic school, or one of the names of God which has been selected for the occasion. Apart from the names which the village *fakī* ordinarily utters during his seclusion, the men may also opt for *subhāna Allah* ('praise be to God'), *yā Muīnu* ('you, who helps') or *yā Latīfu* ('you, the gracious'). Every 124,000 utterances are said to represent *bīr* (the well). In order to call rain the men must recite at least seven 'wells'. Each man makes a mark in the sand for each rosary he has recited. From time to time one man, who keeps the total count, adds up the number; a rosary is laid aside for each thousand of God's names pronounced. The *fugarā* and literate men do not recite God's names but read the Koran. During *du 'a* the men make tea bought with money collected among themselves.

The more 'wells' that are achieved the better is the chance of bringing on the rain, and quite often the total of seven 'wells' is exceeded even if the *du 'a* lasts as long as five days. For each 'well' achieved, a notch is carved in a piece of wood hung in the mosque. The number of notches serves as a witness of previous achievements in which the men take great pride.

At the end of the *du 'a* a *karāma* of one or two goats is usually held at the waterhole or in the village mosque. The meat is prepared and consumed by all the men who participated in the ritual. The *karāma* ends with the saying of *al-fātha*: the men recite the opening sura of the Koran, or just the first two opening verses if they do not know the whole sura, holding their hands with palms up in front of their chests or faces and then rubbing their faces at the end of the recitation.

The village *fakī* also goes into seclusion for a week or two to chase away birds or locusts from the fields but, unlike the *du 'a* for rain, this *du 'a* is not an annual occasion and the Koranic verses which he recites are less standardised and vary greatly among individual *fugarā*. Although each one may favour a different verse, the verses which are seen as appropriate for the occasion are always those which refer to birds or insects.

The village *fakī* is not a ritual specialist exempt from ordinary daily work. Like other villagers, he cultivates his fields and tends his livestock. He receives only a modest reward for his services to the community in the form of the dues in kind or money, and only occasionally may he be given some millet, flour, oil or sugar for a special service rendered. As, perforce, he cannot weed his fields when he is in seclusion, he receives about seven or eight pounds of grain or the equivalent in cash from each household in the village for his *du 'a*, and a communal work party is organised every year to weed his fields. As virtually all the men and women from the village take part, all his fields are usually weeded in a single day.

A village *fakī* may also occasionally write amulets, perform divinations or write Koranic verses on a wooden slate to be washed away with water which is then drunk as a medicine. But these last three activities are more often performed by other *fugarā* than the village *fakī*. Different *fugarā* tend to specialise in a particular activity or have acquired the reputation for being good at it and their services are sought by people from far away and become a lucrative source of income.

Amulets

An amulet (*hijāb*, protector; pl. *hijbāt*) consists of a piece of paper on which the *fakī* copies from his *umbatri* a text appropriate for its purpose. The text consists of some Koranic verses, some of the ninety-nine names of God, the names of angels and *junūn*, and some astrological formulae and signs. The verses and formulae for any particular amulet are chosen on the same principle of 'sympathy' which guides the selection of verses for rain prayers (see Osmal el-Tom 1987). The sheet of paper is folded several times into a small square which is then sewn into a leather bag or sometimes covered by a piece of cloth. This is not done by the *fakī* but is the responsibility of the client himself who usually asks a local saddler to do the job. The leather bag is tied to a piece of string and worn around the arm, across the chest or around the neck. Camels, donkeys and horses sometimes wear amulets hung around their necks. An amulet for protecting a house is hung unfolded and uncovered above the door. Other amulets may be buried, burnt, hung from the roof of a hut or inserted into its wall.

Amulets are normally written to order but ready-made *hijbāt* are also sold by some *fugarā* in local markets. With a few exceptions, an amulet need not to be written for a particular individual to be effective and even a stolen amulet does not lose its power. The Berti never throw away amulets and they are regularly inherited; when a particular amulet is needed, it is often borrowed. Nevertheless, most *fugarā* detest the sale of ready-made amulets and they claim that only bad *fugarā*, who do not have enough clients, resort to it. This practice is bad, they say, because religious knowledge should never be sold. When a *fakī* works for a client, he never asks for a fee and it is left to the client to decide how much he wants to pay. The price of particular amulets is, however, more or less standardised and varies according to the amount of writing involved. Most clients automatically pay the standard price. Not only because they may require his services in the future, but also because offending a *fakī* could be dangerous – the 'secrets' which he knows may be used for malevolent as well as benevolent purposes.

Probably every adult Berti has at least one amulet and people who possess three, four or five of them are quite common. A few individuals have as many as fifty and there are some who claim to possess even more. The amulets are used for a variety of purposes, the most common having standardised names by which they are ordered. Some are effective against a wide range of dangers or misfortunes; for example *hijāb hifiz* (from *yahfaz* – to protect) which is used against sorcery, the evil eye ('*ēn*) and diseases caused by *junūn*, or *hijāb hirāsa* (protection) which protects babies and small children against devils and diseases. Some amulets are used as protection against weapons. The most popular among them is *hijāb hadīd* (iron) which protects against knives; others are *hijāb bundug* (rifle) and *hijāb tasrīf* (from *yissarif*, to miss the target). To remain effective, these amulets must be taken off if their wearer has illicit sex or is involved in any other forbidden act which is polluting. *Hijāb angalat* (from *yangil*, to bend) immobilises the arm of an attacker.

Amulets are used not only for protection but also to bring about various desired ends. *Hijāb sūq* (market) or *hijāb jālib* (from *yajlib*, to bring) are used particularly by merchants to attract customers and almost every merchant keeps one in his shop. Similar to these are *hijāb riziq* (wealth) and *hijāb burda* (from *bārid*, cold) which are used to bring about wealth, prosperity and general well being. The last is worn particularly by men involved in a court case to secure its favourable outcome. *Hijāb arkabi* (from *yarkab*, to ride) makes sure that the man who wears it will not miss his target and it is favoured by hunters. *Hijāb mahabba* (love) is used particularly by young men to attract a girl's affection. Others protect against dangers on travels, ward off enemies, protect against diseases, etc. Many people have two or three amulets of the same kind. It is, for example, quite common for a man to have several amulets to protect him against weapons so that, should one of them fail, the others will still be effective.

Amulets are used not only for benevolent but also for malevolent purposes. *Hijāb nijēsa* (from *nijis*, polluted) helps a man to commit adultery and at the same time protects him against any weapon with which he may be attacked in consequence, except a rifle. *Hijāb batūta* is used by men who want to commit adultery or steal something because it puts people off their guard and makes them fall asleep or lose their consciousness for a while.

There are numerous stories told about the effectiveness of amulets, particularly those which protect against weapons. These amulets are sometimes tested for effectiveness, although this practice is viewed with disapproval. Not only is one's faith in a *hijāb* necessary for its efficacy, but the *hijāb* contains 'the name of God' which must not be doubted. It is not the amulet as such but the 'name of God' which it contains that brings about the desired end. Doubt in the amulet thus means doubt in the power of God, and that is something unthinkable. Any particular failure of a *hijāb* is explained by reference to the state of pollution in which the person who wore it must have been and which made it ineffective, to the mistakes which the *fakī* must have made in his writing or to the *fakī*'s inadequate knowledge of all the 'secrets'. These are typical 'secondary elaborations' (Evans-Pritchard 1937) which effectively protect the belief in *hijbāt* from any possible questioning (Horton 1970: 162).

Mihāi

Koranic verses, whole suras of the Koran and other formulae similar to those used in *hijbāt* are also written by the *fakī* on both sides of a wooden slate (*lōh*) and the written text is washed off with water. The collected water is called *mihāi* (from *yamha*, to erase) and is drunk by villagers to cure illness and women's sterility, to ensure safety on long travels, an easy childbirth, success in learning at school or in business ventures and court cases, to protect the client from the effects of malicious gossip, to induce the affection of a woman, or to safeguard health, prosperity and general well-being. Like amulets, *mihāi* can also be used for malevolent purposes, like inflicting leprosy on an enemy (Osman el-Tom 1985: 427–8). Some people drink *mihāi* more or less regularly every few months as a general precaution. Others ask a *fakī* to prepare it for them only in case of a lingering disease or if they think that the evil eye has been cast on them or that they have been attacked by *shētān* or evil *junūn*. When drinking *mihāi*, the patients must not drink beer and they must avoid all polluting acts like adultery and, according to some, all sexual intercourse. The selection of the text appropriate for a particular *mihāi* is guided by the same notions as the selection of texts and formulae for *hijbāt* and rain prayers.[5] When *mihāi* is used for treating children, the appropriate verses and formulae have to be written down on the slate seven times. For the treatment of adults, the verses have to be written down at least forty-one times, or a hundred times if the cure has not been effective. Depending on the purpose of the *mihāi*, the writing may take anything between a few days and several weeks. The *fakī* usually stays during this time as a guest in his client's household and the *mihāi* is often shared by several or all members of the household who drink it from the same container, either at once or in small doses during the day. On the following days new portions of *mihāi* are prepared by the *fakī* and drunk in the same way.

If an epidemic, locusts, drought or outbreaks of fire threaten the well-being of the whole community, a large amount of *mihāi* is prepared to be drunk by all the people in the village. Such *mihāi* is called *jumla* (total) or *wazn al-kitāb* (the weighing of the book) and it involves writing down and washing off the whole Koran. *Jumla* is organised by the village *fakī* who invites other *fugarā* to help him with writing in the village mosque. *Jumla* ends with a *karāma* whose cost is met by all household heads.

The Koran is considered to have an immense power which guarantees the well-being of those who have internalised it. It protects them against evil forces and malevolent practices of others and ensures the achievement of their various aspirations. The widespread use of *hijbāt* and *mihāi* is based on this idea of internalising the power contained in the Koran, the names of God and other sacred inscriptions which would otherwise remain external to the person (Goody 1968b: 230–1). The same idea also underlies the emphasis on the memorisation of the Koran. Through it, it is internalised in the head (*rās*), which presides (*yaras*) over the rest of the body. Committing the Koran to memory is the highest way of its internalising it; this is also why it is believed that reciting the Koranic verses and suras from memory is more effective than reading them from the book. This way of appropriating the divine power inherent in the Koran is, of course, available only to the *fugarā* who have mastered the art of reading and writing. For the illiterate villagers, *mihāi* and *hijbāt* are substitutes for this ultimate religious achievement. Although drinking the words of the Koran is seen as less effective than memorising them, it is more effective than carrying them

---

[5] See Osman el-Tom 1985 for the discussion of texts and formulae used.

on the body in the form of amulets, which may be lost or stolen and thus removed from the person they should be protecting. *Mihāi*, once drunk, can never be dissociated from the body of the patient. This is also the reason why people resort to drinking *mihāi* in cases of illness, after other means of cure, including *hijāb*, have failed.

Divination

Berti men resort quite frequently to divination to find out the where-abouts of stray or stolen animals, the response of a girl's guardians to an intended marriage proposal, the welfare of absent relatives, the future fate of a sick kinsman, the outcome of an intended journey or market transaction and for a multiplicity of other reasons. Most men know at least the rudiments of divination done by interpreting the meaning of figures constructed from dots made in a haphazard way by a finger in the sand. Some men have a reputation as experts in this type of 'sand divination' (*ramul*; from *ramla*, sand) and are often asked by others to perform it for them. However, men perform sand divination only when the problem to which they seek an answer is not too serious. For important problems, the Berti seek divination which they call *sagit* (deduction) or *sagit al-kitāb* (deduction from the book). This kind of divination employs writing and is therefore practised exclusively by the *fugarā*. Each *fakī* usually employs a specific method described in some astrological book which he has copied into his *umbatri*. But the basic method of divination is standardised among the *fugarā*, and is based on ascribing different numerical values to letters of the Arabic alphabet, and on reading the future from people's names, names of the days of the week and other words. The methods of divination taken over from printed Arabic manuals are often modified by the Berti *fugarā* who employ, for example, a simplified method in counting the numerical value of letters and names. Modification is probably most apparent in divination aimed at establishing the cause of a disease. There are seven causes of diseases recognised in the printed books on divination which circulate among the *fugarā*, but the Berti recognise only four (*jinn*, wind, sorcery and the evil eye) and so do the *fugarā*. In the Berti view, disease always comes from outside the body. In consequence, blood, yellow bile and black bile which are mentioned in the printed texts are omitted in the *fugarā*'s handwritten books. Further comparison of these books with the printed texts indicates that only material that does not contradict the cultural knowledge of the Berti is copied (Osman el-Tom 1983).

The divination sessions are conducted in private and many of them are concerned with finding out whether an intended wife will be fertile, whether she will bear sons or daughters, or which one of the spouses will survive the other. Other divination is aimed at discovering the prospects for the recovery of a sick relative, the fate of a kinsman who left the village long ago and from whom nothing has been heard since, the prospects of an intended business venture or journey, or the cause of some lingering disease.

Most often the *fakī* is asked to establish a person's star through divination called *tanjīm* (from *najim*, star). Each person has one of the four stars which correspond to the four elements and he or she is either *nārī* (adjective from *nār*, fire), *riyāhī* (from *rīh*, wind), *mā 'ī* (from *māa*, water) or *turābī* (from *turāb*, dust). The star is established from the person's own and his or her mother's name.[6] Each star corresponds to a certain character. *Mā 'ī* is easy going, comfortable to live with and generally of a lucky disposition; *nārī* is tough and good at maintaining peace and order and consequently this is a good star for a *shēkh*; *turābī* is successful in anything he or she does and wealth comes to him or her easily; *riyāhī* is generous and always willing to help others which often prevents him from accumulating wealth for himself. But it is not so much the character of individual people that matters as rather their mutual compatibility, and the main purpose of the divination is to establish the stars of future spouses: *Al-khēl taljim u l 'awīn tanjim* ('You bridle the horses and you establish women's stars through divination'), the men say. The best is a marriage of *mā 'ī* to *turābī* or of *riyāhī* to *nārī*. They naturally complement one another in the same way as water is needed for the earth to produce and wind for the fire to keep burning. *Mā 'ī* and *nārī* are mutually incompatible as are water and fire and so are *riyāhī* and *turābī* for the wind blows away the dust. Spouses who have the same star are mutually compatible but their marriage is believed not to be as prosperous as a marriage of *mā 'ī* to *turābī* or *riyāhī* to *nārī*.

I asked a number of husbands and wives about their stars. A few admitted to having the same star as their spouse but most couples claimed to be either *mā 'ī* and *turābī* or *nārī* and *riyāhī*, and none of them admitted to having incompatible stars. When the actual couple's stars are established through the method used by the *fugarā*, a considerable number of them have incompatible stars (Osman el-Tom 1983). This indicates that the divination is obviously manipulated to reveal the desirable outcome; a skilful *fakī* can easily do this by varying the spelling of the names from which he reads the stars. The divination thus easily confirms the compatibility of a woman whom a man desires to marry as

---

[6] This belief seems to be widespread throughout the Muslim world. Westermarck mentions it from Morocco where the four stars indicate the person's 'nature' (1926, vol. 1: 129).

well as the incompatibility of a woman he does not want to marry. I
know men who successfully avoided marriage to girls chosen for them
by their fathers on the grounds that divination revealed their stars to be
incompatible.

The Berti hold ambivalent views about their *fugarā*. On the one hand,
the services they provide in divination and in writing amulets and *mihāi*
are positively appreciated. The *fugarā* are also admired for the danger
to which they expose themselves in handling 'hot' verses while providing
their valuable services. The *fakī*'s ability to write is admired as a great
achievement and the writing which he does is seen as hard work, more
tiring than strenuous manual labour. On the other hand, the *fugarā* are
treated with suspicion. They know the 'secrets' which can be put not
only to beneficent but also maleficent use and they are often suspected
of helping others to commit adultery, theft, sorcery (*sihir*) or other
undesirable or immoral acts, or of helping them to acquire wealth by
illegitimate means or even helping them to kill others. The famous
fugarā whose services are widely sought are often quite rich and they
emulate the merchants in their lifestyle, abstaining from any manual
labour and relying on hired herders to look after their animals and on
wage labourers to weed their fields. The means through which they have
acquired their wealth are suspected and it is widely believed that they
employ dangerous *junūn* as their helpers.

Karāma

Most religious rituals in Berti society are performed by the *fugarā*.
Individual religious rituals, with the exception of the Ramadan fast, are
not ascribed great importance by the Berti. Collective rituals, like *du 'a*,
are of much greater significance to the majority of the illiterate villagers.
Of even greater significance are the periodic offerings to God (*karāma*)
which are by far the most important religious rituals in Berti society,
through which most villagers actively and regularly proclaim their faith.
Karāma is for them the central ritual element of their adherence to
Islam. The participants at a *karāma* are usually inhabitants of the
village, but its organisers may be members of one family or household
rather than the whole village community. I will first describe instances
when the members of the village community act as the communal
organisers of a *karāma*. Any disaster is a sign that God is angry with the
people and must be placated by an offering. *Karāmas* are made in order
to bring about rain, to ensure a good harvest, to avoid illness, etc.
Communal *karāmas* are also arranged by the village during some
Muslim festivals. Each village arranges a *karāma* about once every two
months. If there is no apparent reason to perform an offering, a *karāmat*

'*āfiya* is held, which is an offering to secure the health of all members of the village community.

The impulse to perform a *karāma* may come from any man in the village. This usually happens during the early afternoon rest in the village mosque, when he remarks that there has been no *karāma* for a long time and that it would be good to have one; he may also suggest a reason why one should be held. The other men usually agree and a search begins for a suitable animal. The sacrificial animal at a *karāma* arranged by the village community is usually a young bull. It is bought at the market or from a villager with all the household heads sharing the price.

The bull is slaughtered on the open space in front of the mosque. Generally there is one man in each village who regularly undertakes this task, as a rule one of the great elders (Holy 1974: 122) who prays regularly, though he need not be a *fakī*. The sacrificer says *bism il-lāhi Allāhu akbaru* ('in the name of God, God is the greatest') three times and, facing east, kills the bull by cutting its neck arteries with his right hand. Next he washes the muzzle, penis and rump with water from a clay ablution jar, also pouring some into the neck wound. This is called *tahāra* (as is the ablution before prayer) and the bull is then *tāhir* (cleansed). *Tahāra* is performed only with animals killed for sacrifice; it is not part of an ordinary slaughter, which is otherwise performed in the same way.

Figure 3 Men slaughter a bull for *karāma*

Skinning and butchering the animal is the work of all the men in the village. The portions of the bull are carried to the mosque shelter where wicker doors, used to close the entrance to the fence surrounding a homestead, have been brought. The meat is laid out on them and later carved there. All the meat from the head, including the chopped up bones, is boiled in a pot of water in which the stomach has been washed. The boiled meat from the head, the brain and the shanks are then grilled on a wire grid and later eaten in the mosque by the men who did the carving.

The meat is divided equally into as many portions as there are households, the portions being weighed on scales made from two gourds, and then set on the hide laid out in the mosque. After weighing out meat from the back, rump and haunch, which is considered the best, the brisket, lungs, heart, liver, kidney and stomach are similarly divided. Each household receives a little of each. The intestines are then twisted into a skein and cut so that each household in the village receives an equal portion. Finally, the skeleton is divided. First the ribs are separated and divided, then the bones from the legs and spine are chopped and shared out equally.

A *karāma* is always held on a day when it does not conflict with any regular or planned activity. During the weeding season a *karāma* is held on a Friday, the day of rest, so that everyone may participate. If one is by exception held on a day when the fields are weeded, usually one man from each kin group in the village takes part.

Sometimes only goats or sheep are sacrificed instead of a bull. If at least three goats or sheep are killed their meat is divided in the way described above. If there is too little meat to be divided, it is consumed communally. Part of the meat goes to the men of the village who prepare it and eat it together, keeping part of it separate for the boys, who also consume it communally. Smaller portions are given to the women for their communal consumption.

In thanks for a heavy rain after a prolonged dry spell during the rainy season, the village community arranges a *karāma baraka* in one of the fields. Women from all the households bring millet gruel, which is eaten in separate groups by the men and women of the village involved in weeding.

A *karāma* may also be given by a household head, for example when there is an illness in the family, in a case of difficult childbirth, at a child-naming ceremony on the seventh day after a birth, after the death of a kinsman, or to celebrate the return of a member of the household who has been away for a long time. The women from the household prepare millet gruel and generally a little meat. After the meal, tea is usually served to the participants. Goats or sheep are killed only rarely, for example at *karāma* held a week after the birth of a child, particularly a son. Except in this case, a *karāma* is always held after the sun has set. The head or another member of the household goes around the village and invites the neighbours. Less significant *karāmas*, for example, *karāmat 'āfiya*, are attended only by the men of the village, who eat the meal in the guest-shelter in the organiser's homestead, in the yard in front of the shelter, or sitting outside the homestead in front of its entrance. More important *karāmas*, for example, those on the death of a kinsman, are also attended by women, who have their meal apart from the men. They usually gather together in the back part of the yard in front of the hut in which the woman cooks.

Karāmas are also held by individual households during some of the Muslim feasts. At *'īd al-dahīya* a ram or goat is sometimes killed, but the more frequent form is millet gruel from each household eaten by the men of the village together. The men spend the day going from one homestead to another so as to take part in the *karāma* of each. The women usually have their *karāma* together late in the afternoon. Each woman takes a dish of gruel to one homestead where they eat together. In the same way individual households prepare *karāma* for all inhabitants of the village at the *'īd al-maulid*, the commemoration of the prophet's birthday; the sacrificial food is again millet gruel. A communal sacrifice, usually of a bull, is also arranged by the whole village on *'īd al-maulid*.

A special type of *karāma* is arranged for the children of the village by individual households during the weeding season. This is held before the weeding begins on a Monday or Friday. The sacrificial food is *belīla*, salted millet boiled in water. The children from the household giving the *karāma* bring out food into the open space in front of the homestead with the cry *'iyāl ta 'ālu āklu karāma* ('children come and eat *karāma*'). This *karāma* is eaten by small boys and girls together.

The local religious orthodoxy
The Berti not only do not care much about the performance of daily prayers but their adherence to Islam also involves a reinterpretation of some other Islamic rules. Most of them, including some *fugarā*, drink millet beer, which forms an important part of their diet. Beer takes three days to prepare and attending to the three batches at their different stages of fermentation is an important part of women's daily chores. The Berti justify their beer consumption by explaining that the Koranic prohibition on alcohol does not apply to it, but only to the spirit

which is occasionally distilled from the beer gone sour. Some of them also argue that it is only *harām* (ritually prohibited) to sell beer but not to drink it as long as it does not make people drunk and does not make them behave violently. The beer has a very low alcohol content and people rarely get drunk on it even when consuming large quantities frequently. Some men do not touch millet gruel for weeks on end and subsist only on beer and occasional meat; they say that beer is like diluted gruel anyway and has the advantage over it of not only satisfying hunger but quenching thirst at the same time.

The segregation of the sexes, a characteristic feature of many Muslim societies, is not adhered to very rigidly. Women, of course, eat separately from men although husband and wife often share the same dish in the privacy of their home. The inner part of the homestead, where the hut in which the woman cooks is located, is a female domain but male neighbours can enter it even if the man of the house is away. Women stay separate from male company only when there are male guests in the household whom they do not know. Inside the house or when working in the fields, women were often stripped down to the waist and did not attempt to cover their breasts even in the presence of strangers; this custom is, however, dying out and nowadays only an occasional old woman may be seen with bare breasts. All women, however, still move around the village with their hair uncovered and work without any head cover in the fields and at the well. They cover their hair only on festive occasions and in the market. Women work jointly with men in fields and at wells and women would stop and chat without any embarrassment with men on their way to the market or to the field. Young men and women from the village regularly get together late in the evening to chat or play riddles, and although adult men tend to come together and chat after an evening meal while women stay in the house or visit one another, mixed impromptu evening parties, at which men and women come together to listen to a story-teller or just simply to chat, are not uncommon.

In contrast to the Islamic code of practice, cases of adultery are settled by swearing an oath and the payment of a fine. Premarital pregnancy is not uncommon and, although it is seen as shameful, it has no long-lasting repercussions for either the child or the mother. The child is brought up by the girl's parents as one of their own and is later usually adopted by her brother. In the Berti system of naming, a person's own name is followed by the name of his or her father. The illegitimate child bears the name of his or her mother's brother, even if the genitor is known. By the time the child grows up his or her illegitimate status is usually forgotten, or at least ceases to be of any concern. Similarly, with the lapse of time, the girl's premarital pregnancy will cease to be a bar to her marriage.

Individual and collective prayers, *karāmas*, fast during Ramadan, payments of *zaka*, pilgrimage to Mecca and rituals accompanying birth, circumcision, weddings and funerals, which I shall describe later, are seen by all the Berti as parts of Islamic religion (*dīn*). With the exception of a few school leavers the Berti also see the divination performed by the *fugarā*, the wearing of amulets and the drinking of *mihāi* as religious activities. Their status as perfectly orthodox Islamic practices derives from the fact that all these actions are seen as having their origin 'in the book'. For the illiterate villagers, there is only one book, the holy Koran, and it is automatically assumed that because *hijbāt* and *mihāi* are copied by the *fugarā* from a written text, they are of Koranic origin. So are the *fugarā*'s divinations for they also stem from 'what is written'. Anything that is written must have been approved by God and his Prophet and is by definition orthodox; the phrase 'it is written (*fī maktūb*) is often heard as the legitimation of the religious status of a specific practice.

These practices are locally distinguished from events and practices which the Berti classify as *'awāid* (sg. *'āda*) and which I gloss as customary rituals. Unlike the religious practices, the *'awāid* are not mentioned in the Koran, *hadīth* or the texts which the *fugarā* have assembled in their *umbatris*. As they thus do not derive from 'what is written', the Berti do not see them as part of what they consider to be Islamic orthodoxy.

Even the illiterate villagers are nowadays aware that the books which the *fugarā* use are different from those brought by children from school or from the printed matter which circulates among those who have been to school, but they do not see them as different from the Koran itself. The *fugarā*, or at least the 'good' *fugarā*, are, of course, aware that not everything that is written down in their *umbatris* comes from the Koran. But the instructions for preparing *hijbāt* and *mihāi* and for conducting divinations were written by reputed religious scholars whose status as good Muslims is beyond doubt. It is only proper for the *fugarā* to follow faithfully their advice which does not contradict in any way what is written in the Koran. On the contrary, the printed books are full of references to Koranic verses and the advice of their authors is based on a deeper understanding of the Koran and its 'secrets' than the *fugarā* themselves possess. The good *fugarā* are aware of the differences between prescriptions which are of Koranic origin and prescriptions and recommendations which originate in *hadīth* but, in their view, the extracts which they have copied from printed books into their *umbatris* have exactly the same status as *hadīth*. These views about what constitutes the written word, in which the proper Islamic beliefs and practices are encoded, legitimise the magical and astrological Islamic lore as an integral part of religion. The books on divination, astrology and the interpretation of dreams, which are part of 'what is written', perpetuate an alternative to the Koranic message which is, however, not simply the result of the villagers' illiteracy militating against their 'proper' understanding of God's message. These books have spread alongside the Koran itself and as elsewhere in the Muslim world (see, for example, Karim 1981), among the Berti too, the spread of Islamic piety was accompanied by the spread of magical and astrological Islamic lore. In their own way, the Berti confirm Lewis's view that 'Islam is . . . not the "religion of the book", but rather, the "religion of the books", a package of written compendia that in their catholic profusion facilitate the diffusion and rediffusion of so-called pre-Islamic survivals' (Lewis 1986: 107).

Unlike the illiterate villagers and the *fugarā*, some Berti who have been educated in schools draw a clear distinction between the Koran and other religious books and the books which the *fugarā* use as guides for divination and for writing *hijbāt* and *mihāi*. They refer to the latter as 'yellow books' due to the cheap yellow paper on which they are printed and they reject them as incompatible with the Muslim faith. They see amulets, *mihāi* and particularly divination as non-Islamic superstitions. Paradoxically, rather than having any influence on the views of the illiterate Berti and the *fugarā*, their opinion generates suspicion about the value of modern school education. Most villagers feel that school education leads people away from proper religion and instils in them heresy which goes as far as doubting the truth and sacredness of that 'which is written'.

The persistence of beliefs and practices which deviate not only from Islam as it is interpreted by religious scholars but also from Islamic orthodoxy as it is locally defined and understood, is commonplace in Muslim societies. These beliefs and practices have often been seen as elements of magic and animistic religion surviving from pre-Islamic times under the veneer of Islam. Such is the view not only of Muslim reformers aiming at ridding Islamic practices of all undesirable accretions but also of many anthropologists and sociologists (cf. Wester-marck 1933; Tubiana 1963; Ferchiou 1972). Lewis recently pointed out the problematic nature of such explanations and argued that beliefs and practices which deviate from local Islamic orthodoxy may be traced either spatially or temporally and that these two dimensions are apt to interpenetrate and coalesce (Lewis 1986: 94–107).

Berti ethnography again appears to give credit to this view. As we shall see later, some of the *'awāid* have close parallels in rituals performed at the sultan's court or elsewhere in Darfur which, on the basis of existing historical records, preceded the spread of Islam. Others have their parallels in beliefs and customs reported from Islamised African societies south of the Sahara as well as from North Africa and from elsewhere in the Middle East. In their case, it is not altogether improbable that they might have spread together with Islam itself in much the same way as the spread of magical and astrological Islamic lore accompanied the spread of the Koranic message. They may thus be post- or even pan-Islamic rather than pre-Islamic. Contacts through trade, pilgrimage and, recently, labour migration could have facilitated their widespread distribution.

The tolerance to locally unorthodox beliefs and practices is usually explained by reference to Islam's 'truly catholic recognition of the multiplicity of mystical power' and the fact that the Koran, though insisting on the uniqueness of God, 'itself provides scriptural warrant for the existence of a host of subsidiary powers and spirits' whose existence and effectiveness, 'whether as malign or beneficial agencies, is not disputed' (Lewis 1966: 60; see also Trimingham 1980: 81–2).

However, this 'tolerant nature' of Islam does not explain why beliefs and practices which deviate from the locally defined orthodoxy appeal to specific sections of society. Accounts of the conversion to Islam and studies of Islam in tribal and peasant societies suggest that women particularly maintain such beliefs and practices (see for example Lewis 1966: 60ff.; Gellner 1968; Eickelman 1976: 132; R. Tapper 1979: 164–5; Trimingham 1980: 47). The picture that emerges is informed by the view that non-Islamic beliefs and practices which persist in Muslim societies are survivals from the society's pre-Islamic past. It is a picture of uneven rates of conversion: men uphold the Islamic faith, women are affected by it to a much lesser degree or have fused its basic tenets with traditional beliefs to a much greater extent than men (Trimingham 1980: 46; Davis 1984: 21, 23). The differing participation of the sexes in the ritual activities of the community is often expressed in terms of religion being the prerogative of men and magic of women (Westermarck 1933: 34, 62, 92; Barclay 1964: 266; Eickelman 1976: 132; Bourdieu 1977: 41, 89; Fernea 1972: 388–9; R. Tapper 1979: 164–5; Friedl 1980: 163–4) or through the emphasis on the involvement of women in spirit possession rituals (Lewis 1971; Constantinides 1977; Morsy 1978). Lewis argues persuasively that it is not justifiable to explain spirit possession rituals in Islamic communities as manifestations of pre-Islamic survivals (1986: 98–106). In fact, we do not need to assume that the differing participation of men and women in the ritual activities of the community reflects either the survival of pre-Islamic beliefs and practices or different rates of conversion. The reasons for the differing participation lie in the pattern of gender relations characteristic of Muslim cultures, and the view that the burden of religious orthodoxy is carried primarily by men who, through their own religious devotion, are also responsible for the religiosity of their women. There are numerous reports on women being either discouraged or prevented from taking active part in public religious rituals (Lewis 1966: 64; Fernea 1972; Dwyer 1978a: 16–17; Beck 1980: 44–5, 50; Trimingham 1980: 62, 74, 83; Friedl 1980: 162–3; Wikan 1982: 59). The resulting image of Islam is a strongly masculine one and 'most writings about Islamic belief and practice concern male, not female, participants, although general recognition of this is still not made by most writers' (Beck 1980: 39). As Dwyer noted, this masculine image of Islam had been so compelling that the impact of women upon Islam has been largely ignored (Dwyer 1978b: 585). We are only gradually gaining a better understanding of the involvement of women in Islamic religion from recent studies of religious beliefs and practices of women in Muslim societies (Fernea 1972; Dwyer 1978b; Beck 1980; Friedl 1980; Tapper 1983; Tapper and Tapper 1987). These studies show that women are not necessarily less concerned than men with religious duties, for the ritual practices in which they come to be involved fully compensate them for their exclusion from public Islamic rituals monopolised by men. The result is the emergence of distinctive male and female rituals, or possibly even distinctive male and female styles of religiosity. This 'sex-linked religious pluralism' has generally been interpreted as reflecting the frustrations which women feel due to their subordinate position in a male-dominated society (Beck 1980: 51–2; Lewis 1986: 100–2) and some analysts have gone so far as to suggest that the more segregated men and women are, the greater is the likelihood that women will develop their separate rituals and ceremonies (Fernea 1972: 390–1). These explanations help us to understand why women have developed their own forms of religiosity and why they have their own Islamic rituals which differ from those of men; they also help us to understand why women are the main carriers of non-Islamic beliefs and practices which persist in Islamic settings. They do not tell us, however, anything about the meaning and significance of such beliefs and practices in the overall system of notions which constitute the culture of the society in which they exist.

The neglect of the latter question is conspicuous in most anthropological studies of belief and ritual in Islamic societies. It seems that the main reason for this is the failure to link together the two areas of research interest in which much progress has separately been achieved in the past decade: gender and practised Islam (N. and R. Tapper 1987: 71). As it is generally assumed that in Muslim societies women are subordinate in secular social life as well as in the sphere of ritual, the studies of 'popular Islam', i.e. Islam as understood and practised in specific communities, have paid virtually no attention to the beliefs and practices which are perceived as deviant from the local Islamic orthodoxy. Their relation to the mainstream of Islamic practices remains largely unrecorded and certainly unanalysed. Ferneas suggested some time ago why this may be so:

Perhaps Western Orientalists have considered Sufism in its myriad forms to be the exhaustive popular response to the formalities of orthodox Islam. Yet as anyone knows who has been attentive to the patterns of behavior and belief in Middle Eastern villages (or towns, or cities), these worlds are full of holy men and women, shrines, incarnate forces of good and evil, evil eyes, incantations, and ceremonies, all of which help to make up a cosmological outlook in which formal Islam plays an important but by no means exclusive role. Thus, our ignorance of the special religious role of Middle Eastern women is only a subcategory in our general lack of knowledge of popular belief systems. (Fernea 1972: 391)

The result of this is that the existing anthropological studies of Islam are characterised by a concentration on only those beliefs which are held in common by all elements of society; for the most part, they lack any sensitivity to the differentiation of interests and beliefs within a society. As it is men who define the local orthodoxy, the studies of Islam as it is locally understood and lived by still show the bias to which Ardener drew our attention some time ago: 'a bias towards the kinds of models that men are ready to provide (or to concur in) rather than towards any that women might provide' (1972: 136). As long as this attitude persists, the contending views expressed in practices and beliefs seen as unorthodox are assigned to a non-real status; in terms of Ardener's metaphor, they are 'mere black holes' (1975: 25) in the universe as defined by the dominant Islamic ideology. Of course, this attitude runs counter to the anthropological premise, recently stressed in the context of an 'anthropology of Islam' by N. and R. Tapper, 'which insists that understanding depends on consideration of *all* the various beliefs and practices of a single community' (1987: 72). They suggest that 'different aspects of a religious system may be the province of one sex or the other, and an understanding of any particular Islamic tradition depends on examining *both*' (Ibid.). Ferneas formulated the problem in similar terms:

We must also consider that all men pass through the world of women, and as they wait to take their places as young men in a man's world, they cannot help but be influenced by the example of their mothers, sisters, aunts, and grand-mothers. Thus the opportunity for women to influence the shared conception of Islam has never been lacking, despite the conspicuous absence of most forms of joint ceremonialism. To be properly understood, Islam as lived today must be viewed through the contributions of both men and women among the faithful. (Fernea 1972: 401)

An additional reason why the total array of beliefs and practices of particular Islamic societies remains poorly understood stems from the fact that anthropological studies of these societies have failed almost completely to pay any attention to symbolism and symbolic classification (the major notable exceptions are Chelhod 1973; Bourdieu 1977 and Ahmed 1984). Because models and ideologies that differ from the dominant ones typically expressed by men who are the society's official spokesmen, are often expressed in symbolic form, they have remained undiscovered and unrecorded.

As in many other Muslim societies, among the Berti the customary rituals (*'awāid*) are more distinctly the concern of women than men, whereas the religious rituals are predominantly male affairs. These two classes of rituals thus obviously express certain views of men and women and say something about the relations between them. Before discussing the commonsense knowledge that underlies the customary rituals, in the next chapter I describe the models of gender relations which the Berti hold.

2

Men and women

The model of gender relations explicitly expressed by Berti men is that of male dominance and female subordination. This is the model which is most forcefully asserted and most often invoked. It tallies well with the patrilineal ideology of the Berti and with their notions about kinship distance according to which kin related through men are seen as closer than the genealogically equidistant kin related through women.

The notions of the greater importance of men and lesser importance of women are expressed metaphorically in the often heard saying *rājil giddām, mara wara* ('the man is in front, the woman behind'). This saying summarises what is seen as the appropriate form of women's deference towards men as well as the leadership role of men: it is often quoted by both men and women to explain and justify the fact that men make all major economic and political decisions and, in their roles as fathers, brothers and husbands, are charged with responsibility for the conduct and morality of women. It informs a great deal of everyday behaviour of men and women in public: when the husband and wife go together to the field, well or market, he walks in front and she follows a few paces behind or, more typically, the man rides a donkey and the woman follows on foot. If a woman is to cross a man's path, she stops and lets him cross in front of her; if a man and a woman are to enter a household, he always goes first through the gate. If a man and a woman ride the same camel, the man sits on the saddle and the woman sits behind him, on the camel's back. The relations between the sexes expressed in the model of male dominance and female subordination also inform the temporal sequence of various actions. Men are served food first and only then do the women serve themselves, both when ordinary food is served and when a communal meal is arranged during festive occasions. This range of examples could be extended.

Gender symbolism

The explicitly asserted notions of the greater importance of men and lesser importance of women are corroborated by certain aspects of gender symbolism. When left and right are used as symbolic vehicles for expressing the relations between men and women, men are associated with the right and women with the left. But rather than right and left, it is bones and flesh that are the main symbolic vehicles for expressing the preeminence of men and the subordinate position of women. The association between bones and masculinity and flesh and femininity derives directly from the theory of procreation according to which the bones and sinews of the child are created from the sperm and the child's flesh from the woman's blood. The sperm and menstrual blood get mixed into a clot inside the womb which grows bigger and bigger after each subsequent intercourse. After about two months sinews appear inside the hitherto undifferentiated clot and thereafter bones gradually develop within the sinews. In accordance with the Koran (23:14), the Berti maintain that only after the bones have been formed does the flesh of the child begin to grow around them and the sinews.

The sinews and bones provide not only support for the outer flesh. They are seen as an active and the flesh as a passive part of the body: the movement of the body emanates from sinews; the sinew moves the bone and the flesh follows the movement of the bone to which it is attached. This notion is supported by common experience: a person with a flesh wound is still able to move around but anyone who has broken a bone is no longer able to move his arm or leg.

This theory of the mechanics of the body is projected into the image of the social order through the mediation of the symbolic association of men and women with bones and flesh respectively. That a man goes in front and a woman behind then becomes much more than a particular social convention: it is natural and it cannot be otherwise because 'men are bones and women are flesh' (*rujāl udām, awīn laham*).

Just as the flesh of the child cannot start forming inside the womb before the sinews and bones have developed, so it cannot exist later without the support of the bones. The skeletons of dead animals lying around each village are pointed out as ready proof of the durability of the bones and perishable nature of the flesh.

The notion of the primacy of bones over flesh becomes an appropriate metaphor for expressing the closeness of kinship. The Berti recognise all those to whom they can trace genealogical connection as their kin (*ahal*). Within this category, kinship distance is evaluated in terms of genealogical distance from ego, but kinsmen are closer than genealogically equidistant kinswomen and any connection traced through a man is closer than that traced through a woman. Thus of two genealogically equidistant kin, the one who is paternally related is closer than the one who is related maternally. The Berti express this idea metaphorically by saying *ubahāt udām, umahāt* (or *akhwāl*) *laham* ('the paternal kin are bones, the maternal kin (or maternal uncles) are flesh') or literally by saying: '*Amm agrab min al-khāl, ubahāt agrab min akhwāl* ('the father's brother is closer than the mother's brother and paternal kin are closer than maternal kin (lit. maternal uncles)').

The greater importance of men and lesser importance of women is not only explicitly asserted and symbolically expressed through the association of men with bones and women with flesh. It is also evident in certain customary practices following the birth of a child. Although, as a rule, men desire boys and women desire daughters, only the birth of a boy is celebrated as *gisma kabīr* (a great gift from God). It is greeted by *izāna* (the shouts of *Allāhu akbaru*) and possibly by the father firing a gun. When a girl is born, women make *zagharāt* (ululation). For the neighbours these are not only clear signs that the woman has delivered, they also inform them immediately about the sex of the baby. The father celebrates the birth of the first child by slaughtering a goat for the neighbours; this, however, is very often not done when the first born is a girl. On the other hand, a man who has only a daughter or daughters may kill a goat when his wife has at last given birth to a boy.

Gender relations and the sexual division of labour

Although women accept the leadership role of men explicitly asserted in the men's model and fully subscribe to the symbols of maleness and femaleness which legitimise it, they nevertheless explicitly assert a different model of gender relations, particularly when they are among themselves and when they are either criticising men's actions or laughing at their expense. It is a model which depicts men as dependent on women. This model is not only explicitly expressed by women; it is also made clearly manifest to both men and women through the division of labour between them.

There are tasks which can be, or customarily are, performed by only one sex. Only men slaughter animals, attend to camels and sheep at pasture and only men spin cotton, sew, make leather bags, ropes and wooden utensils. Most of the tasks which are customarily performed by women can be performed by men if there is no woman available for them. Thus only women harvest, but a man can do so if there is no female labour available in the household: he cuts the millet stalks with an ordinary knife instead of the special harvesting knife which is an implement handled solely by women. Only women winnow the threshed grain; again a man can do that in emergency. It is, however, always shameful for him if he has to resort to winnowing and he takes special care not to be seen by others when doing it. Only women husk millet in wooden stamps-mills, grind flour, cook meals and brew beer.

There are thus tasks for whose performance women depend on men and tasks for whose performance men depend on women. The mutual dependence of the sexes on one another is, however, not symmetrical, and it is this asymmetry which the women's model emphasises. When portraying men as dependent on them, women invariably stress that a woman can easily live on her own, as indeed many do, either temporarily when her husband is away from the village, or permanently if she is divorced or widowed. When there are only women present in the household and they want to kill a chicken to entertain unexpected guests, they ask either a neighbour or any passing man to do it for them. Fresh meat is rarely eaten by the Berti and slaughtering is very rarely done. Furthermore, meat can always be purchased from the butcher's in the market without resort to one's own slaughtering. The dependence of women on men is thus only occasionally made manifest in the existing division of labour; moreover, it can easily be alleviated through the culturally recognised alternatives. When a woman who lives on her own needs a leather bag, a rope or a utensil which only men manufacture, she can buy it in the market. If she has camels or sheep which have to be grazed outside the village, she is certainly wealthy enough to be able to hire a herder.

Unlike a woman, a man cannot live on his own. Although he could harvest his own field and thresh and winnow the grain all by himself, he cannot cook his own food and brew his own beer. A man at most brews tea, at least occasionally. He himself buys tea and sugar; its regular purchase in the market accounts for a better part of each household's recurrent expenditure, which the man is able to control more effectively if he himself directly controls the money spent on tea and sugar. He himself resorts to brewing tea if he is anxious to control not only the direct expenditure on this commodity but also its consumption. Even if he entrusts the women with making tea, he usually keeps sugar and tea in his trunk or bag and allocates it in modest quantities to his wife or daughter to do the brewing.

Apart from occasionally brewing tea, men cook only the meat of sacrificial animals for communal ritual consumption. They must, of course, resort to cooking when they are temporarily without women, either on pasture with sheep or camels or when travelling. In the latter case, they are always particular to camp outside a settlement where they can cook for themselves without being seen by others.

It is unthinkable for a man to do everyday cooking; it would be a clear indication that he has failed to maintain a woman to care for him as a woman should for a man. As food and beer have to be prepared daily, the men's dependence on women for the performance of these tasks is made manifest continually and more directly than the women's dependence on men. Moreover, there are no culturally accepted alternatives to the preparation of food in the household: although beer can be obtained from the market, cooked food cannot.

The asymmetry in the mutual interdependence of the sexes which the women's model of gender relations emphasises, manifests itself in yet another important way which the women are always ready to point out. The man's status as an elder who has a right to take part in settling disputes, i.e. his status in the public domain, depends on his being *rājil be bētu* (a man with a house) i.e. on being the head of his own household, in which his daily sustenance is provided for him by his wife.

It is the man's role in the public domain and the general domestic orientation of women that is being emphasised in the men's model: men dominate because women hold no position of authority in the public domain. Only men travel far afield while women stay at home all the time. The overall passivity of women, which accounts for their subordinate position, is expressed by saying that a woman does not fight (*al-mara mā 'indu aza*) nor carry out litigation (*al-mara mā 'indu gadīya*); even if she is involved in a dispute or the case concerns her directly, she is represented by a man, either her father or husband, under whose protection she is.

The women's model clearly privileges the domestic domain; women have power over men, not only directly because of their monopoly over the processing of food, but also indirectly in that it is the man's status within the domestic domain that is the basis for the ascription of his status in the public domain. For this reason women can see themselves as making the men what they are. A man without a wife has no status in the public domain. He acquires it only after he has been married and established his own house. If he then subsequently gets divorced, he does not lose his status of an elder, but his prestige certainly becomes significantly impaired.

I have already pointed out that the source of the woman's power is her monopoly over the processing of food. A woman acquires this power and thus becomes a fully adult member of her sex only after she has been associated through marriage with a particular man and, through this association, acquired her own domestic fire which is the symbol of her independent existence. Until her marriage she is not a woman (*mara*) but a girl (*binei*). An adult unmarried man is not referred to as a boy (*walad*) but as a bachelor (*'āzib*). As such, he is not yet a full man; he becomes one only when he has his own house. Just as a woman acquires her power only through her association with a particular man, a man acquires his authority only through his association with a particular woman. Women thus depend for their power on men and men for their authority on women.[1]

But this relationship is again not symmetrical. The status of a woman as the mistress of her own fire which enables her to lead her independent existence is not affected by her subsequent divorce; after her divorce she does not revert back to the status of a *binei* fully subject to the authority of her father. She becomes *'azaba* (divorcee), who can maintain her own independent household (as most divorcees do) virtually for the rest of her life and who controls all her own economic transactions as well as all her subsequent relations with men, either as lovers or future husbands. If she remarries, and even if her new husband has never been married before, her new house (if the husband does not simply move in with her) will not be built in a ritual way as her first house was, nor will her new hearth.

Unlike a woman, a man after divorce reverts to what he was before his marriage – an *'āzib* (bachelor) with a concomitant loss of prestige awarded to proper elders, i.e. *rujāl be bētum* (pl. of *rājil be bētu*). Whereas a woman needs to be married just once to be for ever after a fully adult member of her sex and, in fact, as a divorcee gains a considerable degree of economic autonomy which a married woman does not enjoy, a man has to be continuously married to qualify as an adult member of his sex. If he does not have his own house, he can regain his full status in the public domain only in advanced age when the fact that he is an elder of a group of his own descendants (even if he lives as a dependent in a household of one of his children) is more important than the fact that he has no house of his own, and when his status as a *shāib* (an old man) becomes more significant than the fact that he is technically an *'āzib*.

The existence of female power in male-dominated societies has been recognised and given due attention in numerous studies of gender relations. Analytically, it has mostly been presented as part of women's strategy to subvert the all-pervasive male dominance or as their defence mechanism against it (cf. Cronin 1977; Ullrich 1977). More generally, women's refusal to cook or sexually to cohabit with their husbands has been pointed out as a usual strategy to which women resort to gain their

---

[1] I use the term authority in the sense of 'the right to take certain decisions' and power as the 'ability to affect or secure such decisions as one wishes, although these decisions are either not allocated as rights, or are the rights of other persons' (Smith 1960: 19).

way in the face of men's dominance or as a strategy to sanction men's actions or conduct which they consider inappropriate (Paulme 1963; Cohen 1971; Strathern 1972: 27, 45–46; Rosaldo 1974: 37; Lamphere 1974: 99). The Berti women too exploit their power in the course of their strategic behaviour. The woman's favourite stratagem in a dispute with her husband, or when she feels that she has been maltreated by him, is to refuse him sexual access and to refuse to cook for him. The latter is publicly much more telling than the former, for sexual inter-course is an act properly carried out only in the privacy of one's own house whereas men whose homesteads neighbour on one another often eat together either in the guest shelter of one home or in the open space outside the homestead's fence. This communal meal starts after the dishes have been brought from all the respective households either by the men's wives or by the boys who already take their meals with other men. Although it is not polite to comment on it openly, the fact that a dish has not arrived from a particular house is noted by all and the situation becomes more humiliating to the man concerned the longer it persists. The man's situation is not immediately obvious if he takes his meals with other male members of his household inside it. But he cannot, of course, go on without food forever, and a man who is eventually forced to seek his nourishment elsewhere than in his own house displays his dependence on a woman by publicly manifesting his defeat by her.

When a woman refuses to cook for her husband, she does more than merely inconvenience him: she challenges or indeed effectively defies the authority which he holds over her. Their control of the processing of food thus provides Berti women with more than a convenient strategy through which they can keep male dominance within bearable limits. They clearly construe it as giving them power over men and, seizing upon this notion, they construct their own model of gender relations: men may be strong, they may be in front and they may hold authority over women but it is only through their ultimate dependence on women that they are what they are. Women may not be free agents but then neither are men: they have to operate within the limitations set up by women's control over the processing of food.

Both men and women are aware of one another's models and they are thus faced with the problem of accommodating the alternative model within the terms of their own to be able to maintain the latter's credibility. One of the possible ways of solving this problem is to deny the credibility of the alternative model by seeing it as a fiction not sustained by the known facts. Rogers (1975) has analysed this solution to the perceived discrepancy between men's and women's models of gender relations in peasant societies where, she argues, women explain away the men's model of male supremacy as 'myth' which it is just simply convenient for them to subscribe to openly so that they can maintain their 'real' power. The problem with this analysis is that the analyst has to take sides in the actor's dispute and concur with either the women's or men's view as the 'true' one. It would be possible to arbitrate in this way on the validity of the views expressed by Berti men and women, and to follow the strategy of most analyses of gender relations, in which their quality has been evaluated in terms of men's and women's respective control over strategic resources (Friedl 1975; Rosaldo 1974; Sanday 1974), or in terms of their exercise of political or ritual power. To see the control over resources or the exercise of political or ritual power as determined directly on the basis of sex would be, however, too simplistic in the case of the Berti. Only the right to make political decisions is ascribed to a person directly on the basis of sex, in the sense that this right is not granted to women and that only a man can be an elder. But here again it is not merely the elder's sex that is decisive but also his status as a household head.

The control of strategic economic resources is not ascribed on the basis of a person's sex. It accrues to the household head who need not necessarily be a man; when a woman is the head of her own household, her control over the household's resources is equal to that of her male counterpart. The woman, however, assumes the position of a household head only when there is no male to occupy it. Even then she can never assume the role of a village elder, which automatically accrues to any male household head. Although the Berti women can thus assume certain typically male roles, in direct comparison to men, the possibilities open to them are still greatly circumscribed. In this respect the relationship between the sexes could be seen as distinctly asymmetrical. But I see the weakness of such a conclusion as deriving from the necessity to introduce into the analysis some measure of objective significance of certain facts that goes beyond the Berti's own perception of their significance.

That a different perception is involved in the Berti's own view of the situation is suggested by the fact that, if not verbally, then certainly in their behavioural practice, both men and women fully admit the validity of the other's model. Women accept their subordinate position and in doing so admit and reaffirm the dominant role of men; they do not deny men their authority over them. Equally, men recognise and accept their dependence on women and in so doing admit and reaffirm women's power. In their practical attitudes, both sexes thus subscribe to a different model of gender relations than the one which they assert verbally. The credibility of the verbally asserted models, which is perpetually undermined by this practical attitude, is maintained through the imposition of specific meaning on the myth which deals explicitly with the origin of gender relations.

It tells that a long time ago, there were people called Farkh al-Ganān (or Abunganān) who lived up on a hill. They were all women and their children were all female.[2] They were tall, big and strong, their bodies covered in hair. They hunted wild animals in the plain below the hill by simply chasing them and living on their meat which they ate raw as they had no fire.

One day they saw a strange light glittering in the plain below the hill. They were frightened and ran up the hill to hide themselves. Next day, the light was there again. The Farkh al-Ganān were curious about it and went to investigate. They came upon a group of riders; they were all men and their horses were all male.

The light which so frightened the Farkh al-Ganān was a fire. The men were sitting around it cooking their food on it. They gave the Farkh al-Ganān some to eat. It tasted much better than the raw meat and the Farkh al-Ganān asked the men for the fire so that they could use it too for cooking their food. The men said that they would give the Farkh al-Ganān the fire if they would give them their daughters for wives who would bear them children. The Farkh al-Ganān agreed and so they exchanged their daughters for fire with the men.

The myth is a short, simple and straightforward story. It has not the elaborate, repetitive structure which, according to Lévi-Strauss, is typical of myths. Even so, it exhibits a scheme of 'oppositions governing its organization behind the mythical "discourse"' (Lévi-Strauss 1966: 136): above/below (the women on the hill, the men in the plain), nature/culture (animal existence of the hairy women without fire, the cultural existence of the fully human men with fire), wild/domesticated (women hunting wild animals, men riding domesticated horses), raw/

---

[2] The female sex of the original inhabitants of the hill is not only explicitly stated in the story; it is also clearly implied in their name (Farkh al-Ganān), which is the name of whitish pigeons living in the mountains. When mating, they make a sound which reminds the Berti of women wailing after a death. The Berti believe that these birds were originally women who went on lamenting the death of their husbands long after the funeral instead of accepting it as God's will. God was angry with them and punished them by transforming them into birds. There exists also a vague notion that the birds are descendants of the people who originally inhabited the tops and slopes of the hills. This is also the reason why the Berti do not eat them.

The word *ganān* has no meaning in itself but *farkh*, although used for both sexes in its sense of 'children' (*farkh al-jidād* – domestic chickens; *farkh al-hamām* – young pigeons) has a clear connotation of femininity like *awlād* (lit. sons), although also used for both sexes in its sense of 'children', has, nevertheless, clear connotations of masculinity. *Farkha* is also a female slave.

cooked (women eating raw meat, men eating cooked food), asexual/
sexual reproduction (the women bear children on their own, the men
need women to bear them children), etc. I do not intend, however, to
analyse the 'syntax' of the myth (Lévi-Strauss 1970: 7–8) and to unravel
the ultimately unverifiable hidden meaning of the myth encoded in the
interrelations among the elements of its underlying structure of binary
oppositions. I propose instead to concentrate on its 'message', i.e. its
subject   matter   (Lévi-Strauss   1970:   199)   or   what   Willis   called
'"conceptual-affective structure", itself formed from the basic "bricks" of
mythological thought – sets of binary discriminations' (Willis 1967: 521).

   Probably the most important message of the myth is that the source of
female power does not lie in women's nature and does not stem from
anything that is inherently or naturally feminine and over which neither
women nor men exercise control. It is socially constituted and rests on
women's control of specific cultural resources, and not on the forces of
nature. This control, in its turn, is the result of the original transaction
which occurred when men and women were brought together for the
first time.

   While both men and women agree on the source and nature of the
female power, they substantiate their respective models by imposing
different meanings on the transaction described in the myth.

   In the following discussion, I consider the myth first from the male
and then from the female point of view.

Female power and the male model of gender relations

Men can be fully aware of the women's power and feel no need to deny
it because the myth clearly implies to them that it was men who gave
women their power in the first place. It shows that the fire, which makes
possible the female monopoly of the processing of food on which their
power rests, was given to them by the men. The myth not only
establishes men as the original masters of fire; it also puts across the
message that they surrendered their control over it to women voluntarily. Hence everything the women are today is due to men. In this
respect, the myth clearly attempts to explain away the contradiction
between the model of gender relations according to which men dominate women and the model according to which they are dependent on
them. It suggests that men have been dominant all the time and that
even those aspects of gender relations which seem to indicate that
women have some power over men are really understandable only
within the context of the all-pervasive dominance of men over women.
Any power the women may hold over men, they hold because the men
ceded it to them.

The women, however, did not obtain the fire for nothing; in exchange for their access to it, they gave themselves to men. This exchange ended the independent existence of the sexes and the apparent ability of women to reproduce themselves without men: the women lived on the hill with their children who were also all female; the myth does not tell anything about the men's children but it clearly implies that they had none before they met the women, and could have none, otherwise there would be nothing they needed the women for. From now on, the complementarity of sexes in reproduction has been established. This too can be seen as the result of the men's wishes: the women received fire in exchange for surrendering forever their apparent ability to reproduce themselves and by making themselves dependent on men in the discharge of their reproductive power.

Even though female power may be seen as confirming the ever existing male dominance and superiority, for it exists only because men agreed to it in the first place, such power nevertheless perpetually challenges the asserted men's dominance which can be maintained only if men succeed in controlling it, i.e. if they succeed in doing what they had successfully done in the mythological past. To control female power is at once the men's main problem and the price they have to pay for having acquired their children through their transaction with women. In practice it means that they can sustain as credible the model of their dominance only insofar as particular men continually succeed in controlling the power of particular women.

In the existing analyses of female power in male-dominated societies, this dominance (unless perceived as a 'myth') has been conceptualised as something taken for granted and accepted by both men and women; it has been conceptualised as basically non-negotiable and women have been seen as mobilising their power, or resorting to it, merely in defence against the dominance of men.

This is certainly not how the Berti conceptualise the relationship between men and women. For Berti men, particularly, male dominance is an ideal that exists in actuality only insofar as it has been successfully negotiated; it is as if the Berti men were saying that a man *should* be in front and *is* in front if he successfully manages to do so against the ever-present opposition of female power. It is rather that female power is taken for granted and accepted by both men and women as an ever-present, non-negotiable force and men dominate only insofar as they successfully manage to curb or control it. This makes sense, of course, once we realise that power is probably the only attribute whose possession cannot successfully be pretended; it exists only as long as it is real. On the other hand, men's authority over women, and any other authority for that matter, has to be perpetually claimed and exists only insofar as it has successfully been claimed by some and recognised by others. I would suggest that this is also the reason why the men's model is more often and more loudly asserted than the women's model. The Berti men speak and the Berti women, for the most part, do not, not because the men dominate and the women are subordinate, nor because men are articulate and women inarticulate, and even less because it is in their nature to do so. The men speak because they cannot afford not to if they want to sustain the notion of their dominance; women do not speak, or at least not as often as men do, because they do not need to (cf. Weiner 1976: 233).

Within the context of the women's model of power relations between the sexes and the male model of authority relations, it also makes sense that polygyny and great numbers of children are seen as signs of a man's prestige for they are also signs of his successful management of his relationship with a particular woman or women, made possible through his effective control of female power.

Although the manifestations of women's power are limited, the means by which a man is able to cope with a woman who refuses to yield her power are even more restricted. He has no monopoly of control over anything a woman cannot obtain without his cooperation. He can, of course, withhold sex as a woman can, but then he is harming himself and not the woman for he is refusing himself children. If everything fails, he can divorce his wife. The asymmetry of the divorce right which accrues only to the husband but not to the wife, as is typically the case in Muslim societies, has again been seen by a number of analysts as a manifestation of male dominance. This interpretation is construed on the basis of specific cultural experience according to which divorce leaves the woman destitute, and on the unwarranted presupposition of its universality. The Berti cultural experience is distinctly different. For them divorce is the ultimate sign of the man's failure to control his wife. It is the sign of the victory of her power over his authority. He has lost and he also suffers most. While a divorced woman can go on living on her own, a divorced man has to attach himself to his mother or sister, at least for his sustenance if not in terms of his actual residence in her household. He can manage to obtain his sustenance from his own household only if there is an adult daughter in it who can cook and brew beer for him. Whatever the case, divorce for him means changing his dependence on one particular woman for a dependence on another; it makes the validity of the female model blatantly obvious.

I mentioned before that female power is conceptualised not as deriving from women's nature but as socially constituted. The myth suggests that women hold it because it was granted to them by men in the course of the transaction which took place between them. As it is power that has been relegated, its exercise involves responsibility and its abuse by women to get their own way is seen by men as irresponsible behaviour. Because men experience women's power when, in their view, women have abused it, they tend to see women as generally irresponsible. *awīn mā lēhum gharat kabīr* ('women do not care much'), the men say. In its turn, this irresponsibility of women provides the rationale for the men's control over them. That women hold power is thus, on the one hand, an outcome of men's dominance and superiority while, on the other hand, women's power makes the male dominance a necessity.

Male authority and the female model of gender relations

Just as men are fully aware of the women's power and do not try to deny it, the women do not try – even privately – to deny men's authority; they recognise and accept it. To be able to do so, they have to reconcile their view that they hold power over men with their other view that men have authority over them and they have somehow to answer for themselves the obvious question of why they accept the dominant position of men when at the same time they claim to hold power over them.

It is again the myth about the origin of gender relations that provides the women with an answer to this question. As I mentioned before, the myth clearly establishes that the source of women's power is not their nature but their monopoly over the control of fire established in the course of the original transaction between the sexes. While the myth reassures the men that they have not lost their control over fire as a result of the women's cunning but handed it over to them in an exchange from which they came out as winners for they gained through it their ability to have children, it reassures the women that the original exchange was not forced on them by the men either. The myth clearly implies that the women themselves longed for the cultural existence of men and in this it reminds them that it was their wish to abandon their animal-like existence and, through acquiring fire, to become full human beings as the men were. They acquired the fire from the men, not simply because men gave it to them of their own accord and hence can take it again from them should they so wish, but in exchange for their procreative power. By agreeing to bear men their children, the women paid for it. From the time of the mythical transaction between the sexes, the children have belonged to the men and their patrilineal affiliation is the cultural expression of this fact.

That children belong to their father and not to their mother, as the

Berti usually express it themselves, is on the one hand the result of the mythical transaction, and on the other hand the source of men's authority over women and of the senior men's authority over junior men. Thus the father has authority over his sons and daughters, and the husband has authority over his wife because his rights in her were transferred to him by her father. The Berti express the asymmetry of the conjugal relationship by saying that it is a man who marries a woman and not a woman who marries a man. Like female power, male authority too is perceived not as natural but as socially constituted; in this context it is logical that the brother–sister relationship is the most egalitarian of all cross-sex relationships.

The women existed independently of men before the mythical transaction took place but they lived without culture in an animal-like state. Through this transaction they acquired their control of fire which enables them to exist independently of men in a fully cultural and human way; men lost the possibility of their independent existence in the exchange. Through surrendering their control of fire to the women in exchange for the possibility of having children, the men became dependent on women both for their sustenance and for procreation. By making men dependent on them, women acquired their power over them. But even nowadays a woman can lead an independent existence only after she has been associated through marriage with a particular man and, through this association, acquired her own domestic fire and hence the means of her independent existence. In this respect, each marriage re-enacts for each individual couple the original mythical transaction between the sexes. The contemporary practice thus rein-forces the message of the mythological story that the power over men which women enjoy results from a specific transaction between men and women and is part of the reciprocity between them. Women gained power in the mythological past and have power now only through their dependence on men; they have to recognise male authority because it is only through their dependence on particular men that they gained the monopoly of food processing which is the source of their power. Typically, a woman gains this power only through marriage, i.e. through individually entering into a relationship with a particular man that was part of the original exchange between the sexes described in the myth.

In accepting men's authority, women do nothing more than accept the myth as a dogma (Robinson 1968: 123), for the myth tells that women became full human beings through striking a bargain with men. It is part of their human morality to honour the conditions of this bargain. The men certainly see it in this light: they consider a woman that abuses her power and openly defies her subordinate position not only as an irresponsible but also as an immoral creature. The women's view of men's morality is the same. They too consider men's authority as being conditional on their fulfilment of the obligations which were part of the original bargain between the sexes. They see men's obligation toward and responsibility for their children as the counterpart of their right in them.

Produce not intended for direct domestic consumption is controlled and sold in the market by the male head of the family which forms the domestic group. His behaviour is seen as responsible as long as he uses the money to buy clothes for the family members, to pay the legitimate expenses like poll tax, damages and his sons' bridewealth, or to reinvest it in livestock from which his children will benefit and which will devolve on them through inheritance after his death. His behaviour is seen as irresponsible when he uses the money for buying things for his own personal use (like a horse, a gun or a sword, for example), or when he uses it to pay his own bridewealth for an additional wife. It is typically in situations like these that a woman will exercise her power and refuse to cook for her husband who, in her opinion, has behaved in an irresponsible way.

In the same way in which the man's authority over his wife or daughters guarantees that they will behave in a responsible manner, each man's dependence on a particular woman guarantees that he too will behave responsibly.

The symbols of the interdependence of the sexes

By asserting their own model of gender relations while admitting the validity of that asserted by the other sex, both men and women tacitly acknowledge that the sexes are mutually dependent on one another.

When women explicitly assert the men's dependence on them, they point out that it arises from the fact that only women process food. Because they do the everyday cooking, women also regularly handle and control fire, including the collecting of firewood which is the women's task; men help only occasionally when the logs are too big for a woman to split with an axe. Embers are perpetually kept alive in the hearth on which cooking is done. If the fire goes out, it is hardly ever relit by a match. Instead, glowing embers will be obtained from a neighbouring house and every evening before the main meal of the day is prepared, women and children going around with broken potsherds to ask for the embers from a neighbour are a common sight in every Berti village.

To attend to the fire is a job for women, and a man who does it is like a man who cooks: he is despicable. This, I would suggest, is the reason why the Berti despise blacksmiths and why hardly any Berti men earn their living by making and repairing iron tools. Most blacksmiths among the Berti are from the neighbouring Zaghawa population. From the casual remarks about blacksmiths which he heard in Darfur, Macmichael likewise got the impression 'that it was not so much to their dealing with *iron* that they owe their inherited unpopularity as to their employment of *fire* for the purpose' (Macmichael 1922, vol. 1: 89). Berti men, of course, need to and can use fire occasionally. A man has a fire in his own hut to keep him warm during the winter nights. Men use fire when cooking the meat of a sacrificial animal in the village mosque, when they extract oil from melon seeds which they use for treating leather bags, when they are burning the old straw in the field before sowing or when they are burning down the nests of birds in the fields. Any time men need to light their fire, they start it with embers which a woman gives them from the hearth in her hut. This makes manifest to both men and women that it is women who control fire, and at the same time it makes fire a powerful symbol of men's dependence on them.

Beer also symbolises men's dependence on women, although not as vividly as fire. As I mentioned before, men can obtain beer from the market, whereas for cooked food they depend solely on their wives, daughters and sisters. That beer, nevertheless, has symbolic significance in the context of gender relations and the sexual division of labour through which they are sustained, is attested by the fact that women who sell beer in the market are despised. A beer-seller subverts the women's power by making beer available to men for cash. Because through her actions she undermines female solidarity *vis à vis* men, her conduct is seen as immoral and it makes sense that she is considered a prostitute: sex and food (including beer) is what other women give to men free. As a woman can also refuse to grant them to a man, they are the signs of her power over him. In this context, it is logical that a woman who sells one of them is seen in the same light as the one who sells the other. This interpretation is supported by the fact that it is women rather than men who express more readily their condemnation of those who sell beer for cash. On the whole, men do not see anything wrong with women selling beer, unless they are their kin. That beer-sellers are mostly women who live on their own correlates with the fact that it is often the only source of income for them as well as with the fact that they are less subject to the control of other men and women.

The objects for which women depend on men also have their symbolic significance. As mentioned before, the women depend on men for meat and wooden utensils but they can again obtain both these commodities from the market. From the male point of view, butchers and wood-carvers are analogous to the women selling beer; they too are despised.

The Berti consider both the killing of animals and the cutting of trees as taking life. Both activities are morally justified and seen as necessary as long as they are performed to satisfy personal needs; they become despicable acts when carried out for profit. I would argue, however, that butchers and woodcarvers are despised not because of the profit which motivates them but again because they undermine the men's relationship with women by making available to them commodities for the supply of which they would otherwise be dependent on men. This interpretation is again suggested by the fact that it is men, rather than women, who express their contempt for butchers and woodcarvers.

As it is fire which clearly and vividly symbolises men's dependence on women, which the women explicitly assert and of which the men are often made acutely aware, it is only logical that the myth which explains how men and women came into contact for the first time, also explains the origin or discovery of fire.

In a manner typical of myths (Lévi-Strauss 1967), the Berti myth also contradicts the ethnographic reality to which it is supposed to refer. In it, it is men who use fire to cook and women who procure meat; or at least the myth is silent about the men hunting while specifically mentioning it as the women's occupation. It is obvious that, just as the men transferred their control over fire to women, the women must have transferred their control over the provision of meat to men, so that the division of labour existing in the mythological past could become that which prevails in the present.

Control over three different resources could be seen as the object of the transaction between men and women described in the myth: children, fire and meat. Control over all three of them is significant in shaping the existing relations between men and women. But while the myth is all about the transfer of the control over children and fire, it is completely silent about the transfer of the control over meat. At best it merely implies, but does not spell out that the killing of animals, and hence the ultimate control over the distribution of meat was ceded by women to the men following the coming together of the sexes. It also leaves it unclear whether anything like that happened at all; maybe the food men cooked on their fire was meat and in the mythological past both sexes hunted.

There is thus a clear asymmetry in the explicit attention which the myth gives to control of fire (the symbol of men's dependence on women) and to the right over children (the symbol of men's dominance) on the one hand, and in the explicit attention to fire and meat (the symbol of women's dependence on men) on the other hand. This asymmetry reflects, of course, the present-day relative significance of fire and meat as symbols of gender relations. But considering that meat has, nevertheless, its symbolic significance in the context of these relations, it appears reasonable to assume that there may be more profound reasons behind the deliberate vagueness about the role of meat in the mythical transaction between the sexes.

In the asymmetrical structure of its narrative, the myth seems to justify the relations between the sexes as portrayed in the men's model. By refusing to acknowledge explicitly that women might have ceded their control of meat and their rights over their children voluntarily to the men in the same way in which men ceded their mastery of fire to the women, the myth dismisses from consideration the possibility that the present-day gender relations may be the result of the wishes of both sexes and not only of the men. In this respect, it can be read as a 'sociological charter' (Malinowski 1948: 120) of male supremacy and seen as a 'male' story which puts across the men's view of gender relations which does not necessarily have to be shared to the full extent by women themselves.

Given, however, that the myth is perpetuated by women,[3] it seems to be more accurate to see it as a charter of women's power and as a 'female' story which puts across the women's view of gender relations. If the women made explicit that this control passed from them to men after the sexes had come together for the first time, the original exchange between men and women would cease to balance. It would be one in which the women clearly lost because, in exchange for their gain of control over fire, they ceded to men not only control over children but also control over the distribution of meat. If the control over meat

---

[3] It is perpetuated by women and always told alongside other mythological stories, fairy tales and humorous narratives of amusing events which happened to fictitious contemporaries.

Story telling usually takes place in the late evening. Older boys and girls often meet at a specific place in the village to play riddles in the evening and, particularly on moonlit nights, children play various games in the open spaces in the village often watched by a group of women sitting in front of one of the houses, and often younger men who joined the women to joke with the younger of them. When boys and girls have exhausted their supply of riddles or when the children grow tired of their games, or the audience of watching them, they turn to some woman who is known as a good story-teller and ask her to tell a tale. All present assemble around her to listen. A story-telling session can last for hours with one story following another and with people demanding to hear their favourite ones.

Less frequently a woman will tell stories in the privacy of her house. It is always the children of the house who ask her to do so but the audience consists of all the people in the house and possibly a few visiting neighbours.

Telling stories is by no means a prerogative of older women; a woman of any age can be known as a good story-teller. Men too tell stories. They do so when they are among other men, typically when relaxing after a communal meal and especially when there are visitors around. But their stories are different from those told by women; they are usually accounts of their various travels or narratives of other events in which they were involved.

were seen as part of the original transaction, women would have lost, for they would have yielded more to the men than they received in return.

Ultimately, it is not really important whether we understand the myth as a 'male' or as a 'female' story. What it says about the transaction between the sexes makes good sense both to the women who tell it as well as to the men who listen to it. The silence about meat entering into the original transaction between the sexes suits them both for only if control over meat is not made into an issue, can female power and male authority be seen as balancing out and the notion of sexes as inter-dependent, which is shared by both men and women, be sustained as credible. At the same time, the symbols which are the object of explicit verbal discourse can thus have become truly 'collective representations'. The crucial point is, however, that while anything is capable of being used as a symbol, not everything is so used. When the attention focuses not on the analysis of the symbolic structure as such, but rather on its production, i.e. when the question asked is not 'how are the symbols logically related' but 'what is the logic of symbolic practices', it is no longer sufficient to see the symbolic structure as a 'body of represen-tations seeming to be the production, emanation or reflection of an undifferentiated society or culture', for 'at least in their being employed and uttered, symbolic relations vary as a function of the identity and position of those who use them and of those to whom they are applied' (Augé 1982: 60).

As Augé rightly pointed out, 'one cannot give an exhaustive account of mytho-logics if one simply reads myths' (Ibid.). The logic of symbolic practices embodied in the mythological story can only be grasped when the myth is understood for what it is to those who tell it and who listen to it, i.e. when it is comprehended as a 'charter' in Malinowski's sense. In following Malinowski's sociological insight, we can go beyond his axiomatic assumption of the rationality of the natives' beliefs and conduct and *show* that the various forms of expression of belief are themselves a rational response to their experience. That the logic of symbolic practices is a rational response to the actors' experience holds true, not only for the symbols of gender relations embodied in the mythological story about the first contact between men and women, but also for the symbols employed in the numerous *'awāid* or customary rituals. But here I am already anticipating the chapter.

3

Milk and water

As I have explained earlier, religious knowledge and understanding and the degree of adherence to Islamic prescriptions and prohibitions vary among the illiterate villagers, the *fugarā* and other pious men and women, and among those who have been to school and exposed to at least some degree of exegesis of the Koran and *ḥadīth*. The same variation exists among these three categories with regard to the understanding of and attitude to the customary rituals (*'awāid*). Although they distinguish them conceptually from practices which they classify as religion (*dīn*), the illiterate villagers do not see the two classes of rituals as mutually incompatible or contradictory. Their easy co-existence within the encompassing system of notions constituting contemporary Berti culture is the main problem which I am going to explore in the following chapters. When I describe the knowledge which underlies the customary rituals, it has to be borne in mind that it is the knowledge of the illiterate villagers – both men and women – who still constitute the absolute majority of the Berti. In the last chapter I then describe the views and attitudes of the literate and the pious.

Apart from a few brief invocations occasionally uttered, the customary rituals do not encompass a verbal tradition, a corpus of standardised texts, and there are no myths explicitly linked to them. Apart from the invocation of God's name at the beginning of a ritual performance – which is a standard practice at the beginning of any activity, whether it be eating, sowing, travelling, or whatever – the rituals are carried out in virtual silence. In fact, the silence is frequently seen as a precondition of the ritual's efficacy. Most rituals are carried out through symbolic action rather than defining themselves in explicit instructions and verbal formulae. Thus, the proper understanding of the knowledge from which the rituals stem requires the grasp of the Berti system of symbolic classification as well as the analysis of the symbols which the rituals employ. Such analysis indicates that through their symbolic structure the *'awāid* reflect at least a partially different set of notions from those expressed through practices which are classified as *dīn*.

Gender relations, symbolic classification and customary rituals

The saying that a man is in front and a woman behind, which metaphorically summarises the greater importance of men and lesser importance of women, informs also the orientation of men and women in space in ritual situations and their temporal sequencing. During communal prayers, the men stand in rows in front of the rows of women facing east towards Mecca. After the first ears of millet have been brought from the field into the homestead during the ritual called *dukhla*, the grain is crumbled off from them into a winnowing basket jointly by a woman and her husband, or any other man if her husband is away or if she has no husband. When this is done, the man holds the ear with his hand in front of the woman's hand. When boys and girls are circumcised together, boys are circumcised first.

When the Berti are asked in general terms which of the four cardinal points is the most important one, they mention east without any hesitation. It provides for them the primary ritual orientation in that the officiants in various rituals always face east (Holy 1983: 274). But it is not always the direction which one faces that is important. When dancing, the girls always stand in a row facing east and the boys dance in a row opposite them facing west. At first, I found this puzzling. When I asked the dancing men why they are facing west and not east, they replied: 'Why, we want to see the girls of course.' This answer made sense in terms of something that is so obvious that nobody feels any need to mention it explicitly: east is in front and west is behind and since a man is in front of a woman, he must also be east of a woman. This principle informs the spatial orientation of men and women in various ritual situations. For example, during the first stage of the wedding (*fātha*), the representative of the bride sits facing east opposite the bridegroom's representative; the man representing the groom is again in front and the man representing the bride behind him. The same principle informs also the details of other customs. When a newborn baby is a boy, the placenta is buried inside the yard to the right side of the entrance to the hut. As the entrance is always oriented towards the south, it is buried to the east of the entrance; when the baby is a girl, the placenta is buried to the left, i.e. to the west of the entrance to the hut.

Berti lateral symbolism exhibits in its own cultural idiom a general contrast of values in that the right is clearly the auspicious and left the inauspicious side (Holy 1983). When left and right are used as symbolic vehicles for expressing the relations between the sexes, men – as in other Muslim societies (cf. Bourdieu 1977: 142, 157) – are associated with the right and women with the left. So when a man and a woman are seated together, the woman sits always on the left, and when husband and wife sleep together, the wife lies on the left from her husband. When a man and a woman sit together facing east, as they would be positioned in all ritual situations when they are likely to sit beside one another, the woman is also to the north and the man to the south and in this way the woman is again at the inauspicious northerly and the man at the auspicious southerly side. In the same way the wife is at the inauspicious northerly side of her husband when they lie on the bed, for the right position to sleep in is with the head towards the west. People fall asleep lying on their right side and if their heads are towards the west, they face the auspicious south in their sleep. When they get up in the morning, they rise from the bed again facing south.

I mentioned already, however, that bones and flesh, rather than right and left are the main symbolic vehicles for expressing the preeminence of men and the subordinate position of women. One of the notions underpinning the symbolic association of men with bones and women with flesh is the theory of the mechanics of the body in which the bones and sinews are conceptualised as the body's active parts and the flesh as its passive part. In their connotations of activity and passivity, the metaphors of bones and flesh reflect the perception of men as active and women as passive. But rather than bones and flesh, hot (*harr*) and cold (*bārid*) are the most common symbols of activity and passivity, and the words 'hot' and 'cold' are semantically employed to indicate metaphorically activity and passivity in numerous idiomatic expressions. The market is cold when it is poorly attended and the business is slow. A fast donkey is said to walk 'hot' (*yamshi harr*). A poor man has a cold hand; what is implied in this saying is that his hand is inactive: he does not give anything to anybody because he has nothing to give. At the same time the life of poverty is hot because a man who has not enough food in his house has to travel in search of it to distant markets and to his kin in distant villages or has to seek employment as a wage labourer in distant places. A hard life is hot because people hard pressed to make ends meet have to be more active than the more fortunate ones. Any hard and strenuous work is always described as hot: weeding, drawing water from the well, looking after animals at pasture outside the village, distant travel, etc. The fertile soil is hot and an exhausted field is cold. A soft and quiet voice is described as cold, an agitated and loud voice is hot and a quarrelsome person is referred to as hot. Weak millet beer is cold, strong beer is hot: it induces intoxication quickly.

The metaphorical association of hotness and activity and coolness and inactivity makes it possible for the Berti not only to assert that 'bones are hotter than flesh' (*al-udām sukhn min al laham*) but to collapse their perception of the respective roles and activities of men and women and the symbolic association of bones and flesh with gender into the explicitly expressed imagery of men as hot and women as cold (cf. Bourdieu 1977: 112, 157). This notion is not only descriptive of the cultural experience of gender characteristics; it is also normative in clearly ascertaining what the relations between specific men and women should be. It indicates that it is wrong when the values of masculinity and femininity are reversed: the general view is that when the wife is hot by being talkative, quarrelsome and domineering and her husband is cold by being submissive and unable to control and dominate her, their household will not prosper and, most probably, their marriage will not last.

Hot is often considered better than cold when these adjectives are used in their literal meaning: for example, hot meat is always preferable to cold and everybody considers the cold nights in winter to be distinctly unpleasant; the hotter the tea, the better and cold tea is considered undrinkable, etc. However, when 'hot' and 'cold' are used metaphorically, i.e. employed as symbols, coldness is always unequivocally ascribed a positive and hotness a negative value: *Ayi hāja bārid kuwayis* ('anything cold is good') is an expression I have often heard in the context of various ritual performances.

This notion derives from the association of activity with fatigue (*ta'ab*) and inactivity with leisure (*rāha*). Fatigue is undesirable and plenty of leisure is the ideal, although, needless to say, often unattainable. The life of a merchant is the object of general envy and an ideal which ambitious men strive to attain one day: a merchant does not need to weed or to engage in other strenuous tasks; he makes a good living by sending others on errands for him while he himself sits in the cool shade of his shop the whole day chatting with people.

The positive value of coldness and negative value of hotness derive not only from the association of hotness with activity in general, but also from its association with malevolent, harmful or dangerous activity in particular. People with the evil eye, who are able to cause damage by merely looking at persons or things, are described as having a hot eye. The eclipsed sun is considered to be particularly hot because of its malevolent effect on health, well-being and general prosperity. An eclipse of the sun is a sign of forthcoming wars, deaths (particularly of important people) and other misfortunes. Some Koranic verses are hot. A man not well trained to use them in healing or writing of amulets would make himself prone to attack by devils (*shayātīn*) and could become mad if uttering or writing them. These are typically verses which the sorcerers use for their malevolent practices. Also some of the names of God are hot which makes *zikr* (counting of rosary beads) a particularly dangerous undertaking, especially if done on a large scale. The message of the Koran is more powerfully expressed in a handwritten than in a printed book, particularly if the calligraphy is outstandingly beautiful. Such a book is hot and it has to be handled with special care. If an oath is to be sworn on the Koran some people bring their own books for the purpose and if the book is hot, it can be dangerous to the whole village community. It can be brought into the village only after a special *karāma* has been arranged. Before this is done, the book is placed in a tree outside the village. There are stories in circulation which describe how a tree wilted and eventually died after a hot book had been put into it.

The association of men with bones and women with flesh gives rise not only to the conceptualisation of men as hot and women as cold. It is also often pointed out that 'men are bones because bones are hard and women are flesh because flesh is soft' (*rujāl udām 'ashan udām gawī, awīn laham 'ashan laham layyin*). This association and the perceived strength, toughness and endurance of men and the weakness of women are again collapsed into the explicitly expressed imagery of men as hard and dry and women as soft and wet.

Like the opposition between hot and cold, when 'hard' and 'soft' are used as symbolic vehicles for contrasting values, it is always softness which is ascribed a positive and hardness a negative value. A stupid person is said to have a 'hard' head (*rāsu gawī*) and an intelligent person has a 'soft' head (*rāsu layyin*). A common proverb says that 'fear softens the head' (*al-khōf belayyin al-rās*) – it makes people see reason. Less frequently, men are referred to as heavy and women as light. This imagery is explicitly related to the notion of the leading role of men. It has been explained by pointing out that the man is heavy and the woman light because 'the man is in front and the woman behind', and because it is the man who marries a woman and not the woman who marries a man. Nevertheless, in its own terms, the opposition between 'light' and 'heavy' expresses again the same contrasting values as the other symbolic oppositions used to portray the gender relations: 'light' connotes good, auspicious and desired qualities, 'heavy' the opposite.[1]

Unlike other Muslim societies (cf. e.g. El Guindy 1966: 249; Bourdieu 1977: 157), men are associated with odd numbers and women with

---

[1] For example, the eclipse is referred to as the death of the sun or moon. It is a sign that misfortune will befall the world and it is said that 'the earth became heavy' (*wata biga tagīl*).

even ones. For example, in a ritual preceding the harvest, a woman brings an odd number of millet ears from the field if her firstborn child is a boy and an even number if it is a girl. Similarly, an odd number of baskets with grain is brought to the mother at the birth of a boy and an even number when the newly born baby is a girl. At the same time, the Berti talk of odd numbers as bitter (*murr*) and see them as inauspicious whereas even numbers are sweet (*hillu*) and hence auspicious. They justify this belief by reference to Koranic verses which say that God created everything in pairs (particularly Koran 43: 12). In placing a positive value on even numbers and a negative value on odd ones, the Berti differ from most other Muslim societies which generally consider the odd numbers to be auspicious and the even ones inauspicious (see e.g. Westermarck 1926, vol. 1: 141–2 1933: 117–18; Barclay 1964: 222). The exception to the Berti system of classification is the number seven which is the most auspicious number of all. When the Berti explain the reason for this exception to their general rule, they mention that there are seven days of the week and, more importantly, that God created seven heavens (Koran 65: 12, 78: 12, 23: 17), seven earths (Koran 65: 12), seven seas (Koran 31: 27) and seven gates of hell (Koran 15: 44). The number seven plays an important role in the various books from which the *fugarā* learn the 'secrets of the Koran', and the belief in its auspicious qualities is, no doubt, reinforced through the magical Islamic lore which the Berti see as part of religion.

The most common symbolic imagery for portraying gender relations is the opposition between white and black. Again unlike some other Muslim societies (see e.g. Bourdieu 1977: 141, 157; Abu-Lughod 1986: 131, 143; Ahmed 1986: 30; 1988: 187), the Berti refer to women as white and to men as black in numerous contexts.

In the explicit system of symbolic classification, white, cold soft and even are clearly auspicious or, as the Berti express it 'good', 'nice' or 'lucky', in opposition to black, hot, hard and odd which are inauspicious, or 'bad', 'ugly' or 'unlucky'. This symbolic association of women with auspicious qualities and men with inauspicious ones thus presents a different image of the relations between the sexes from that expressed in the model of male dominance and female subordination. But it does more than that: it expresses in symbolic form the gender relations which women assert in their own model, when they depict men as dependent on them. It is difficult to imagine how the set of notions contained in this model could have emerged in a society in which both men *and* women adhere to Islam, which clearly stipulates the preeminence of men; it is not altogether implausible to assume that it predates the conversion of the Berti to Islam. The fact that the Berti have presumably not been exposed to Islam for all that long makes this assumption even more plausible. But whatever the possible historical origin of the notions about the preeminence of women, nowadays they easily co-exist with the Islamic faith and constitute an integral part of Berti culture.

As I explained before, women see themselves as making the men what they are. The same notion is expressed through the symbolic association of women with whiteness.

Any time I asked people why women are white and lucky and men black and unlucky, or in what sense are women white, the exegesis (if it may be called that) invariably was that it is because only women give birth. The response to my inquiries into the connection between 'white' and giving birth was always the same and it can best be indicated by quoting the actual answer of one man:

A woman gives birth to a boy who will grow to become a *fakī*, a ruler, sultan, a rider. A woman is like a pot in which porridge is cooked: its back is black but its belly is white. A woman's back is also black but her belly is white. A woman who does not give birth is like a male (*dakar*). She is black. [At this point the man's son interrupted him and said that all women are white.] A man's back is black and his belly is also black.

This exegesis is rather elaborate by Berti standards. But however brief any exegesis was, it always stressed that a woman gives birth to a *fakī*, a *shēkh*, a ruler or a rider. Invariably only typically male roles were mentioned. The exegesis, whether provided by men or women, quite clearly expresses the same idea which women make explicit when they talk about the relations between men and women and when they formulate the model of gender relations which depicts the women as making the men what they are. This model is also quite clearly expressed through most customary rituals and their symbols, and informs them to a much greater extent than does the model of male dominance and female subordination.

Customary rituals
The customary rituals range from large public events which last several days and which have a distinctly 'alerting' or 'arresting quality' (Lewis 1980: 19–21) to privately performed actions in the domestic setting which are over in a few seconds. They are quite numerous and I shall describe some of them in detail later. Here, to introduce the discussion of ritual symbols and officiants, I mention just three of them as examples.

The bridegroom's entry into the bride's house
Before sunset on the day preceding the bridegroom's first entry into the bride's house, he rides on a female camel or a female donkey from his

house to the nearest *hajlīd* tree (*Balanites aegyptica*) which grows east of the village. If he rides a camel, a small girl (either his sister or one of his patrilateral cousins) sits on it behind him and another woman leads it by its bridle; if he rides a donkey, it is again led by a woman. The groom's head is covered by a white scarf and he holds a drawn sword in his hand. In front of him walk women who beat earthen drums and behind him more women who sing and dance; one of them carries a rolled mat under her arm, one carries a pot of millet beer and another a basket filled with grain on which there are two or three small dishes, one filled with melted butter, another with water and possibly a third filled with milk, if any is available. The bridegroom is accompanied by a large procession of people who came to attend the feast which was held in his village that day. The women ululate and some of them wave palm leaves above the bridegroom; the men brandish swords and sticks above their heads; some men fire their rifles into the air and young men race their camels against the procession to the shouts of *absher* (from *bashar*; to bring good news). When the procession reaches the *hajlīd* tree, it walks round it three times in an anticlockwise direction. After that two women squat on the western side of the tree and, facing east, smear its trunk with melted butter and, if possible, milk. They dig a shallow hole on the western side of the trunk into which they sprinkle some grain and pour water and beer. The mat is then spread west of the tree, so that the

Figure 4 A bridegroom mounted on a camel is led to a *hajlīd* tree by women
beating earthen drums

groom can stand on it facing east, and cut off a small branch with his sword. The branch is put on the grain in the basket. A woman then carries this back to the village accompanied by the procession, singing and dancing.

Next morning before sunrise, the groom is taken to the house of his bride, again riding on a female camel or a female donkey. A woman again carries the *hajlīd* branch stuck in a basket filled with grain. Upon the groom's arrival, a woman from the bride's house anoints the neck of the camel or donkey with milk or melted butter and sprinkles the groom and the animal with water. The groom is lifted from his mount and carried into a temporary shelter built of blankets and pieces of cloth inside the homestead. The bride is brought to him later in the morning. The groom sits in his shelter facing east and the bride is seated on his left side. The groom does not speak until he is asked, by one of the bride's kinswomen, with what he greets the bride. He mentions either a cow, sheep or a goat and this animal, which he then later points out in his herd, is his gift to his wife and becomes her individual property. All present pronounce *fātha* and the assembled *fugarā* may read a few passages from the Koran. After that the bride leaves the groom who remains alone in his shelter for the rest of this and the following day. On the third day, young men and women from the village build a flat-roofed shelter (*rakūba*) in the bride's homestead from poles and straw collected

Figure 5 A man puts an ear of millet, *gongobai*, a *hajlīd* twig and a palm leaf onto the top of the roof of a new house

from the homesteads in the village. Only the green bark with which the poles are tied together and the long twigs on which the straw is tied (and which have to be fresh to be flexible) may be brought from outside the village. Before sunset, the groom and bride enter the shelter. This again is ritualised. Two women facing east smear the middle pole of the shelter with melted butter and/or milk and again dig out a shallow ditch on the western side of the pole into which they sprinkle some millet and pour water. The ditch is then covered with earth into which the women stick the *hajlīd* branch which the groom cut off, palm leaves and an ear of millet. Palm leaves and white strings are tied round the right wrists of the groom and the bride. The couple spend seven days in the shelter; at night they are alone, during the day young men and women from the village come to greet them and to chat with them. After seven days the bridegroom returns to his house. The bride remains secluded in her house which she may leave only after the women have plaited her hair on the fortieth day. From then on, the bridegroom comes occasionally to spend a few days with his wife in the shelter built for them in her parents' homestead until, after a few years, the couple eventually establish their own independent household.

Hut building
A hut is built by men, who complete the whole construction of the conical roof on the ground. Before they begin to thatch the roof, two crossed sheaves of straw are tied to the western side of the roof by a man facing east and then the second thatch, again consisting of two crossed sheaves, is placed in position on the eastern side of the roof opposite the first thatch. When the thatching of the roof is completed, an ear of millet, a *hajlīd* branch and a stick held in a bent position by a piece of string (*gongobai*) are stuck vertically into the head of the roof. Before the men lift the roof on its supporting poles, two women walk round it three times anticlockwise and sprinkle it with water and *dashīsha* (crushed millet mixed with water).

A new mare
When a man brings home a new mare from the market, his wife smears the animal's head three times with milk, melted butter and sometimes *dashīsha*.

Ritual symbols
Whatever the rituals' complexity and whatever the occasions at which they are performed, the Berti see them as being primarily concerned with bringing about the well-being, safety, health, comfort and pros-

perity of those who undergo them or on whose behalf they are performed, or as averting any misfortunes or dangers from them. They are also aimed at bringing about the fecundity of people, animals and cultivated crops. When, for example, women sprinkle the roof of a newly built house or smear the central pole of a shelter, the explicitly stated aim is to ensure that many children will be born to the couple, that they will have many animals which will prosper and multiply, that their crops will grow well and that they will have plenty of grain. When a woman smears the head of the mare which her husband has brought from the market, the aim of her action is both to make sure that her husband will encounter no danger when riding and that the mare will be fertile.

Like the Kwaio, the Berti are 'more concerned with means than with meanings, with results than with reasons, with controlling than with explaining' (Keesing 1982: 49) and any exegesis of how the rituals achieve their envisaged ends is totally missing. The Berti simply do not know how it happens and they do not show any intellectual curiosity in this matter; their attitude is distinctly pragmatic. In their view the rituals achieve their envisaged ends as long as they are properly performed, and people are more concerned with making sure that the right things

Figure 6 Women sprinkle the roof of a new house with water and *dashīsha*

are done at the right time by the right people, than with contemplating why these things are right and why some people are the right people to do them. But even in the absence of explicit exegesis, I do not think we go beyond the Berti understanding when we see the rituals as based on the idea that the natural engendering of life or healthy growth is the source of the ability to engender healthy life, growth and well-being through ritual means. This idea is expressed through a number of instrumental symbols (Turner 1967: 32) to which the rituals resort: water, *hajlīd* branches, millet ears, beer, *dashīsha*, milk, melted butter, flour, palm leaves, white cloth, beads and strings, water melons and cucumbers or pumpkins.

In one sense, water is a paradigmatic token of cold which, for the Berti, is an auspicious quality and in the system of symbolic classification stands in opposition to the inauspicious hot. It was often explained to me that it is sprinkled on people and things to cool them, which amounts to rendering them auspicious. Many times, when informants described how a particular ritual is performed, they mentioned sprinkling with 'cold water' or spontaneously explained that people or things are sprinkled with water 'because water is cold'. However, water becomes an appropriate symbolic vehicle in rituals whose aim is to bring about well-being and prosperity not only because it is cold, and hence auspicious, but also because of its purifying potency and, most importantly, because it is a source of all life. This idea is expressed by the Berti in equating water with a life force of spirit (*rūh*). According to them, all living things – humans, animals, plants – have a spirit and they die when the spirit leaves them. Since spirit is water, death is desiccation: all living things die when they dry up, when their spirit leaves them. The wrinkled skin of old people is the sign of their drying up; their spirit is gradually leaving their bodies. Their legs die first and they cannot walk but the upper part of their bodies is still alive. This is because the spirit is slowly rising from the lower part of the body into the chest until it eventually escapes through the mouth, leaving the body forever with the last breath.

I mentioned before that the Berti consider the killing of animals and cutting of trees as taking life and that these activities are seen as despicable acts when carried out for profit. Similarly, they despise the selling of water which to them is equivalent to trading in life. When I stayed in a Berti village, I hired a young man to supply me with water from the well on a regular basis. Once a woman from the village asked me if I was paying him for his services. When I confirmed it, she opined that the man was wrong in taking money, 'Water is *rūh*,' she said, 'it should not be sold.'

I have never elicited any coherent exegesis explaining why *hajlīd* branches are used in numerous rituals. The clue to understanding their efficacy as instrumental symbols was, however, provided in the way people often talked about *hajlīd* outside the specific ritual situations. It is obvious from this talk that the Berti see *hajlīd* as endowed with auspicious qualities. It acquires this meaning due to the fact that it is the only tree that remains green throughout the whole year. Green itself is an auspicious colour and the qualities of being soft and wet, which the Berti attribute to *hajlīd*, also have distinctly auspicious connotations. Just as women, who are also spoken of as soft and wet, are seen as auspicious in opposition to men who are dry and hard,[2] *hajlīd* is auspicious in opposition to all other trees which shed their leaves during the dry season. The fact that it stays green for the whole year clearly indicates the vitality of its *rūh* which, in turn, makes it an appropriate symbol of life, vigour and health.

Its ability to engender life and health is also suggested by its perceived practical utility. Its bark is used as a medicine for indigestion and internal pains. It was also used for washing cloths before cheap soap became widely available from the market. Its fruit, called *lalōba*, is sweet and it is eaten as a delicacy in much the same way as dry dates, biscuits or sweets bought from the market. After its thin hard skin has been removed, it is also boiled in water to which wheat flour and sugar are added to prepare a sweet non-alcoholic drink called *nīsha*. Its hard inner core is oily. It is bitter but when boiled in water it loses its unpleasant taste and provides emergency food in times of famine which, because of its nutritive value, is generally considered superior to any other emergency food like *makhēt* (*Boscia senegalensis*).

Hajlīd is spoken of as the 'sultan' of trees and the 'best' or 'most powerful' tree of all. One of my informants compared *hajlīd* to the government: *Hajlīd, huwa zayi hakūma. Hakūma mā shadīd? Hakūma fi nās wa hu fi shajar* ('Hajlīd is like government. Is government not strong? Government is among people and it [*hajlīd*] is [like this] among the trees'). The *hajlīd* tree is thus clearly seen as having the ability to sustain people in times of famine and I would suggest that it is precisely its ability to ensure the continuation of life which makes it a suitable instrumental symbol in rituals specifically aimed at ensuring long and healthy life and general well being and prosperity.

It is also pointed out in support of *hajlīd*'s mysterious qualities, that its fruit has the ability to turn blood into water. I was told that if *hajlīd* fruit is thrown into the spilled blood of a slaughtered animal nobody would

---

[2] The symbolic equation of men with dryness and women with wetness has been reported from elsewhere in the Muslim world (see e.g. Bourdieu 1977: 112, 142, 157).

know that an animal was slaughtered for it would seem that water was spilled on the ground. A *hajlīd* tree is never cut down. In fact, the Berti would consider such an act a sign of madness.

The cult of saints plays no significant role in Berti religion but there are a few tombs (*gubba*) of saints in the Berti area mostly visited by women unable to conceive or by the sick who have tried other treatments in vain. The patient walks round the tomb seven times anticlockwise and pours a libation of milk and water into the potsherds placed at the tomb above the feet, head and middle of the buried body. In the same way, a sick person, for whom other treatments have failed, may be taken to two *hajlīd* trees growing close together in the east–west line. Milk is poured at the trunk of each tree and a person accompanying the patient takes him or her by the hand and together they walk round the trees seven times. If the patient shows no sign of recovery, the visit to the trees is repeated after seven days.

Because of its own vitality and the ensuing ability to engender and sustain life, a *hajlīd* twig is stuck into the roof of a newly built house to ensure the health and prosperity of its inhabitants and a *hajlīd* twig is planted on the spot where the placenta or the circumcision blood is buried to ensure the well-being of the newly born child or the circumcised girl. The situations in which *hajlīd* appears suggest that it is used to protect and to bring about desired ends which are mostly beneficent but can also be malevolent. It is, for example, believed that the power of a *hajlīd* tree can be mobilised to kill an enemy by sorcery (*sihir*). The sorcerer again pours milk at the trunk of the tree, walks round it seven times anticlockwise and, facing south, which is the direction of the dead (Holy 1983: 275–6), pronounces the name of his enemy and shouts the curse *Allāhu akbar 'alē. Alla yarmi* ('Be the greatness of God against him. God throws down').

It is not impossible that the notions about the auspicious qualities of *hajlīd* and its extensive use in various rituals predate the adoption of Islam among the Berti, for the cult of this tree was probably common in Darfur before the spread of Islam; Slatin Pasha at least mentions its existence among the Bideyat (Slatin Pasha 1896: 114–6).

What *hajlīd* may do for people in times of famine, millet does year in and year out, Although, objectively speaking, the viability of the Berti economy rests on the successful combination of cultivation and pastoralism and on the integration of subsistence activities with production for the market, the Berti themselves ascribe prime importance to agriculture. To them, it is the basis of all existence and all those who do not cultivate are considered foolish. This is one reason why they look with contempt on the neighbouring pastoral Meidob who grow only a little millet. The Berti attitude to agriculture is strikingly opposed to that of the nomads; for the latter, cultivation is humiliating work, for the Berti it is an activity which brings *ajr* and attracts God's blessing more than any other. I have argued elsewhere that their agricultural ethos is a cultural elaboration of an optimum survival strategy whose rationality may be obscured most of the time but becomes clearly apparent in acute crisis (Holy 1988). The Berti consider themselves autochtonous in the area which they now inhabit in northern Darfur and which, as far as our records go, has always been subject to a considerable fluctuation in rainfall. It seems reasonable to assume that their culture with its strongly expressed emphasis on cultivation as the source of all wealth and the ultimate guarantee of their sheer physical survival, is the result of the Berti's numerous past experiences of natural disasters. Paradoxically the drought and several successive years of total crop failure in the early 1980s distinctly reinforced the Berti agricultural ethos. The importance of millet cultivation for long-term survival was manifestly demonstrated to everyone by the fact that those who relied on pastoralism and the exchange of cattle for grain for their subsistence were worse equipped to survive the drought than those who relied primarily on agriculture and had adequate supplies of grain to tide them over at least some of the years of total crop failure. The importance of agriculture for long-term survival was stressed by informants who pointed out, with obvious satisfaction, that during the drought even the neighbouring nomads, particularly the Zeyadiya Arabs, who rely normally on the purchase of millet from the market, resorted in increased measure to the cultivation of their own food. When the return of the rains made the pursuit of agriculture possible again and the fields were again sown and weeded and the harvest collected and threshed, these tasks were performed with a distinct joy and relish, and people were taking obvious pride in the fact that they had harvested millet to last them for a year and, in some cases, two.

Once we appreciate the importance which the Berti ascribe to millet for their sustenance and physical survival, we can also appreciate why it should become an appropriate instrumental symbol in rituals aimed at securing long life, health and prosperity. Also, once we appreciate that the motivation of water and millet as ritual symbols derives from their ability to engender and sustain life and growth, we can appreciate the motivation of beer and *dashīsha*: they become appropriate instrumental symbols due to the fact that they are both a mixture of these two life-engendering substances.

Other instrumental symbols employed in customary rituals derive their motivation from the overall emphasis on the reproductive powers of women as the source of symbolic creativity or symbolic inducement of growth and life: milk, melted butter, flour, palm leaves and white cloth, beads and strings. Their symbolic significance is explicit. All Berti are able to explain that they are used to achieve the goals of the rituals because they are white. Other specific objects used in rituals acquire appropriate symbolic significance in virtue of their feminine gender (female donkeys and female camels, water bags made of the skin of female goats) or in virtue of being typically female things: flour, butter and also *dashīsha* fall into this category as well as palm leaves from which women plait mats. Water melons, cucumbers or pumpkins which are used as instrumental symbols in a few rituals, have been selected because they are soft and wet and thus again possess one of the qualities by which the Berti characterise femininity in opposition to maleness.

All these objects are particular tokens of the same symbolic whole in which the symbolism of white and femininity clearly give meaning to one another. In this respect all symbolic vehicles used in particular rituals express the same basic idea. Although this is certainly true at the level of the ritual's symbolic meaning, when informants describe various rituals, they put a much greater emphasis on milk than on any other symbol. This is readily understandable. While flour or piece of white cloth, for example, are suitable symbolic vehicles simply because they are white, the way in which milk is motivated as a symbol is much more complex.

In at least one respect, milk is opposed to water and this opposition is expressed in their colour. Milk is white and water is black: 'the water in the well appears to be white but it is black', I have heard. 'White' and 'black' also, of course, symbolise the opposition between the sexes; the sexual opposition between milk and water is also expressed directly by conceptualising water as masculine. That a female cannot procreate without a male was often exemplified by pointing out that the earth does not produce without water; some informants went even further and explicitly stated that the earth is female (*intāi*) and the rain is male (*dakar*).

The relevant oppositions are indicated in the following table in which the terms in each column are linked together through metonymy and metaphor:

milk	water
white	black
earth	rain
female	male

Not only does each term in the left-hand column stand in complementary opposition to the corresponding term in the right-hand column, but all the terms in the left-hand column are particular tokens of the same symbolic whole which stands in its totality in opposition to the symbolic whole expressed by the terms in the right-hand column. As the cohabitation of male and female is necessary for engendering new life, and as the rituals are predicated on the idea that the natural engendering of life is also the source of the ability to engender healthy life, growth and well-being through symbolic means, the opposition between white milk and black water could be taken to indicate the opposition and complementarity of female and male in ritual action. Smearing with milk and sprinkling with water might then be seen as a symbolic expression of the complementarity of the sexes on which the creation of life depends. There is no doubt that the series of oppositions between white : milk : earth : female and black : water : rain : male is part of Berti symbolic thought, but it does not follow from this that the symbolic meanings of water and milk which derive from this opposition also necessarily inform their rituals. Two facts would rather suggest that they do not: the motivation of milk as a ritual symbol and the symbolic connection between water and woman.

Just as water is a paradigmatic token of cold, milk is a paradigmatic token of white and all that it symbolically stands for. Asking why white is auspicious, I did not elicit any coherent exegesis but I was often told: 'White is nice, is not milk white?' Although all women are white and therefore lucky in opposition to men who are black and unlucky, a nursing woman is particularly lucky. It is, for example, a particularly auspicious omen if a nursing woman is the first person one sees in the morning when leaving the homestead.

Apart from smearing with milk, smearing with butter is an important part of virtually all customary rituals. The use of butter is rationalised by pointing out that butter is made of milk. But some people do not realise this motivation of the symbolic practice and use oil, if there is not butter available, or even animal fat, focussing quite obviously not on the fact that butter is but a different form of milk, but on the fact that it is fat. But those who understand the rituals properly do not agree; when animal fat was used instead of butter, I have heard people say that 'the luck is not in the animal, the luck is in the milk' (*bakhīta mā fī bahīma, bakhīta fī laban*).

Milk is, however, an important ritual symbol not only because it is white, but also because of its ability to make people and animals grow and stay healthy. It is precisely these qualities which people stress when talking about it. So they point out that a cow, when it is not milked, calves regularly every two years; a milking cow calves only after three years. A lamb will itself give birth after a year, if it has had full benefit of its mother's milk. If the sheep is milked and the lamb thus deprived of proper nutrition, it will itself lamb only after two years. The nutritive value of milk for humans emerges from its comparison with the ordinary diet of millet porridge and relish. People allege that children who eat only this food after they have been weaned are undernourished: they have thin arms and legs and their bellies are swollen. Children who drink milk are healthy. They mature faster and age slower ('A boy who drinks milk becomes a man in seven years; a boy who eats porridge is not yet a man even at the age of fourteen'). The perceived beneficent qualities of milk are sometimes stretched so far that its pragmatic and symbolic values appear to fuse: 'A man who drinks milk before he goes to search for a stray animal will find it. He will find money in the market and everything he does will be successful.'

Most importantly, the ritual importance of milk derives from the fact that it is a symbol of procreation. A male (*dakar*) is always characterised by not having milk or children: an informant was once talking to me about the star called *sihēl* of which he said: *Hu dakar wihēdu, mā 'indu laban, mā 'indu 'iyāl* ('he is a male alone, he does not have milk and he does not have children').

Like other Muslims (Altorki 1980), the Berti prohibit the marriage between children who have been suckled by the same woman even if there is no genealogical relationship between them. The notion of shared substance, which is implied in this prohibition, emerges also in other contexts and throws additional light on the ritual importance of milk.

The Berti believe that some people rise from the grave after they have been buried and live as *nabātī* (ghosts).[3] They ultimately die and remain forever in the grave only after they have risen seven times. The Arabs Beni Ḥisēn, Beni Halba, Beni Badur, Beni 'Omrān, Ben Atif, Beni Faḍul, Beni Jalāl, Jilēdād, Nasari and Bideriya (in Eastern Darfur) and the Meidob of Urdato clan are all *nabātī*, the Berti say. During the day, a *nabātī* lives in the mountains but at night he comes to the fields to eat millet and water melons and he even enters the village to eat food kept in the yards of the homesteads and to drink water from the storage jars. A *nabātī* looks like an ordinary human being except that he does not blink and, some say, does not greet others. If one meets a stranger at

---

[3] Belief in the reincarnation of people who have died, missed paradise and returned to live a normal human life as ghosts (*ba'ātī*) is widespread in Northern Sudan (Trimingham 1949). Macmichael mentions it as a popular belief in Darfur which 'attributes to all the Fur a power of metamorphosis, and the word *nabātī* there is a common expression of abuse implying that the person to whom it is addressed is in his second existence, that he had died, that is, and instead of dwelling in Paradise, has come back to lead a second existence upon earth' (1922, vol. 1: 103).

night who will not greet, it is a clear sign that he is a *nabātī*. There are numerous stories told about encounters with *nabātī* and the fear of them is one of the reasons why women would never leave the village or even their homestead alone at night. Sometimes a *nabātī* may appear somewhere where nobody knows him, settle down and live together with the people in the villages as one of them. He may marry and have children; when he dies, he will be buried like anybody else but he will rise again from the grave and only from the hole at the gravesite will people know that he was a *nabātī*. There was some disagreement among my informants about whether *nabātī*'s children would also be *nabātī*. Some claimed that if a woman marries a *nabātī*, her children will also be *nabātī* and if a man marries a *nabātīya* (fem. of *nabātī*), his children will be *nabātī*. Others maintained that only in the latter case will the children be *nabātī*. This is because being a *nabātī* is transmitted through the mother's milk. On this point there is unanimous agreement and the belief that a child suckled by a *nabātīya* would become *nabātī* is general. This is also the reason why only close kinswomen and the trustworthy women whose ancestry is not in doubt are chosen as wet nurses of babies whose own mothers have died.

The notion of the creation of relationships through the sharing of milk seems also to be expressed in the prescription that one must never refuse a drink of milk. Any refusal to partake in the offered food is tantamount to the refusal of the relationship expressed through the offer. But it is much worse to refuse milk than to refuse any other food or drink. All my informants stressed that although it is impolite to refuse offered food, it is very rude indeed to refuse the offered milk. For this reason, people who do not want to drink the milk when they are offered some, always dip their forefinger into it and lick it (see Westermarck 1926, vol. 1: 243; vol. 2: 19, 41 for a similar practice in Morocco).

As I already suggested, all the instrumental symbols which derive their motivation from the reproductive powers of women as the source of ritual creativity are particular tokens of the same symbolic whole in which the symbolism of white and femininity are collapsed together. This whole can be seen as produced by a symbolic process in which each symbolising or signifying term is in turn symbolised or signified and this conversion unfolds in a chain in which every new symbolising term acquires the symbolised terms of the previous symbolic processes (Todorov 1977: 245). The creation of well-being, health and prosperity is the acknowledged goal of most customary rituals. If creation is conceptualised as nurture, milk becomes its appropriate symbol and this particular symbolisation unfolds the following chain through the process whereby each symboliser becomes itself symbolised by a new term:

symboliser	milk	white	woman	feminine gender female things
symbolised	creativity	milk	white	woman

The symbolic connection between water and woman results from a symbolic process in which not only is each signifier in turn signifed (*rūh* signifies life and growth and is in turn signified by water) but in which the terms are also linked through homonymy (water signifies *rūh* and cold) and synonymy (water and woman signify cold):

symboliser	*rūh*	water→water	woman
symbolised	life, growth	*rūh*	cold→cold

By suggesting that water is not used as an instrumental symbol expressing maleness, I do not wish in any way to indicate that the importance of male and female principles is altogether denied in ritual action. On the contrary, as the following discussion will show, the fact that it takes a male and a female to engender new life underlies much of the ritual symbolism. All I want to suggest here is that the opposition between milk and water is not marshalled to express symbolically this fact. After we have considered in more detail which particular conceptualisation of reproductive powers informs the ritual action, it will become more apparent why the masculine connotations of the water imagery have to be denied in ritual symbolism and why water, which is seen as masculine outside the ritual sphere, has to be seen as an agent of life and growth, and as such linked with women in the ritual context.

Ritual Officiants

The idea that natural reproductive ability is the source of the ability to produce culturally or symbolically underlies the structuring of ritual actions. This idea is expressed not only in the instrumental symbols which the rituals employ but also in the selection of ritual officiants. It is most strongly suggested by the requirement that those who perform the rituals, whether women or men, must not only be fertile but must be people whose capacity to produce both naturally and socially (i.e. the capacity to produce both people and social relations) has been fairly successful and enduring. Perhaps the most central aspect of their ritual significance is to be found in their name: they must be *sabbar* (from *sabara*; to last), i.e. women or men whose firstborn child has survived and is alive, who have not been divorced from their first spouse and whose spouse is alive.

The ritual emphasis on the reproductive power of men and women expresses in symbolic terms the Berti theory of procreation, according to which both sexes contribute to the child's substance. Such a notion is fully in line with the Koran (86: 5–7) although the Berti go beyond it in specifying that the bones and sinews of the child are created from the sperm and the child's flesh from the woman's blood.

The complementarity of both sexes in reproduction is most directly enacted symbolically in those rituals which are performed jointly by a man and a woman. For example, before a married woman is cere-monially introduced into her new household, the hearth is built in the hut by a man and a woman who are both *sabbar*. The hearth consists of an old pot and two stones which support the cooking pot above the fire. The man and the woman jointly hold in their right hands a knife with a white string tied around its handle, the blade of a dutch hoe, one ear of millet if the firstborn child of the woman for whom the hearth is being built is a boy or two if it is a girl, white palm leaves and a *hajlīd* twig. They circumscribe the spot where the hearth will be built several times with these objects. Then the woman puts in place the old pot, fills it with sand and sticks into it the knife, dutch hoe,[4] ears of millet, palm leaves and the *hajlīd* twig. The man then positions one stone and the second is put in its place by both of them. Glowing embers are then brought into the hut in a censer or on a potsherd, the man and the woman circumscribe them several times with a small bundle of straw which they again hold jointly in their right hands and then the straw is set alight in the hearth to start the fire. During one occasion which I observed, the hearth was built jointly by two women, one of whom was the mother of a firstborn daughter and the other the mother of a firstborn son and two men, one of whom was again the father of a firstbegotten daughter and the other of a firstbegotten son (see p.93).

Another ritual always performed jointly by men and women is *dukhla* (from *dakhal*, to enter) – the bringing of the first ears of the new millet from the field. In some villages, *dukhla* is performed by all households on the same day, in others it is performed independently by individual households. Sometimes, the household head whose firstborn is a boy, and who is referred to as *sīd adlam* (owner of the dark (see p.98) performs it in the second half of the lunar month when the moon is waning and the evenings are dark; the one whose firstborn is a daughter (*sīd abyad*, owner of the white) does it in the first half of the month

---

[4] The bride has received the knife from her father (who also gives her the hoe blade) and the weeding hoe from her husband's father. These are the most important implements used in the production (hoe, weeding hoe) and preparation of food (knife), which is now the new household's own concern. Their origin from both sides of the family symbol-ically indicates both the bridegroom's and the bride's families' concern with the well-being of the new household.

when the moon is waxing and there is moonlight in the evenings.[5] Before *dukhla* has been performed, any millet from the new harvest may only be eaten raw in the field, in the shelter or in the yard of the homestead; it may be cooked and eaten inside the house only after *dukhla*. In some villages, no new grain in whatever form may be eaten before *dukhla*; only small children eat new grain in the field for 'children are like birds'.

Dukhla starts by a man and a woman departing together to the field. As the ritual is performed separately by each household in the village, they are normally husband and wife. They do not symbolise, however, the unity of the domestic group but rather the complementarity of the sexes. This is clearly suggested by the fact that a widow or a woman whose husband is absent from the village goes to the field, either with her son or with another man or boy if she has no son; the boy can even be a baby whom she carries on her back. She selects a tall and well-growing plant in the middle of the field and, facing east, anoints it three times with butter and milk. When doing that she utters the following invocation which clearly indicates the goal of the action: *Bism il-lāhi, arētna bel 'ēsh u 'āfi. Alla yilahigna jadīd at tānī* or *Alla yilahigna sana tānī* ('In the name of God, we hope to be with grain and health. Let God find us another new [harvest]', or 'Let God find us another year'). The man then cuts the first ear of millet from the plant before the woman cuts more ears and puts them on a flat winnowing basket to take them home. When only a small boy who is not yet strong enough to cut the ear is with her in the field, she holds his hand in her right hand and cuts the first ear herself. If the woman is accompanied by an adult man, they anoint the millet stalk jointly. Afterwards the man eats a little of the grain and gives the woman some of it to eat. The woman also cuts some *banu* (Eragrostis sp.) and *marhabēb* (Cympobogon nervatus?) grass and a sorghum stem to bring to the village with the first millet. It was explained to me that *marhabēb* is brought from the field because it is used for making the brush with which the yard of the homestead is swept, and *banu* because a brush for sweeping the grinding stone is made from it. *Banu* is seen as symbolically appropriate also because it is prolific: 'its seeds [lit. children; *awlād*] are small but many' ('*iyālu sughār wala katīr*). Sorghum is used because it is white. In some villages, *banu* and a greyish plant called *shēbi* are brought with the millet. It was again explained to me that *shēbi* is gathered because it is white right from the moment of its germination. *Banu* and *shēbi* are common weeds growing in the fields and Berti refer to them as 'spouses of millet' (*jōz 'ēsh*).

---

[5] For a similar custom among the Bedeira in Kordofan see Aglen 1936: 344.

When brought home, the millet ears are again anointed with milk and butter and then crumbled off onto a winnowing basket. This is done again jointly by the man and the woman so that the man holds the ears with his hand in front of the woman's hand because 'the man is in front and the woman behind'. Then the child from the household takes the basket with the grain and a bowl with milk and butter to all other households in the village asking people to taste the new millet. Everybody takes a few grains from the basket and 'greets' them by kissing them twice before putting them into the mouth and anointing his or her wrist with the milk and butter.

Three ears of millet if the woman's firstborn child is a daughter and four if it is a son, together with the stalk of sorghum, *banu*, *marhabēb* or *shēbi*, are stuck inside the hut into the roof above the entrance and *banu*, *marhabēb* or *shēbi* are also stuck into the straw fence of the homestead on both sides of the entrance and of the entrances in the inner parting walls of the homestead. The first ears from which the grain is crumbled off are not thrown away, but the woman takes them back to the field and sticks them into the plant from which they were cut and ties the plant with a string made of *banu* grass. I shall return to the significance of these practices in the next chapter.

Figure 7 *Dukhla*. A woman anoints a millet plant with butter and milk

The complementarity of the sexes in reproduction is not only seized upon symbolically in rituals jointly performed by men and women. It is also symbolised, although in a different way, in rituals performed only by women.

A strict sexual division of labour accompanies the harvesting, threshing and winnowing of the grain. The harvesting is done by women who cut the ears of the ripe millet with an oblong iron blade inserted into a short wooden handle, which nestles in the palm. The cut ears are laid in a flat, spirally woven winnowing basket (*tabag*), and are transferred to a larger basket (*rēka*) for carrying off to a *jurn*. This is a low platform built next to the clay threshing floor in the field. Its top surface is formed of branches laid close together and covered with a layer of straw and mud. The ears of millet are spread out on this to dry before threshing. The threshing begins after the crop has been brought in from all the fields in the village and it is done by a large working team composed of all the able-bodied men of the village, who use a simple flail consisting of a piece of wood split lengthwise to which a bow-shaped branch is attached as a handle. They thresh in one day the grain gathered in the field of one household and then move on to thresh the grain of other households in turn. The women from all the households in the village winnow the grain of the household which was threshed the previous day and on subsequent days they move on to winnow the grain of other households in the same order in which it has been threshed.

Specific ritual practices accompany the winnowing. A woman from the household whose grain is to be winnowed carries to the field the glasses for drinking tea, the winnowing baskets and the brooms for sweeping the threshing floor which consist of a bundle of stalks of the *marhabēb* grass tied together by a piece of string. These things are put into a large basket (*rēka*) into which the woman also puts two small balls made from ashes from the hearth mixed with water: two if her firstborn child is a daughter, and three if it is a son. These are called *tigil an-nār* – 'the heaviness of the fire'. A small stone, three or four pieces of *lalōba* (the fruit of the *hajlīd* tree), a little bit of the grain from the previous year which has been stored in the household, a bundle of *banu* grass, and possibly two or three *kabbūs* (small balls made of millet flour mixed with water) are also placed into the basket. I shall return again to the significance of these objects in the next chapter. When they reach the threshing floor, the women first 'greet' the threshed grain. They sit or squat next to the grain and chaff which was swept by the men the previous day from the threshing floor and piled into a heap on its eastern edge. They put both hands with palms down on the heap and then again using both hands, scoop up a little of the grain, blow or spit on it and say

Alla addīna tērāb ('God give us the seed'). Anybody else who approaches the threshed grain 'greets' it in the same way.

The winnowing is inaugurated by two women sitting down in front of the heap of grain and chaff facing east. Their heads are covered by one piece of cloth and they hold in front of them two flat winnowing baskets on which there are the *tigil an-nār* or *kabbūs*, a small stone and the *hajlīd* fruit. One woman holds the bundle of the *banu* grass with her left and the other one with her right hand and they jointly sweep some grain and chaff from the heap on the winnowing baskets. The baskets are then overturned onto the heap and the procedure is repeated once more. Then the baskets are filled full with grain and chaff and the grain, together with all the objects which were put on the baskets, is again poured back on the heap. The woman whose grain is being winnowed sticks the bundle of the *banu* grass onto the top of the heap.

Two flails are then put on the threshing floor next to one another so that the head of one points to the north and the head of the other, to the south. The brushes made of the *marhabēb* grass and the bundle of the *banu* grass are placed beside the flails. The two women start winnowing the grain so that they jointly hold in their hands one winnowing basket filled with grain, raise it above their heads and slowly pour the grain from it so that the wind blows away the chaff. The grain is poured on the

Figure 8 Two women start winnowing the grain by jointly using one winnowing basket

flails and bundles of grass lying on the threshing floor. When the first four baskets have been winnowed in this way, they are placed upside down on the heap of the clean grain. Then the two women continue to winnow, using another basket, until the flails, grass and winnowing baskets have been fully covered by grain.

The winnowed grain is left to 'cool' while all the women sit away from the threshing floor drinking millet beer. After a while they proceed to 'open' the grain: they sweep the grain from the baskets and flails back onto the heap of grain and chaff on the eastern edge of the floor and they then turn over the baskets. The chaff which has stuck to the inside of each of the four baskets represents camels, cows, sheep and goats. It is seen as indicative of how the various animals of the household will prosper in the following year.

After the grain has been 'opened', the general winnowing starts, each woman working independently with her own basket until the last four baskets have been filled with grain and chaff. The two women who inaugurated the winnowing stand facing each other on the threshing floor and the grain from the four baskets is poured over their out-stretched arms. They catch some of it in their hands and spread it on their arms and faces as if they were washing themselves, as they recite: *Arētna bel 'ēsh, arētna bel-laban, arētna bel-matara, arētna bel-mōya* ('Let us be [seen] with grain, let us be with milk, let us be with rain, let us be with water').

A steady easterly wind usually blows during the threshing and winnowing of grain and it blows the chaff away towards the western edge of the threshing floor. There is still some grain left in the chaff and to loosen it off, the women re-thresh the heap of chaff and then winnow it once more. Before this is done, one of the women who inaugurated the winnowing picks up a flail and, holding it like a hoe, walks over the chaff from north to south and back again, digging holes in exactly the same way in which they are dug during sowing. The other woman follows in her steps, sprinkling a few drops of water from a gourd into each hole and dropping into it a few grains of millet from the winnowing basket. She then covers the holes by sweeping chaff into them with the bundle of *banu* grass. This action is accompanied by the following invocation: *'Ēsh min wēn? 'Ēsh fī arāsha, alma fī sama. 'Ēsh min wēn? 'Ēsh Fulān, alma fī sama* [or *alma min sama*], *alma min Alla.* ('From where is the grain? The grain is from the gardens in the watercourses, the water is in the sky. From where is the grain? The grain is the grain of So-and-So [the name of the male head of the household], the water is in the sky [or, the water is from the sky], the water is from God'). Then the two women sweep the chaff over the holes with grass brushes while imitating the sound of the falling rain. All the other women also imitate the sound of rain and put the empty flat winnowing baskets over their heads as if protecting themselves from it. Sometimes a woman may sprinkle water from her mouth over them.

When all the chaff has been re-winnowed, the two women sit again in front of the heap of clean grain facing east and fill two winnowing baskets. They then hold one of them and together push it up and down the heap to the rhythm of the following song: *Wālī, hē, gandūl ash-shabāb, addīna lel-arbāb* ('Guardian, he [of] the millet ear of the youth, give us to the owners [of the field]'). The basket is then emptied onto the heap and left lying turned over on top of it. A few grains are sprinkled on its bottom. The same is done with the second basket. An empty pot in which millet beer was carried to the field is then brought and the two women grasp it by its mouth and, pushing it up and down the heap, fill it with grain before burying it inside the heap. This action is accompanied by a spoken or sung invocation: *Dukhn as-sāfī, jur al-wādī wa ta'āl lēna* ('Good millet, run with the watercourse and return to us'). Other women sit at the heap facing east and, with their brushes, sweep grain over the pot so that it is completely covered. A bundle of *banu* grass and a brush used for sweeping the threshing floor are then stuck on top of the heap and all the women leave the threshing floor to drink tea and millet beer.

After this short break, the clean grain is put into bags made of cow hides which the men then load on camels and bring to the village where it is stored in underground pits. The woman whose grain has been winnowed and who is always one of the two women performing the rituals, sits down in front of the heap facing east. She has to work silently and, to prevent herself from speaking, she sometimes places a short millet stalk into her mouth, holding it between her teeth. She fills a large basket with grain and then the other women sweep a small amount of grain from it onto a flat winnowing basket from which they pour it into the bag; they repeat this operation several times until the large basket is empty. The large basket is filled once more and the grain is transferred from it into the bag in the same way. Afterwards the women scoop the grain onto their winnowing baskets straight from the heap and pour it into the bags.

When winnowing the grain, the women work with their heads uncovered and with the wraps, which they wear over their dresses in public, removed. Before performing each ritual action, they wrap themselves over and cover their hair. If they do not finish winnowing and filling the bags with grain in one day, they turn the winnowing baskets over on the heap of winnowed grain and sprinkle a few grains on them before leaving the threshing floor for the night.[6] The baskets are also turned over in this way any time the women leave the threshing floor temporarily to drink beer or tea. Men are not allowed near the threshing floor while women are winnowing unless they pay them a small sum of money.

Two women are required to officiate, not only during the rituals accompanying the winnowing, but during all the rituals which women perform, with the exception of simple actions sometimes performed in the domestic setting. For example, when the ritual consists of smearing a tree or shrub with milk and butter when the newly born baby or a circumcised girl are taken out from the village for the first time, the action is always performed jointly by two women. The two women are chosen because of their sexual identity symbolised by their procreative ability: although her own sexual identity is not being manipulated, a woman whose firstborn child is a son (*um wilēd*, mother of a boy) is symbolically male due to the sex of her offspring and in the ritual context, clearly stands for maleness. Equally a woman whose firstborn child is a daughter (*um binei*, mother of a girl) stands for femaleness. The point that one woman must be *um binei* and the other one *um wilēd* was often explicitly stressed when women were advised on how a ritual should be properly conducted. All my efforts to elicit from the informants the rationale underlying this practice invariably provoked disquisitions on the 'facts of life' along the lines that a man alone and a woman alone do not reproduce; only a male (*dakar*) and a female (*intāi*) together reproduce. Such exegesis not only stresses the mutual contribution of men and women to reproduction, but it also indicates that it is indeed reproduction as such that gets symbolically enacted in the ritual performances.

Even though in one of their aspects the rituals dramatise the reproductive complementarity of men and women, their overall emphasis is on the reproductive powers of women as the source of ritual creativity. Most of them are either exclusively women's affairs and women perform them even if men are the object of them or, in ritual performances, men themselves are represented by women. If both sexes participate in a ritual, women are usually the main officiants and the men's role is often reduced to that of spectators.

Macmichael mentions that the ritual officiants among the Berti 'are old women who hold the right from mother to daughter, but the daughter does not practise until she has had children or is advanced in years' (1922, vol. 1: 65). The rituals are performed at stones and trees

---

[6] The same custom has been reported from the Beja in Kordofan (Aglen 1936: 344).

which are referred to as *maḥāllát 'awāid* (places of customs or customary rituals) and consist of sacrifices of sheep and offerings of meat, milk, fat and flour before the beginning of the rains and before the harvest to ensure a good crop. 'One informant denied any idea of a spirit or animal living below the sacred tree or rock, but others on the contrary held there are *afárit (sing. afrī* an (evil) spirit) there, though they had no notion of their shape or form or attributes. The old women, they say, talk to these and stroke and soothe the stone' (ibid.).

The expression *maḥallāt 'awāid* has nowadays no meaning to the Berti. There are no rituals of any kind performed at particular rocks and trees and there are no rituals performed at the beginning of the rains or before the harvest which would resemble those mentioned by Macmichael. If such rituals ever existed, they have completely disappeared. According to Macmichael they were in decline already in the second decade of this century when he was collecting his data: 'those Berti who have acquired some measure of civilization by contact with the Arabs are inclined to regard the whole matter as a superstition, and it seems to be only among the ruder type living among the Tagabo hills that the rites are still practised (ibid.).

Macmichael mentions sacrifices and offerings at stones and trees not only among the Berti but also among the Meidob where old women make offerings of milk, fat, flour and meat at special rocks to induce rain (Ibid.: 63–64), among the Fur, where sacrifices are made by old women to malignant local spirits to ensure good rains at stones and trees also known as *maḥallāt 'awāid* (ibid.: 100–1), as well as among the Zaghawa, Bideyat, Daju, Birged (ibid.: 73–4) and Tunjur (ibid.: 127).

Macmichael's information on rituals among various Darfur peoples derives from his interviews of single informants who were often educated men who described to him customs and beliefs of other tribes than their own (see ibid.: 73–4) and who might well have attributed to them beliefs and practices which they did not really possess but which seemed to fit with the informants' preconceived views of their 'backwardness'. The resulting image of a set of ritual practices common throughout Darfur may thus be more a result of Macmichael's methodology than of ethnographic fact. As detailed anthropological research into the ritual practices and their associated beliefs of specific peoples in Darfur is still lacking, it is difficult to be sure about the accuracy of Macmichael's information. The important ritual role of women which emerges from Macmichael's description is, however, corroborated by sound historical evidence, according to which women played an important role in the sultan's succession ritual and generally acted as ritual experts at the sultan's court (O'Fahey and Spaulding 1974: 143–4, 150;

O'Fahey 1980: 19–20). It is not inconceivable that the ritual prominence of women at the sultan's court reflected their prominence throughout Darfur and that the present-day ritual role of Berti women may well be a specific manifestation of a cultural pattern characteristic of Darfur as a whole about which we, unfortunately, still lack adequate information.

Berti men, of course, also perform specific ritual roles. They officiate either in rituals which involve the performance of a task which can be done only by them like, for example, a sacrifice, or if an activity ordinarily done only by them is ritualised. The female reproductive power can be seen, however, as the source of symbolic creativity even in rituals which are performed by men.

One of these rituals is the 'opening' of the well at the beginning of the dry season when water has dried out in the surface pools and shallow wells dug in the riverbeds, and has to be drawn again from deep permanent wells. Although this ritual is classified as *'āda*, unlike most other customary rituals, it involves a sacrifice and, for that reason, has to be performed by a man. He stands on the western side of the well facing east, chanting suitable Koranic verses, if he knows any, while other men bind stalks of water melons and pumpkins or cucumbers to each corner of the wooden frame which covers the mouth of the well and to the stakes in the frame. He then places *kabbūs* (cylindrical pieces of dough, about 15 cm long and 3 cm thick, made of millet flour mixed with water) to each corner of the well and, standing again on the western side of the well facing east, he pours a little milk into the well. After that, he sacrifices a goat on the western side of the well, slitting its throat so that the blood flows into the well (for a similar practice in Morocco see Westermarck 1926, vol. 1: 319–21). Then he draws up the first bag of water. Before this ritual has been performed, nobody would dare to use the well for fear of exposing himself to danger. The ritual is to ensure that there will be enough water in the well for the whole year, to prevent all disasters, and to ensure that neither man nor beast will fall into the well.

A man also ritually inaugurates the weeding. Weeding is done by a kind of dutch hoe which is pushed forward so that its crescent-shaped iron blade burrows under the ground to cut the roots of the growing grass. Millet seeds are always planted in rows which run from east to west and weeding is always done from south to north, irrespective of the shape and location of the field, for it is much easier if done across the rows of millet rather than parallel to them. If the weeding were done parallel to the rows of millet one would have to stay bent down for a long time while weeding by hand round the plants, which the Berti consider very tiring. When people weed across the rows, the bending down is done at intervals instead of continually. Both men and women weed and the division of labour is such that men dig furrows in the unbroken soil and women then 'kill' the grass in between the furrows dug by men, for weeding in between the first furrows, where the hard-packed soil has already been disturbed, is much easier than cutting the roots of grass in unbroken soil. A man is chosen to inaugurate the weeding season because it is typically men's work to cut the first furrows with the dutch hoe in the unbroken soil. Before the general weeding starts, one man from the village goes to his own field and, with his dutch hoe, digs seven short furrows. He starts his weeding at the western end of the field, digging the first furrow from west to east; the next, north of the first, is dug from east to west; the third, north of the second again from west to east, and so on, with the final furrow being dug, like the first, from west to east. Seven furrows are dug not only because seven is the most auspicious number in Berti culture but also because, with an odd number of furrows, the digging can both start and finish in the auspicious easterly direction. After the seventh furrow has been dug, the man starts 'killing' the grass between the furrows, reversing his movements. The first furrow to 'kill' the grass is dug south of the last one from east to west, the next from west to east, until the last furrow is made from west to east between the first and second main furrows. The man then returns to the village announcing: *Sammētu* ('I have started'). The following day, general weeding begins with each person making seven furrows in his own field in the way described above. After this regular weeding proceeds in the south-north direction. When weeding is ritually inaugurated, it starts and finishes in the auspicious easterly direction. The goal of this particular action is not merely to remove the grass which will enable the millet to grow; any weeding would achieve that. The action is *'āda* and its goal is to ensure a good harvest and the general prosperity and well-being of the household; it is not merely an instrumental but a symbolic action and it acquires its symbolic significance by being the reversal of the normal procedure.

Threshing of the harvested millet is also ritually inaugurated and this is again done by a man, for threshing is the men's work. Millet is threshed in winter, when the wind always blows from the east. The men do the threshing in such a way that they stand in a row facing west and, starting on the eastern edge of the threshing floor, slowly move westwards beating the ears with their flails; the loosened chaff is blown away from them by the prevailing wind. When threshing is being ritually inaugurated, the procedure is again reversed. Three ears of millet are placed on the eastern edge of the threshing floor in an east-west direction, together with a water melon and a cucumber. They are threshed by a man facing east and, after this simple ritual has been performed, the general threshing starts.

A man is also chosen to perform the simple ritual of placing the first two thatches on the roof of a house, because only men thatch roofs.

The man who officiates in all the above-mentioned rituals has to be one who displays symbolically female attributes. He has to be *abu binei* (father of a girl), that is a man whose first begotten child is a daughter. His appropriateness as a ritual officiant derives from the following chain of symbolic processes in which each symbolising term is in turn symbolised:

symboliser	milk	white	woman	*abu binei*
symbolised	creativity	milk	white	woman

In this chain each new symbolising term acquires the symbolised terms of the previous symbolic processes (Todorov 1977: 245). Thus white takes on, through the intermediary of milk, the 'meaning' of creativity, even though there is no direct symbolic relation between them. In consequence, the white cloth wrapped around the top of the roof of a newly built house or a piece of string tied round the handle of the knife during the building of a new hearth, can be seen as carrying the same symbolic meaning as the milk or butter with which people and objects are anointed during various ritual performances. *Abu binei* becomes an appropriate person to perform a ritual whose aim is to bring about future well-being, safety, health or prosperity because he too takes on, through the intermediary of woman, white and milk, the 'meaning' of creativity even though there is no direct symbolic relation between them. He takes on also, of course, the meaning of white and is, in consequence, referred to as *sīd abyad* (owner of the white) or sometimes as *sīd gamra* (owner of the moon; moon being perceived by the Berti as white), although, being a man, he is not related metonymically to the white milk as a woman is. *Abu binei* is not only a term in the chain of milk–white–woman, but also a term in the chain mentioned above:

symboliser	*rūh*	water→water	woman	*abu binei*
symbolised	life, growth	*rūh*	cold→cold	woman

In this chain, again, *abu binei* acquires the symbolised terms of the previous symbolic processes and, through the intermediary of woman and water, takes on the 'meaning' of cold; the Berti say that 'his shadow is cold' (*dullu bārid*) or that 'his back is cold' (*daharu bārid*).

Abu binei and woman belong to both symbolic chains and so link them together into one symbolic whole which the Berti express by asserting that women are white, cold and soft. It is a whole in which the symbolism of white, cold and femininity are collapsed together and inextricably linked by the overarching notion of auspiciousness which the Berti express by asserting that women are good, nice and lucky. All the concrete objects which are particular tokens of this symbolic whole stand in opposition to black, hot and maleness which are again fused in their explicitly asserted quality of inauspiciousness.

As a symbolic token of auspiciousness, *abu binei* stands in opposition to *abu wilēd* (father of a boy). The latter is *sīd azrag* (owner of the black) or *sīd adlam* (owner of the dark); his shadow is hot (*dullu harr*) and he is inauspicious or unlucky. *Sīd abyad* is believed to have a generally lucky disposition which is manifested in everything he does. It is believed that the household of such a man will prosper and wealth will come easily to him. *Sīd azrag* is not as likely to be blessed with prosperity, wealth or a stable marriage. Because of his auspicious character, *sīd abyad* is chosen not only to perform certain rituals, but to inaugurate any work to ensure that it will be successful. So *sīd abyad* is the first one to lift up a flail when men thresh the harvested millet; he digs the first hole for the posts of a house when men of the village build it together and, when the wooden structure of the roof has been completed, he ties the first thatch onto it. When men travel in a party, for example in search of a lost animal, when driving sheep or cattle for sale in Omdurman, when seeking work as wage labourers, or when going to a distant market, they will meet with success if led by a *sīd abyad*. In the past, this applied particularly to men going to battle. Nowadays, the party travelling to rock-salt deposits in the desert should particularly be led by a *sīd abyad* so as to return home safely. *Sīd abyad* should start to saddle and pack the animals, he should be the first to mount his camel, start the cooking when the party camps at night or start pouring the water from the bags. A village founded by a *sīd abyad* will prosper and it is likely to grow bigger and to last longer than one founded by *sīd azrag*.

Apart from being 'lucky' through his association with symbols of auspicious connotations, the father of a daughter is 'lucky' in an immediate and practical sense. Although it is a son's moral obligation to support his father in his old age, the Berti argue that a man will be better looked after by his daughter. It is, after all, a woman who cooks and brews beer, they say, and if the father is looked after by his daughter, he can always be sure that he will not go hungry. If he is looked after by his son's wife, because he has no daughter to take care of him, he may be neglected by her when her husband is not around to remind her of her duties, because she is not as strongly attached to him as she is to her own father (Holy 1990).

The auspicious character of a *sīd abyad* derives from the fact that although he is a man, symbolically he represents femaleness, in exactly the same way as a woman whose firstborn child is a boy (*um wilēd*) can, under certain circumstances, act as a man. Like all Muslims, the Berti do not eat the meat of animals which have died without being slaughtered, or which have been killed accidentally. But if an animal is about to die, they rush to slaughter it before it dies so that its meat can be consumed. When there is no man around whom a woman can ask to slaughter a dying beast, she sometimes does it herself. If she is a mother of a firstborn daughter (*um binei*), only she, and possibly, her husband will eat the meat; everybody else will consider it *nijis* (ritually unclean). But if she is a mother of a firstborn son (*um wilēd*), the meat is treated as if the beast were slaughtered by a man; it is considered *halāl* (ritually clean) and will be eaten by anybody.

Customary rituals and gender relations
The importance attributed to the sex of the ritual officiants or to the sex of their firstborn or firstbegotten child, the insistence on their being *sabbar* and the symbolic meaning of the actions they perform, all suggest that the rituals are predicated on the idea of procreative power as the source of all creativity. The explicitly asserted theory of procreation stresses the contribution of both sexes. The woman forms the child's flesh from her blood, but she is only a co-contributor to its substance; its bones and sinews are the result of the man's contribution. The fact that it takes a man and a woman to produce a child underlies much of the ritual symbolism. However, the explicitly asserted theory of procreation which postulates semen and mother's blood as creating the child's substance is not at all symbolically elaborated. On the contrary, the ritual symbolism replaces the notion of semen and blood as the source of the child's substance with the notion of milk as the substance-creating agent. In this emphasis on the creative power of milk, the ritual symbolism stresses the preeminent role of women, for lactation is of course, a uniquely female characteristic. If a woman does not create the child alone, she alone makes it grow through nursing it. The milk symbolism thus clearly emphasises the nurturing rather than the strictly procreative aspect of reproduction, and hence stresses the feminine creativity: although a man and a woman are needed to produce a child, only a woman can suckle it and thus keep it alive after it has been born. This stress on female creativity is also expressed by the fact that

water is not used in the ritual context to express maleness but is linked with women, as I argued in the previous section. This is achieved through de-emphasising its colour (black) which links it with maleness ('men are black and women are white') and emphasising its cold quality which links it with femaleness ('men are hot and women are cold').

Men are, of course, aware of the powers of women to create naturally in all societies, and in many societies in which men try to assert their supremacy over women through ritual means, an important aspect of rituals is the symbolic attribution of procreative power to men, and a symbolic devaluation of the natural procreative ability of women (see, for example, Bloch 1986: 92); alternatively men may be concerned with bringing the natural procreative ability of women under their ritual control (see for example La Fontaine 1972; Middleton 1982: 138–9). Nothing like this can be detected in Berti rituals. Both in their selection of the officiants and the symbols which the rituals employ, either the complementarity of both sexes in procreation or the reproductive power of women alone is dramatised. This would suggest that only in certain societies are men concerned with denigrating women's creative powers or with appropriating creative powers to themselves through ritual means: those in which the religious ideology is undifferentiated, and in which men have to ascertain their ritual creativity within one complex of cosmological notions to which both men and women subscribe. Although it would not be appropriate to construe Islam as a 'counter-point ideology' (Poewe 1981) among the Berti, for both men and women subscribe to the basic tenets of the Muslim faith, a considerable division of ritual labour is clearly drawn along sexual lines and roughly corresponds to the conceptual distinction between customary and religious rituals. As men are in charge of major religious rituals, they have no need to bring the customary rituals under their control or to assert their dominance in them. Through performing the religious rituals, they concern themselves, independently of women, with the same aims with which the women are concerned in customary rituals. Furthermore, only the religious rituals are understood as orthodox within the dominant Islamic ideology. In consequence, they come to be seen not only by men, but also by women, as more prestigious, and ultimately as more important, than the customary ones. Through this conceptualisation, men manage to appropriate for themselves the kind of ritual activity that matters most and succeed in persuading themselves that women are lesser creatures than men, and that it is not in their nature to be as deeply religious as men are. Perhaps this view suits women as well, for it enables them to express freely and strongly a different model of gender relations from the one Islam itself puts forward in its emphasis on the preeminence of men.

In those societies, including Islamic ones, in which men attempt to subject women's creative powers to their control, women's powers are typically conceptualised as both beneficent and dangerous (Bourdieu 1977: 128–9); Abu-Lughod 1986: 125–33) and men assert their dominance in ritual through emphasising the dangerous aspects of women's powers and through construing women as polluting. Typically, the polluting aspect of menstrual blood is emphasised (Bourdieu 1977: 126; Abu-Lughod 1986: 129–30). Nothing like this happens among the Berti, with the result that women's powers are construed in customary rituals and their symbolism as exclusively beneficent.

The onset of menses is not ritualised. It is merely taken as a natural sign that the girl has become capable of bearing children and that she can be married. In accordance with Koranic injunction (2:222), the Berti abstain from intercourse during menstruation. A menstruating women is certainly *nijis* (polluted) until she has washed herself and her clothes after the blood flow has ceased; like anybody else in a state of ritual pollution, she does not pray and she does not fast during Ramadan. If there is another woman in the household who can grind flour, cook and brew beer, a menstruating woman abstains from the performance of these tasks; she also does not work in the field or go to the well if another woman can take her place. If there is no one else to perform her chores, she grinds flour, cooks and brews beer after she has washed her hands and forearms; she also attends to all other work outside the homestead except that she does not go to the market where it might be detected that her clothes are stained with blood, which would put her to shame (*fadīha*). But she would not be seen as endangering others through being in an impure state; people would just simply say that she is *denī*, which is a term normally used to denote a sloppy woman in general, or a bad, careless or inefficient housewife in particular. Even when a menstruating woman abstains from her normal chores, she is not confined to her house and she moves freely around the village. On the whole, menstruation is seen as a temporary incapacitation, as a recurring indisposition or illness, more or less in line with the Koran (2: 222).

The Berti do not put any significance or emphasis on the act of defloration. Although ideally it is expected that a bride will be a virgin, no proof of her virginity is required.

When talking of blood, the Berti emphasise the dangerous aspects of human rather than specifically female blood, and they certainly do not conceptualise female blood in itself as more dangerous than the male one. Any shedding of blood creates a state of ritual pollution. It has to be emphasised, however, that it is the quantity of the blood shed that matters, not the fact that it is female blood; the blood shed during a boy's circumcision is as dangerous as the blood shed in childbirth. Women, of course, shed blood more often than men and in consequence they are more often in a state of ritual pollution. Because only women give birth and because a lot of blood is shed during childbirth, they also expose others to danger more often than men do. But in this respect, the difference between the two sexes is merely a difference in degree, not in kind. What the symbolism of the customary rituals emphasises is clearly the difference in kind, for which milk, through its association with the uniquely female aspect of nurturance, becomes the appropriate symbol. If we appreciate this emphasis on the difference in kind between men and women, we can also appreciate why it is not blood but milk that is, for the Berti, the symbol of female creative power, in spite of the theory of procreation according to which a woman makes the child's flesh out of her blood.

4

Village and wilderness

The preceding chapter was concerned with the interpretation of the meaning and motivation of the instrumental symbols employed in customary rituals. In offering this interpretation, I concentrated on the rituals as instrumental acts aimed at achieving specific goals. Most rituals so far mentioned precede the performance of a seasonal activity or set of activities like weeding, harvesting, threshing, winnowing of the harvested grain or drawing of water from the well during the dry season of the year. Other rituals accompany the construction of a new house or the construction of a hearth inside it. The goals of all these various rituals are quite explicit. Most Berti are able to state that the rituals are performed to bring about a good harvest, to make sure that no danger will befall those who are going to draw water from the well or to ensure the health, prosperity and well-being of those who will inhabit the new house. A ritual is, however, not only an instrumental act but also a 'culturally constructed system of symbolic communication, that is to say, its cultural content is grounded in particular cosmological or ideological constructs' (Tambiah 1985: 129).

In this chapter, I consider the customary rituals from this point of view. The cosmological constructs which they express are most clearly brought into focus in those rituals which are concerned, in one way or another with the crossing of the boundary between the village (*hilla*) and the world outside the human settlement (*khalā*). These rituals are again aimed at achieving specific goals through the manipulation of various instrumental symbols. The informants' explanations of the goals and the explicit exegesis of the meaning of the symbols indicate that the crossing of the village – *khalā* boundary is a situation of heightened danger.

The village and the world outside it

The distinction between the village (*hilla*) and the world outside it (*khalā*) seems to be drawn in what are basically spatial terms and in this sense it only comfortably corresponds to the analytical distinction between culture and nature. In a certain sense, the village is the realm of culture in that, unlike nature, it has been created by people, and in that life within it is regulated by the social and moral order that is qualitatively different from the order that regulates events in the world outside it. But *khalā* is not simply nature: the fields that have been carved by people out of nature are in the *khalā* and so are wells and cattle camps which have also been built by people.

One way in which the Berti think of the difference between the village and *khalā* is in terms of the opposition between safety (*amāna*) and danger or misfortunes (*masāib*). They point out that *khalā* is the place of *masāib*. The fields, the bush, the rocky outcrops and the desert are places in which people encounter a direct physical danger in the form of snakes, hyenas and leopards. People indicate the dangerous qualities of the desert by mentioning men who got lost and died in it. The well, on which a number of rituals centre, is definitely seen as a place of danger. People and animals occasionally fall into it and get injured or killed; people and animals also frequently get injured in the commotion at the well, upon which up to a dozen of villages depend for water. But wells are seen as dangerous not only in this direct physical sense but also because they are mysterious places. Some of them are up to forty metres deep and carved through solid rock. They are believed to be the work of people who lived in the mythological past and who were endowed with abilities which present-day people do not possess. Some are said to have been dug by the legendary giant Nāmadu who was the 'king' of the Berti before the arrival of Islam; only a giant could have accomplished a task which is beyond the comprehension of those living now. Numerous stories are told about mysterious creatures sometimes seen in a well, typically a huge white snake believed to be a *jinn*.

Like other Muslims, the Berti believe in the *junūn* (the Berti Arabic plural of *jinn* which is itself a plural in classical Arabic) which are distinct from ordinary beings of everyday life and the existence of which is attested to in the Koran. They claim, for example, that the *fugarā* who practise sorcery (*sihir*) are able to do so because they have solicited the cooperation of a *jinn*. On the whole, however, they stress the harmless nature of the *junūn* which clearly distinguishes them from the *shayātīn* who are always seen as malevolent and dangerous, The snake in the well may be mysterious but the fact that it is referred to as a *jinn* and not a *shētān* signals its harmless nature.

The desert, like the well, can also be seen as dangerous by virtue of its weird and mysterious quality. The men who have been in it comment in their narratives, not only on the lack of water there or the oppressive heat during the day and the bitter cold at night, but also on the strange silence and the lack of any life; what seems to impress them most is the fact that there are not even flies there, which they take as a clear sign of how completely devoid of any life it is.

The belief that the world is populated by *junūn*, which is common throughout the Muslim world, is not strongly elaborated in Berti cosmology. On the other hand, the belief in the existence of the malevolent and dangerous *shayātīn* is pervasive, and the main danger of the world outside the human settlement derives from the fact that it is a world inhabited by *shayātīn*. Many of the characteristics which the Berti attribute to the *shayātīn* are similar to those which Moroccans attribute to the *jinn* (see Westermarck 1926, vol. 1: 262–301; 1933: 5–7; Crapanzano 1973: 138–40) and which are widespread throughout the Muslim world (Westermarck 1926, vol. 1: 366–90). Thus the Berti claim that the *shayātīn* are more numerous than people and some say that they too have their villages, cattle and wells. However, a more prevalent opinion is that they constantly move around and have no fixed abode; in this respect and also because they are invisible, they are like wind. They live off people's cattle. If somebody has a large herd of cattle but does not give milk to other people, does not make sacrifices and wears torn and dirty clothes, it is because his cattle is a *shētān*'s herd. Some Berti suggest that blind people can see the *shayātīn* and the general belief is that they are also visible to animals, particularly dogs, donkeys, horses and camels. When dogs occasionally bark without an apparent reason, it is because they see a *shētān*, and when camels or horses suddenly run away, it is because they saw a *shētān* and became frightened.

Although, unlike animals, ordinary people cannot see *shayātīn*, they can occasionally hear their noises which resemble human chatter but are incomprehensible to the humans. The *shayātīn* can change into cattle, goats, gazelles or dogs. Many men tell stories about encountering a *shētān* when hunting: they shot a gazelle, and although they did not miss, the gazelle ran away unharmed even after it had been shot several times; it was not an ordinary gazelle but a *shētān*.

There are several kinds of *shētān*. *'Ārid* or *iblīs* is a particularly dangerous one; people grasped by *'ārid* become paralysed; they cannot walk and use their arms and hands. A *fakī* has to smear the blood of a sacrificial animal on their forehead to rid them of the *'ārid*. If an ordinary *shētān* grasps a person, such a person becomes mad (*mishōtan*). People grasped by *shayātīn* talk to themselves and their speech is incoherent. There are male and female *shayāṭīn*. A male *shēṭān* which grasps women is stronger and more dangerous than a female one which grasps men. One will not be grasped by a *shēṭān* if one encounters it but is not afraid of it. Although women are more easily frightened than men, the Berti observe that many more men than women are mad and they ascribe this to the fact that men venture alone into the *khalā* more often than women do; women go only to the fields, to the well and to collect firewood but, unlike men, they do not travel alone anywhere else.

Unlike people, *shayāṭīn* do not live on the earth but either below or above it. So they congregate in wells, particularly the deep ones, and they live in antholes which are referred to as their houses. When a person travels alone, he or she avoids coming near an anthole, particularly at noon or after sunset when the *shēṭān* is most active. However, the favourite abode of the *shayāṭīn* are tall trees like *harāz* (*Acacia albida*) and *sarha* which grow on the banks of the water courses. When people travel alone, they avoid tall trees and they always take rest in the shade of a small tree. They would camp in the shade of a tall tree in the riverbed only when travelling in a large group. The *shayāṭīn* also live on the tops of mountains, hills and rocky outcrops.

Not all places in the *khalā* are equally dangerous and when men are at pasture with camels and sheep and they sleep in the open, they immediately move to another place if one of them has a particularly bad dream, which is taken as a sign that the place in which they stay is a dangerous one. Also a cattle camp is moved to a different location if it proves in a similar way to have been built in a bad place. On the whole, hills, rocky outcrops and riverbeds with their tall trees are much more dangerous than the open sand dunes on which people farm, because tall trees, which might be frequented by *shayāṭīn*, are rare in the open country.

According to Macmichael, placating malignant spirits at rocks and trees was a main feature of pre-Islamic ritual throughout Darfur (Macmichael 1922, vol. 1: 63–5, 73–4, 100–1, 127). It is hence not inconceivable that when the rituals were replaced by Islamic practices, the spirits which were believed to live under the rocks or in the trees came to be described as *shayāṭīn*. Macmichael mentions a Fur belief that the spirit, which lives under a stone where rituals are performed to placate it, is a 'devil (*shaitán* or *gin*)' (1922, vol. 1: 100). Such 'Islamisation' of mysterious spiritual creatures of pre-Islamic origin might have been facilitated by the beliefs that the *jinn*, whose many characteristics are attributed by the Berti to the *shayāṭīn*, live under and above the ground which are prevalent in Morocco (Westermarck 1926, vol. 1: 264, 282; 1933: 5; Crapanzano 1973: 138) as well as in other areas of the Muslim world (Westermarck 1926, vol. 1: 371).

The opposition between the safety of the village and the dangers of *khalā* is expressed in the details of custom and ritual practices, most of which clearly dramatise the crossing of the *hilla – khalā* boundary. Such crossings occur in two ways. Firstly, the people move physically in and out of the village and both the movement out and the movement in are regulated by appropriate rituals. Secondly, in its material aspect, the village is made of things that originated in the *khalā* and the food which people eat also has to be brought into the village across its boundary. This movement from the *khalā* into the village is again regulated by ritual.

Both kinds of boundary crossing are necessary but dangerous. The dangers involved in them are seen as deriving from the exposure of the people (the beings of the *hilla*) to *khalā*, which occurs either when the people leave the village and enter the *khalā*, or when they re-enter the village after having been exposed to the *khalā* and the things from the *khalā* are brought into the village. The dangers are mitigated by customary rituals performed at the time of the first movement across the boundary.

Crossing out

A ritual accompanies the first movement of a child out of the village forty days after its birth when it is taken by its mother for the first time to the well, to the field and to collect firewood. Before this ritual is performed, the mother can leave the village alone but must not carry the baby with her.

When the mother goes to the well for the first time with her child, she carries a small basket with boiled millet (*belīla*), a small bowl with butter and some *kajāna* (fermented dough from which beer is filtered). At the well, any man whose first child is a daughter (*abu binei*) is summoned. The mother sits on the western edge of the well facing east with her child in her arms. The *abu binei* lifts water from the well in a bag made of the skin of a female goat and places it three times on the head of the mother and the baby. A little water is poured into the boiled millet which is then mixed with butter and the man anoints the mother's and the baby's foreheads with it three times. He then smears this mixture on all the four corners of the wooden frame at the mouth of the well. All people present anoint their wrists with butter and *belīla* and the women utter *Alla addīni ŋaŋa* ('God, give me a child'). The water which was lifted from the well is poured into the *kajāna* to make beer which the women then filter either into one of the watering troughs or into a bag in which water is carried into the village and all those present at the well are invited to have a drink. The purpose of the ritual is to make the well a safe place for the child to visit in the future and particularly to protect the child from the *shayātīn* which congregate there.

On the fortieth day the mother, carrying her baby, is also taken by other women from the village to collect firewood. The women go to a *kitr* shrub (*Acacia melifera*) around which they walk three times. A woman who is *sabbar* and whose firstborn child is a daughter (*um binei*) and another woman whose firstborn is a boy (*um wilēd*) sit down west of the shrub and, facing east, smear its trunk three times with *belīla* mixed with butter. They then dig a shallow hole close to the western side of the trunk and pour into it a few grains of millet, water and millet beer. They anoint the mother's hair and the head, wrists and feet of the child with butter saying *Alla ya'mil lēk kurāk dushāsh* ('Let God make you soft feet'). All women who are present also anoint their hair with butter. A piece of bark is peeled off from the shrub with a sharp stone; a knife must not be used. The bark is torn into thin threads which are then tied together into a small tassel and fastened to the string of the amulet which the child wears round its neck. Another tassel is fastened to a plait on the right side of the mother's head and all women who accompany the mother also tie such tassels into their hair. The mother herself does not collect any wood; it is collected by the women who accompany her. They tie it into a bundle which they put on the mother's head to carry back into the village. Only after this ritual has been performed can the mother venture out of the village carrying the baby with her.

If the ritual is performed in winter when the millet is ripening, the mother and her baby are also taken on the same day to the field where a strong and well-growing millet plant is selected in the middle of the field. Two women sit down west of it and, facing east, smear it with milk and butter. They then cut off a well-formed ear, crumble off a few grains from it and place it into the baby's hand. All the women present eat a few grains saying: *Jiddan Alla maragākum u Alla yirajikum* ('Thank God for having brought you out and let God make you prosper'). This invocation clearly indicates the conscious goal of the ritual. If the mother and her baby were taken to collect firewood before the harvest has commenced, the ritual in the field is performed separately at the time of the harvest before the mother starts cutting the ripe millet in her field.

When boys and girls leave the village for the first time forty days after circumcision, they are also first taken to the well where they undergo a similar ritual as that performed for a new-born baby; the girls are also taken to collect firewood, but not boys as collecting firewood is exclusively a female task. In both instances, the ritual is concerned (1) with protecting those who leave the village against the dangers of the *khalā* to which they are going to be exposed; (2) with cooling, blessing or rendering harmless the things of the *khalā*; and (3) with controlling the exposure of the baby or circumcised child to them:

1. At the well, *abu binei* smears millet grains mixed with butter three times on the baby's or child's forehead. All women present at the well, including the child's mother, also smear their heads with millet and butter; the men anoint their right wrists.

    When the baby or the circumcised child is taken for the first time to the field or to collect firewood, its head and its wrists and feet are again anointed with butter. All women attending the ritual anoint their heads with butter and they also anoint the head of the baby's mother.

2. The water from the well is lifted by an *abu binei* in a bag made from the skin of a female goat. The man smears millet mixed with butter on to the four corners of the wooden frame of the well.

    Before the firewood is collected, a green *kitr* shrub is smeared with butter.

    In the field, millet stalks are again smeared with milk and butter.

3. The bag with water lifted from the well is lowered three times on the head of the baby or circumcised child, and in the case of a baby, also on the head of its mother.

    When collecting firewood, the bark of the *kitr* shrub which has been smeared with butter is torn into threads from which a tassel is made and tied to the amulet hung around the baby's neck. Each woman ties a similar tassel to her hair.

    In the field, a few grains are crumbled off an ear of the millet previously smeared with butter and placed into the baby's hand. All women present eat a few grains.

The rituals accompanying the first movement out of the village are predicated not only on the notion that inherent dangers reside in the *khalā* but also on the notion that it is necessary to be protectively acclimatised to them. The ritual actions are clearly concerned with bringing a person who is being newly acclimatised to the *khalā* into a ritually controlled first contact with it. The practices follow 'the model of homeopathic vaccination or prophylaxis' (James 1988: 120) and they are distinctly sympathetic: when exposed in a ritually controlled way to the substances which are symbolic of the *khalā* (water, bark of the *kitr* shrub, the grain still growing in the field), the person's defences against the dangers inherent in it are being built up. The dangers of the *khalā* can then be faced in the future if a person has been fortified against them by this ritually controlled first contact with them. This interpretation is supported by one detail of the ritual: the peeling off of the bark of the *kitr* shrub with a sharp stone, i.e. an object which itself originates in the *khalā*. Although all the Berti who commented on this action stressed that a knife must not be used, none of them was able to explain why. However, this prescription seems to fit logically the prophylactic purpose of the ritual and it is not unreasonable to assume that it originates in the idea that if a knife, i.e. an object which belongs conceptually to the domain of the village, was used, the bark would be 'tamed' or 'contaminated' by the qualities of the village and thus lose its dangerous potency which it has to retain to make the ritual action effective.

Crossing in

The ritual practices that accompany the crossing of the boundary in the opposite direction, i.e. the movement from *khalā* into the village, are concerned with cooling, blessing or rendering harmless the things that move in.

Thus, when a house is being built, before the thatched roof is lifted on the supporting poles, women sprinkle it with water and *dashīsha*. More elaborate ritual practices accompany the building of a house for a newly married couple which is referred to as *bēt ʿāda* (the house of the customary ritual). It should be built from the straw and wood collected from other households in the village or neighbouring villages, i.e. from material that has not been brought fresh from the *khalā* but has originated from within the village. This house is *bēt nār* (the house of the fire) around which other structures will gradually be built to form the household. It is not only the core of the future household but the place in which the woman gives birth and in which, therefore, human life originates. The idea here seems to be that this very essence of the life that is culture should not originate by culture appropriating nature but should originate within culture itself. In the house, which is the symbol of culture *par excellence*, culture reproduces itself without acknowledging the existence of anything that lies outside it. Consistent with this notion is also the precaution taken against the house reverting to 'nature' after it has been built. This would happen if it was left exposed to the dangers which may penetrate it from outside the village. The *bēt* 'āda is always built some time before the bride moves from the household of her parents to live with her husband in their own independent household. To make sure that a *shetān* will not enter the house before the couple start living in it, it may not be left empty after it has been built. Immediately after its construction has been completed, a small bowl filled with water and a small plate filled with millet is brought into it and put on a shelf built of branches on the inside of the roof. A fire which is then left to die out, is also immediately started inside. Although the bridegroom continues eating and working in the household of his parents, he starts sleeping in the new house right after it has been built, for under no circumstances must the house be left empty at night.

Water and firewood are generally brought into the village without any restrictions, but the first water from which the newly married couple will drink is ritually brought in. Usually during the 'day of counting the bridewealth' (*yōm al-hisāb*), which normally takes place before the groom starts cohabiting with the bride in the shelter of her parents' household, or during the day when he moves to the shelter with her for the first time, his father or brother brings two bags of water on a female donkey from the well; the bags have to be made from the skin of a female goat. Their mouths are not tied with a leather or bark string as is normal, but with white cotton thread. The head of the donkey is anointed with butter before the bags are removed and they are sprinkled with water before the water from them is poured into the storage jar.

A ritual called *dukhla*, discussed in the previous chapter, is again clearly concerned with the controlled movement of the new millet, which originated in *khala*, into the village. Before the ritual has been performed, any millet from the new harvest may only be eaten raw, in the field, in the shelter or in the yard of the household; it may be cooked and eaten inside the house only after *dukhla*. The boundary marking in the ritual is quite obvious. The first ears together with a plant called *shēbi* and *banu* grass are stuck into the roof of the hut above the entrance, and *shēbi* and *banu* are also stuck into the straw fence of the household on both sides of the entrance and on both sides of the entrances in the inner parting walls of the household. The first ears from which the grain has been crumbled off are not thrown away but taken back to the field and stuck into the plant from which they were cut off.

When a man returns for the first time from the desert with rock salt, certain rituals are performed. Their goal can be seen as rendering him harmless after his prolonged stay in the desert, the utmost *khala*, as well as to render harmless the rock salt which originated there. The camel on which the man rides is led from the outskirts of the village to the homestead by a white turban cloth tied to its bridle. The man is anointed with butter and *dashīsha* and the women of the village sprinkle water on him and on the camel on which he is riding. The leather bags with rock salt are marked with white spots and also smeared with *dashīsha* and sprinkled with water. The man cannot enter the house right away. He is carried from the camel to a shelter in his homestead, in which he stays for seven days before entering the house. This again is ritualised. The man is seated on a mat in the yard of his homestead and a woman puts white butter on his hair. Young women from the village come one after another and smear it with their heads. Afterwards women carry the man into the hut and put him on the bed. A woman anoints his right wrist with *dashīsha* and covers his head with white cloth. Then she again smears the bags of rock salt with *dashīsha* and sprinkles *dashīsha* on the assembled crowd. Only after that are the bags opened jointly by a man and a woman or two men and two women. A man takes pieces of the rock salt from the bags and throws them into the crowd; everybody present tries to grab a piece. This particular piece will then be added to the rock salt from which a drink is prepared for the animals.

All the customary rituals which I have mentioned in this chapter indicate the importance of the boundary between the village and *khalā*, which can be seen as marking the boundary between the zone of safety and the zone of danger. The village acquires its significance as a place of safety by standing in conceptual opposition to the world outside it, or by being what the world outside it is not. People leaving the safety of the village and entering the potentially dangerous world outside it, accomplish the move by being ritually protected when crossing the boundary and by being first exposed to the things of the *khalā*, which have themselves ritually been rendered harmless.

When the movement occurs in the opposite direction the ritual is clearly concerned with rendering harmless the things of the *khalā* and the people who move from it into the village. This concern is perhaps most clearly expressed in the way in which the new grain, the basis of the staple food, is brought from the threshing floor in the field for storage and consumption in the village. As I mentioned in the previous chapter, certain objects are brought to the threshing floor when the grain is winnowed. These are first of all two or three *tigil an-nār* (small balls made of the ashes from the hearth mixed with water), and/or two or three *kabbūs* (small balls made of millet flour mixed with water, which are also sometimes referred to as *tigil an-nār*). Other objects include a small stone, and some *hajlīd* fruit. As I have explained, before the winnowing starts, these objects are buried in the heap of grain and chaff. They are not removed from the grain when it is being winnowed and they remain in it when it is packed into the leather bags and eventually brought into the village and poured into the storage pits. The explicitly stated reason for adding the *tigil an-nār*, *kabbūs* and the stone to the grain is to make it 'heavy' so that it would not be blown away and would last longer. The fruit of the *hajlīd* tree is added because *hajlīd* is 'lucky', 'nice' or, in ther words, auspicious. The motivation of the *tigil an-nār*, *kabbūs* and the stone is, however, more complex and does not derive simply from the fact that they are 'heavy'. The Berti also state that the *tigil an-nār* and the *kabbūs* represent the grinding stone. In fact, they are deliberately shaped to resemble it in miniature. One of the balls is always flattish and larger than the others. This is because it represents the large flat grinding stone cemented to the floor of the hut (*murhāka*) whereas the other ball or balls are smaller and round because they represent the stone (*binei murhāka* – the daughter of the grinding stone) which the woman holds in her hands when grinding. The actual stone which is buried in the grain must not have been picked up in the field but brought from the village; it too is said to represent the stone with which the woman grinds flour (*binei murhāka*).

All the objects to which the grain is exposed before it is brought from the field have a strong association with the village or, more specifically, with the hut. Not only are the *tigil an-nār* and *kabbūs* said to represent the grinding stones, but they are made of materials which have themselves originated in the hut: the ashes and flour. The bundle of *banu* grass which is stuck into the grain any time when it is not being handled by the women is ordinarily used as a brush for sweeping the flour from the grinding stone. The stone must be one brought from the village. The *hajlīd* fruit also fits into the image, for the *hajlīd* tree, as I will explain later, is used in ritual action as a symbol of the village.

The symbolic actions which accompany the bringing of grain into the village thus seem to be motivated by the same concerns which guide the first movement of the child out of the village into the *khalā*. In the latter case, the objects symbolising the *khalā* are used to acclimatise the child to the dangers it will face outside the human settlement. The grain originates in the *khalā* and, by virtue of this fact is potentially endowed with a dangerous quality. Through its exposure to objects which in their appearance and substance as well as in their name (*tigil an-nār* – heaviness of the fire), are clearly associated with the village, its potentially dangerous quality is 'tamed' before it is brought across the village boundary. The symbolic action which accompanies this movement may be seen as aimed both at making it last a long time and converting it from a thing of the *khalā* into a thing of the village. Even if the Berti mention explicitly only the former goal, and are silent about the latter, I do not think that in my interpretation I go beyond their tacit knowledge, for both goals are logically implicated. In fact, the former presupposes the latter, for only when properly stored in the village can the grain last a long time.

The hut: the place of safety and women

The relation between the village and *khalā* is, however, more than a simple opposition. *Khalā* as a whole is a place of danger in comparison with the village but some places in the *khalā* are more dangerous than others. In the same way, the village is a place of safety in comparison with the *khalā* around it, but the hut at the centre of the homestead is a place of greater safety than the rest of the homestead, and the homestead itself is a place of greater safety than the rest of the village. If we think about the Berti cosmology as ordered by the notions of 'inside' and 'outside', there are degrees of inside and outside. If the village as a whole is inside, within it, the hut with the hearth, which is the centre of the homestead, is more inside than the rest of the homestead (the man's hut, the flat-roofed shelters, of which one is a guest-house, and the yard of the homestead), and the whole homestead, surrounded by its straw fence, is more inside than the open space of the village. On the outside, there is a similar gradation with the fields and well being less on the outside than the riverbeds, rocky outcrops, hills and mountains, and with the desert being on the edge of the world and as such, the very opposite of the centre of typically human existence that lies inside the hut within the homestead. The Berti world can be depicted as a structure of concentric circles around the hut which lies in its centre, the outer circle being the desert, the very periphery of the world into which humans occasionally penetrate.

This cosmological scheme is again expressed in the details of custom and ritual practices. So, for example, the rituals accompanying a man's return from the desert are concerned, not only with his crossing of the main boundary between the village and *khalā* , but also with his crossing of all the boundaries within the village: he is led in a ritual way into the village itself, then into his homestead where he stays in a shelter for seven days while the bags with the rock salt remain unopened, and ultimately he is carried inside the hut and the bags he brought are opened. The same concern with the boundaries within the village is expressed in bringing the first millet from the field: before the ritual is completed, new millet may be eaten in the yard of the homestead, but must not be brought inside the hut.

These two rituals suggest that the hut is the place of ultimate safety. Not only is it constructed from material gathered from within the village rather than from material assembled for this purpose in the *khalā* but also every precaution is taken so that it will not be exposed to any danger from the outside before the couple start living in it. The movement of people and objects from the *khalā* into it is accomplished only after their dangerous quality has been reduced by their gradual movement across the other boundaries that lie between the hut and the *khalā* outside the village.

The hut which lies conceptually at the very centre of the Berti universe is a female domain *par excellence*: it is the place in which the woman cooks, sleeps and gives birth to her children. This hut is the first structure of the homestead to be built and it is the only part of the new homestead built before the *rahūla* (from *rahal*, to move), the final stage of the wedding process when, after the full bridewealth has been transferred and the wife's trousseau has been assembled by her mother, the couple finally establish themselves in their own household as an independent domestic group. The association of the hut with the woman is clearly expressed in the way it is constructed. Provided that the bride has not had a house built for her before, which is the case if it is either her first marriage or if her previous marriage ended in divorce while she was living in her parents' household, the house is *bēt 'āda*: it is built from material collected from other households in the village, the upper part of its conical roof is wrapped in white cloth and its top is adorned with palm leaves and a branch of a *hajlīd* tree. The husband's status does not

Figure 9 A bride is led to her new house by a turban cloth tied round her neck

determine whether the house will be built as *bēt 'āda* or not. Even if he has never had his own house before but his wife has, the house will not be a *bēt 'āda*.

Even if it is her house, under the ideal of virilocal residence the woman and not the man who moves into it is the stranger. Being an incoming stranger, the bride has to be ritually introduced into her new house. After her trousseau has been displayed in her parents' homestead, its items publicly counted (and often nowadays a written list of it compiled), it is packed by the groom's kinsmen onto a camel or camels and the bride, all clad in white, is led from her parents' house by the groom's brother or other close kinsman, using a turban cloth tied round her neck. The bride is sprinkled with water by one of her kinswomen. The analogy with other customary rituals would suggest that the bride, who is now for ever leaving the safety of her community, is being rendered immune to the dangers that face her outside its boundaries. The bride is put on a standing camel by the groom's kinsmen and the camel is led to the couple's new house using a turban tied to its bridle. Upon arrival, the camel and the bride are again sprinkled with water, the camel's forehead is anointed with butter, the groom's kinsmen lift the bride down from the camel and she crawls into her new house led again by the groom's brother or other close kinsman using a turban cloth tied round her neck. I was told that, in the old days, the bride crawled on a piece of white cloth spread on the floor of the hut between the entrance and the bed at the rear. The aim of these practices seems to be to render harmless any potential danger which the stranger bride might be carrying with her.

During the first week the bride does not cook, this being done by her husband's sister. It is only after about a week that the hearth is ritually built in the new house and the bride herself starts cooking. She still does not grind her own flour, using flour and other foodstuffs which she has brought as part of her trousseau. A few days after she has started cooking, the grinding stone is built for her by the women of the village, and she thereafter runs her own household as any other wife. Her gradual establishment as a fully-fledged mistress of her own house seems to parallel the gradual re-entry into the house of a man returning from the desert or the gradual move of the new millet into the house.

All these actions suggest a motivation by concerns similar to those which guide the movement of people from the safety of the village into the potentially dangerous *khalā*. In the same way people need to be protected against the dangers they face when venturing into the *khalā* for the first time after their birth or circumcision, and have to be gradually exposed to the things of the *khalā* in a ritually controlled way, the safety of the house has to be protected against contamination that could be brought into it by things that are dangerous by virtue of having originated in the *khalā*, by people who have been exposed to the *khalā*, or by those who may be dangerous simply by virtue of being strangers. The things which have been brought in from outside the village, and people who enter or re-enter the hut after their prolonged stay in the *khalā*, again have to be rendered harmless through the performance of appropriate rituals.

Village and women

I suggested in the previous chapter that the prominent role of women in customary rituals derives from the rituals being predicated on the idea of procreative power as the source of all creativity. But it seems that their prominent role in customary rituals also derives from the symbolic association between women and the village, which appears to be a logical extension of the already-mentioned symbolic association between a woman and the hut.

The Berti certainly see women as more closely associated with the village than men: when describing the difference between men and women, one of the things they invariably mention is that a woman, unlike a man, stays at home all the time and 'does not go anywhere'.

When a house is built, men construct its wooden frame, thatch the conical roof and raise it on its supporting poles. Women then thatch the round wall of the house and later build the straw fence around the homestead. This division of labour is not adequately explicable simply in terms of practial rationality. It is understandable that lifting the heavy roof is left to men; it is hard work and it taxes the strength of the men to its limits. But there is no apparent reason why men could not finish the whole job, and this suggests that the division of labour is symbolically motivated: it is symbolically appropriate for women to construct the wall and the fence which are the physical boundaries of what is perceived as female space.

If women stand for the village, their significance in the ritual re-entry into the house of a man returning from the desert may go beyond what I have said so far. The women smearing the butter on the man's hair with their heads and later carrying him into the house, can be seen very much like the other instrumental symbols (butter, water, *dashisha*, white cloth) used during the ritual, and the acts which they perform can be seen as being aimed at the removal of the dangers which the man may be bringing with him. But if the women symbolise the village, these acts may equally well dramatise his gradual establishment of contact with the village and his gradual and controlled re-introduction to the things inside it after his exposure to the dangers of the *khalā* – a theme of gradual acclimatisation to the domain which a person is entering, which we have already seen dramatised in other customary rituals.

Day and night

The distinction between the village and *khalā* is drawn in spatial terms and quite a number of customary rituals are indeed concerned with crossing the physical boundary between the village and *khalā* or between the hut and the world outside it. The opposition between the village and *khalā* is, however, also paralleled by the opposition between day and night. Certainly the night is seen as the time of increased danger. The Berti say: *Ahal al-lēl aktar min ahal an-nahār* ('The creatures of the night are more numerous than the creatures of the day'), and they point out that all the dangerous animals like snakes, hyenas, lions, jackals and foxes appear at night. Night is also the time of *nabātī* and *shayātīn*. The common Sudanese invocation *Alla najīna min masāib al-lēl u an-nahār* ('God save us from the misfortunes of the night and day') is, to the Berti, proof that there are more dangers at night than during the day. They say that all the night creatures are *majārim* (criminal), and they point out that thieves too burgle houses or steal grain from storage pits only at night: 'A man without bad intentions does not move around at night; he travels during the day.' People travel at night only when it is absolutely necessary; ordinarily, people set out on a journey in the morning and they interrupt their travel at night. Women, unless accompanied by men, would never venture out from the village at night for fear of encountering a *nabātī* or *shētān*. A woman alone would not even move from one house to another within the village at night; when women go to chat with neighbours, they always move in pairs or small groups; a woman alone would at most quickly slip to her next-door neighbour at night; she would certainly be reluctant to visit alone a house at the other end of the village.

Day is the time for work and night is the time for rest. The Koranic verses (78: 10–11), rendered by the Berti as *Lēl libāsa, nahār ma'āsha* ('The night is a cloak, the day is for livelihood') are often quoted in support of this view. Sometimes, people have to work at night of necessity. Threshing the harvest from one field has to be finished in a day so that men can start threshing the harvest of another neighbour the next day, and consequently threshing often continues well into the night. Towards the end of the rainy season when there is only a little water left in the well, people often have to wait for hours for enough to accumulate at the bottom of the well and they often have to draw it at night. But they refrain from sowing and weeding after sunset in the belief that by continuing after dark with the work which should properly be done during the day, they would adversely affect the future harvest. There is also a belief that if grain were pounded in mortars at night, the people of the village would gradually move to other places and the village would cease to exist.

The physical boundary between the village and *khalā* has of necessity to be crossed: people have to go to the fields, wells and markets, animals have to be driven out to pasture, and firewood, building material and food have to be brought into the village from outside. All this traffic across the boundary ordinarily occurs during the day. But the boundary between the human settlement and the world outside it has to be maintained clear and distinct at night, the time of increased danger. Thus men returning with rock salt from the desert have to enter the village before sunset; if they reach their village after the sun has set, they have to spend the night outside it and enter it the next morning after sunrise.[1] The grass or straw for thatching and the thorny branches for building cattle enclosures must not be brought into the village after sunset; they have to be unloaded outside the village and brought in the next morning. Some people are of the opinion that they can be brought into the village even after sunset but must be left overnight outside the entrance to the homestead and brought inside the next morning after sunrise.

The prohibition on bringing grass, straw or thorny branches into the village at night fits logically into the Berti cosmology. They are the material for building the fences – the actual physical boundaries which separate the homesteads from the open space of the village and the first boundaries which humans have to cross during their life. It is through this crossing that the human infant – the product of nature – enters the community of fellow men and joins for the first time the moral community of human society. The physical boundaries of homesteads thus separate the hut, the domain of 'culture' *par excellence*, from the 'nature' outside it as well as the 'nature' inside it from the 'culture' outside. If seen in this way, it logically fits that it is the women who construct the straw walls of the huts and the fences around them. Just as the fences mediate between 'nature' and 'culture', so women mediate

---

[1] The notion that a village must be entered only at the appropriate time of the day by travellers or those coming either for the first time or after a long absence seems to be widespread in Darfur. But probably not everywhere is it stipulated that the village must be entered before sunset. Nachtigal reports that when the caravan with which he travelled in 1874 from Wadai to Darfur approached Kobe, they camped in a nearby riverbed during the day 'because custom requires that arrival in a village should be timed for the evening' (Nachtigal 1971: 251). From his description it appears that they then entered Kobe after nightfall (ibid.: 252).

between the two domains, for only women are involved both in 'natural'
and 'cultural' creativity.

Physical and conceptual boundaries

When talking about the village, the Berti stress not only that it is a place
of safety (*amāna*), but also a place of mercy (*rahma*) and of privacy and
modesty (*sutra*; from *satar* – to cover or shroud parts of the body which
are not to be seen). *Rahma* implies first of all food and drink: *Al hilla
fōgu rahma, fī khalā mā fī shī* ('There is mercy in the village; in the
wilderness, there is nothing'). *Rahma* is a quality produced by women,
for only women process food and both sexes admit that women possess
greater *rahma* than men.

When talking about *sutra*, the Berti make it clear that it is the fence
which lends the homestead this quality and that every homestead should
have a proper fence so that no one can see inside it and no animal can
enter it. Sick people who cannot leave the house can relieve themselves
in the latrine in the yard without being seen and can thus preserve their
modesty. 'The house without a fence is bad or ugly (*shēn*) for everybody
can see what goes on inside it; it is like a person without clothes. *Sutra* is
again a quality produced by women: men build the hut but women
construct its straw wall and the fence around it which separates the hut
from the outside world and makes it a place of *sutra*.

If *rahma* and *sutra* are the typical qualities associated with the life in
the village, and if these qualities are produced by women, one can
readily understand why women themselves are a symbol of the village.
The Berti also associate *hajlīd* closely with the village; while they see *kitr*
as the most typical tree of the *khalā*, they see *hajlīd* as the most typical
tree growing inside human settlements. They point out that goats feed
on its fruit, spreading it into the village where the trees then sprout.
They are not cut down as they provide valuable shade and an abandoned village site can always be recognised by its *hajlīd* trees. In various
rituals, the *hajlīd* tree is employed as a symbol of the village and I have
mentioned before that in different contexts it can also be seen as symbol
of femininity. Its multivocality is the result of the substitution of one
symbol for another: if women and *hajlīd* stand for the village, then
logically women stand for *hajlīd* and *hajlīd* stands for women.

I have so far paid specific attention to rituals and customary practices
which are apparently concerned with the crossing and maintenance of
the boundary between the village and *khalā* and between day and night.
But there seems to be more involved than the distinction and mediation
between these physical and temporal domains. In fact, these domains
themselves can be seen as concrete symbols of a more general and

abstract conceptual opposition. At one pole of this opposition stands the unique world of humans who are God's animals and the highest of all his creatures: *Insān bahīma rabbina* ('A human being is God's animal') and *Beni Ādam sultān al-jasad kullu* ('A human being is the sultan of all bodies'). Only they produce (*nātij*), understand (*fāhim*) and 'know God' (*ba'rfu Allah*) and only they are discerning (*bāsir*) and able to differentiate between *halāl* and *harām*, proper and improper, good and evil. Only they marry properly, purify themselves after the performance of polluting acts, bury their dead and only they pray, fast, make sacrifices and go either to heaven or hell after death depending on how well they have obeyed divine instructions when alive. Their moral order is opposed to the amorality of other creatures who only walk around, eat, copulate, do not understand, are *nijis* (unclean) and eventually simply die. The divinely ordained way of life of the humans which is the life of safety (*amāna*), mercy (*rahma*) and propriety or modesty (*sutra*), is opposed to the anti-divine and anti-social life in the natural world outside human society which is populated by dangerous or potentially dangerous beings of which the most powerful and most dreaded are the *shayātīn*. The basic conceptual opposition in Berti cosmology is at once the opposition between creative humans and non-creative non-humans, God and *shētān*, reason and the lack of reason, safety and danger or misfortune (*masāib*), purity (*halāl*) and pollution (*harām, nijis*). The village and *khalā* are merely concrete symbols of two major conceptual domains which can be variously expressed through the opposition of the following terms:

village	*khalā*
day	night
safety	danger
rahma	deprivation
sutra	amorality
creative humans	non-creative non-humans
reason	lack of reason
halāl	*harām*
God	*shētān*
pure	polluted (*nijis*)

Customary rituals are not concerned merely with regulating and controlling the movement across boundaries. Many of them are concerned with the maintenance of a clear and distinct boundary not only between the village and *khalā* and day and night but also of the boundary between the two major conceptual domains of which the village, *khalā*, day and night are the concrete metaphors. Let me sketch here some corroborating evidence which clearly indicates the presence of this concern in Berti culture.

A major conceptual opposition in all Islamic cultures is that between what is ritually clean and permitted (*halāl*) on the one hand, and what is ritually polluting and hence forbidden (*harām*) on the other. The Berti, like all other Muslims, subscribe to this opposition which they clearly articulate verbally. According to the Islamic doctrine as they understand it, the camel is a clean animal and its flesh is edible; a donkey or horse, on the other hand, is *harām* and eating its flesh is forbidden. Equally, sex within marriage is *halāl* but any sexual intercourse except that between husband and wife is *harām*. The latter category includes both pre-marital sex and all illicit or adulterous sexual relations. But pre-marital sex and adultery are, in fact quite frequent. Being *harām*, they are dangerous and a man involved in any kind of illicit sexual relation has to take certain precautions if he is to avoid the dire consequences of his act.

If a man travels on a donkey or a horse to visit the woman with whom he has illicit sexual relations, no danger ensues. If, on the other hand, he travels on a camel, the camel will die, or, if it gets stolen, he will never find it again. Also his cows, goats and sheep will die for, like the camel, they too are all clean animals and, as the Berti say, they avoid *harām* (*mā bidōru harām*). Why these animals die is explained by drawing a parallel with mixing bitter and sweet substances: the bitter does not become sweet as a result, but the sweet always becomes bitter. For example, a bitter melon (*hamdan*) is eaten only by donkeys and horses which themselves are *murr* (bitter)[2]; it is never eaten by camels. If one mixes a bitter melon with an edible one, the latter itself becomes bitter. Equally, if one buys a stolen animal with money which was earned honestly and which is hence *halāl*, all one's wealth becomes *harām*.

Underlying this belief is not so much the idea that actions which are *harām* are dangerous as such, but rather that danger ensues when the boundary between *halāl* and *harām* is blurred and that it is always *harām* which spoils *halāl* whereas *harām* is not made *halāl* by being exposed to or mixed with it. The same idea clearly motivates the efforts to keep clear and distinct the boundaries between other conceptual domains.

The state of ritual pollution places people where they do not belong conceptually and in many respects it is equivalent to them being in the

---

[2] The Berti often used the word *murr* (bitter) in the sense of *harām* (ritually forbidden) or *nijis* (polluted). For example, the *shētān* is often characterised as *murr*.

khalā. A severe state of pollution is induced by their exposure to human blood. As I have explained earlier, the Berti see human blood as dangerous. Animal blood is not dangerous in the same way and butchers, who are constantly exposed to it, do not need to take any special precautions.

Human blood is *makrūh* (disapproved; in the sense of something that is to be avoided). Precautions have to be taken when it is spilled. This can happen either accidentally (such as when one injures oneself or others) on purpose (such as when illness is cured by letting blood by an incision in the skin) or as an unavoidable consequence of circumcision or birth. Any time blood is spilled it has to be buried in the ground. This is rationalised by pointing out that otherwise chickens might eat it and if one ate a chicken which had fed on human blood, it would be as bad as eating human flesh. Also flies get attracted to human blood left uncovered on the ground and then transfer it onto the food which people eat. It is not only blood that has to be buried lest it returns to the human body through food. Excrement and nail parings are also buried for the same reason. Only hair, after it has been shaved off, may be left on the ground uncovered. Birds pick it up to build their nests but it does not attract flies and no animal eats it.

Because a lot of blood is shed during childbirth, 'the blood of birth' (*dam wilāda*) is particularly dangerous and people who have come into contact with it are in the state of ritual pollution, or *nijis* as the Berti express it. They are prone to being attacked by a *shētān*, for a *shētān* is attracted by anything that is *nijis* (*shētān bidōru nijis*). In terms of the spatial metaphors of the village and *khalā*, through which the Berti represent to themselves the basic conceptual oppositions underlying their cosmology, people who are *nijis* are in the same position as if they were in *khalā*. This makes perfect sense if we recall that in one of its aspects *khalā* is seen as a place of danger because it is where *shayātīn* live and that the purpose of the numerous customs which accompany the movement of things and people from *khalā* into the village has often been stated by the Berti themselves as preventing the *shētān* from entering the village.

The rituals which are triggered off by the polluting aspect of the 'blood of birth' are clearly motivated by the same concerns as the rituals accompanying the crossing of the physical boundary between *khalā* and the village. I mentioned before that the safety and purity of the house has to be protected against contamination by things that originate in the *khalā* or by people who are re-entering the hut after their prolonged stay in the *khalā*. The same concern is expressed in rituals that accompany a person's re-entry into the hut after his or her exposition to the dangers of the 'blood of birth'. Such people have to establish or re-establish contact with the objects inside the hut in a gradual and ritually controlled way. In the case of childbirth a woman cannot re-enter the hut because the delivery always takes place inside it. However, as I shall describe later, she is ritually brought into a renewed contact with the things of the hut. This suggests that a woman polluted by the blood of birth is conceptualised as being outside the human community. This is further suggested by the fact that she can leave the hut to relieve herself only at night. When she goes at night, no boundary crossing is implied as it would be if she went out and re-entered the hut during the day. Conceptually she is on the opposite of the boundary from the rest of the people in the village; as she is 'out' of the village already, none of her actions should imply that she is actually crossing the boundary between the village and the world outside it. As she is conceptually outside the boundary, she can cross it only by coming in, and that must be done during the day.

The rituals triggered off by the polluting effect of the 'blood of birth' thus clearly dramatise the crossing of a conceptual, rather than merely a spatial or physical boundary. They indicate that people polluted by the 'blood of birth', although physically fully within the village, are conceptually outside it, and their re-entry into it has to be ritually controlled.

The temporary exclusion from human society and a ritually controlled re-entry into it is most clearly apparent in the case of a couple who have a stillborn child. When the child is born dead, the polluting effect of the blood of birth, to which every woman who gives birth is exposed, is aggravated by the fact that the couple have created the ultimate marginal being: one that passes into the afterlife without having entered human society and led a fully human life. Both parents who have been involved in its creation are perceived as dangerous to the village community and by virtue of this subject to ritual treatment.

When a woman's child is born dead, she and her husband stay confined for a week in the hut in which she delivered. During all this time, the man wears his cap as a protection against *shētān*. The couple do not speak to anyone and nobody comes to greet them. The woman does not cook and the couple eat food brought to them by neighbours who leave the dish in silence outside the door of the hut. On the seventh day, the couple and another couple who have had a stillborn child or one which died soon after birth, go to the nearest *hajlīd* tree. If the tree grows outside the couple's homestead, the woman is led to it completely wrapped in white cloth. She carries a kid, if there is one, and water is sprinkled on both the woman and her husband. The couple split one of the branches of the tree and tie it together again with a piece of string.

The couple and the tree are sprinkled with water. The branch is inspected after three days and if the split has not healed, another branch is split and tied together. Only after the branch has healed can the couple leave their house. The fact that nobody speaks to the secluded couple or greets them indicates quite clearly that they are seen as being outside the human community; the fact that the woman has stopped cooking and performing all the other tasks which women in the village ordinarily perform also indicates this. The couple are allowed to rejoin the community only after the split branch of the *hajlīd* tree has healed.

If the *hajlīd* tree is seen as the symbol of the village, the significance of the splitting and healing of its branch becomes quite transparent. If the branch does not heal, it is a sign that the couple are still dangerous to the community at large. Its healing is a sign that their danger is over; they can now re-enter the community without carrying any danger or pollution into it. No actual crossing of any physical boundary is involved and such a crossing is only symbolically enacted through the visit to the tree. But that a boundary has been crossed is also indicated by the time of day at which the ritual visit takes place. I have mentioned before that the boundary between *khalā* and the village can be safely crossed only during the day; when informants described to me how the ritual at the *hajlīd* tree is performed, they always stressed that the ritual must take place *before* sunset.[3]

The basic notion which gives meaning to the customary rituals and determines the occasions on which they are performed is that of fundamental opposition between two major domains into which the world is divided. This opposition can be expressed in various terms and it is not so much revealed in a coherent body of stated beliefs as rather embedded in the rituals themselves. These then become the main medium 'for transmitting meanings, constructing social reality, or for that matter creating and bringing to life the cosmological scheme itself' (Tambiah 1985: 129). They do this through resorting to concrete images of the village and *khalā* which are symbols in the sense that they stand for, or are concrete metaphors of, more abstract cosmological concepts

[3] The ritual response to stillbirth differs from the response to other abnormal births – miscarriage, the birth outside the hut and the birth of twins – which I discuss in Chapter 8. In the case of a miscarriage, which occurs up to about the sixth month of pregnancy, no human life has been created because the Berti consider the foetus to be a person from about the sixth month, after which a miscarriage is seen as a stillbirth. In the case of a birth outside the hut, a human being was born in the wrong place, and in the case of twins, two human beings were born instead of one as is normal. These births thus involve either a creature that is not yet human or a proper human being or beings born under abnormal circumstances. The stillbirth differs from these abnormal births in that the woman gives birth to a marginal human being that passes into afterlife without ever joining the human society. This, I would suggest, is the reason why it triggers off a different ritual response from the other abnormal births.

which are dimly felt rather than clearly articulated in Berti cognition. While being metaphors for the more abstract cosmological concepts, the images of the village and *khalā* are themselves represented in the ritual performances by specific concrete objects. These can again be seen as symbols in that they are to some extent arbitrary; thus numerous other subjects than those which have been actually selected, could have been chosen to symbolise the village or *khalā*. However, the arbitrariness of chosen symbols is circumscribed in that concrete objects are selected which are linked through metonymy or synecdoche to the domain which they represent. In that respect they can be seen as clearly motivated and one can envisage the process of symbolic construction as metonymy and synecdoche expressing, in concrete images, the entailments of an over-arching metaphor.

The *kitr* shrub and its bark, the stone used to peel it off, the firewood, the field and the millet plants which grow on it, the well, thorny branches, straw and various other objects are concrete images which symbolise the *khalā* through metonymy or synecdoche. The *khalā* itself then symbolises, through metaphor, the world which lacks human reason and the knowledge of God. Similarly, women, the *hajlīd* tree, the hut and the thorny branches, the straw and grass from which fences are built, are concrete objects which symbolise the village through metonymy or synecdoche. The village itself again symbolises through spatial metaphor all the different values pertaining to the life of humans as moral beings who 'know God'.

When the Berti express their abstract cosmological notions in terms of spatial metaphors of village and *khalā*, they employ a cognitive process which is probably universal. It is a process through which 'sense is made of the human world via the human understanding of the object world' (Gudeman 1986: 43). This is a process through which the non-physical is conceptualised in terms of the physical; that is, the less clearly delineated is conceptualised in terms of the more clearly delineated (Lakoff and Johnson 1980: 59, 108–9). Just as the concrete objects which stand for the village and *khalā* are clearly motivated, these spatial metaphors themselves are not without motivation. Their motivation is rooted in experiential basis arising from interaction with the physical environment (ibid. 18, 56–57). Thus, for example, when the Berti are explaining why *khalā* is dangerous, they always resort to narrating their experiences of dangers encountered there in the form of snakes, leopards and hyenas.

By manipulating the concrete symbols which stand for village and *khalā* in their ritual practices, the Berti express through imagery the abstract values which they find difficult to put into words. There is no escape from this 'logic of the concrete' even in the exegesis which also always resorts to concrete symbols or images. For example, it typically employs the image of the *shētān* – one of the concrete images that stands for the world which lacks human morality, reason and the knowledge of God. Thus I was told several times that there are many *shayātīn* in the *khalā* but only a few in the villages, for they avoid houses in which Koran is read and, particularly, they avoid *masīd* – the place for collective prayers and sacrifices. A *shētān* will not enter a village alone; it can be brought into it only by people. Many people explained that the purpose of the prohibition on bringing thorny branches, grass or straw into the village at night, or on entering the village after sunset when returning from the desert, is to prevent bringing a *shētān*, who is particularly active after sunset, into the village. In the morning after sunrise, the *shētān* will rise and leave the thorny branches or straw, which it is then safe to bring in. Others do not subscribe to the view that *shayātīn* live only in the *khalā* but argue that they are omnipresent. 'Even as we now talk, the *shētān* is hovering around us and only the angels protect us from him', I was told. 'It is true that a *shētān* avoids houses where people read the Koran but as many people do not read the Koran or pray regularly, there is a *shētān* in their houses; he eats and drinks with the people.' However, even those who dispute that a *shētān* would be brought into the village with thorny branches or straw after sunset, still resort to concrete images in their exegesis of this custom. They say that bringing in straw and thorny branches at night would 'spoil the village' (*bakharib al-hilla*): people would gradually leave it and settle elsewhere.

By expressing in writing the ideas which the Berti express through concrete images, I have inevitably made these ideas appear not only more abstract but also more coherent and systematic than they appear in Berti consciousness. Because of the unavoidable difference in the anthropologist's and actors' medium of expression, my interpretation may appear not to be supported adequately by the actors' explicit exegesis. There is, however, further ethnographic evidence which suggests that the rituals are indeed concerned with keeping the divinely ordained way of life of the moral human community separate from anything that originates in the world which is devoid of judgement and self-restraint characteristic of human existence, and with controlling the intrusion of the latter domain into the former. This has to be done to avoid the corruption of the uniquely human domain by the anti-divine and anti-social forces which dominate the world outside human society for, just as *harām* can never be turned into *halāl* but *halāl* is always turned into *harām* when exposed to it, human morality can never overcome the amorality of the non-human world but can itself only be corrupted by any uncontrolled exposure to it. I shall return to this topic again when I discuss the rituals which are explicitly concerned with keeping separate the two major conceptual domains.

5

Custom and religion

By expressing the knowledge that procreation is a joint enterprise but that making people grow and giving them health and personality is essentially a feminine role, the customary rituals elaborate in their own way the idea made explicit by women when they talk about themselves as making the men what they are, and thus formulate a different model of gender relations than that of male dominance and female subordination. It is a model which depicts men as dependent on women. The validity of these two models has different sources.

The validity of the model of male dominance and female subordination derives from the fact that it is understood as part of the Islamic tradition and hence as ordained by God. It is frequently justified by reference to the Koran which stipulates that 'men are in charge of women, because Allah has made the one of them to excel the other' (Sura 4: 34) and that 'men are a degree above' women (2: 24), and it is legitimised by reference to the well-known Koranic injunctions according to which the inheritance shares of women are half those of men (4: 11), and according to which two women have to testify in place of one man (2: 282). Although this model is expressed verbally more often by men than by women, women are not only aware of it but subscribe to it in their everyday conduct without any reservations. They share it with men because, like them, they also fully subscribe to the tenets of Islam in which this model is perceived as having its origin. Obviously, as the dominance of men over women is seen as part of the divine order, women cannot, and hence do not, challenge it openly. This also makes understandable the fact that the view of men as dependent on women is elaborated mainly in symbolic form and expressed more strongly or more often, in ritual actions than in explicit verbal statements (Ardener 1972).

The model of men as dependent on women derives its validity from the everyday commonsense experience of both men and women. It is, however, also justified by the fact that many of the notions expressed through the symbolic structure of customary rituals can easily be reconciled with the Islamic tradition. Thus, for example, the Berti clearly see the idea of the purifying potency of water as deriving from this source. They readily mention that, in accordance with Koranic injunctions (4: 43, 5: 6), water is used for ablution before prayer, for purifying a sacrificial animal and generally for removing ritual impurity. Koranic verses (21: 30, 25: 40) are also quoted in support of the idea that water is the source of all life, and equating *rūh* with water is also seen by the Berti as having its origin in the Koran (25: 54). The notion of milk as a symbol of procreation is also justified by reference to the Koranic allusion to semen and milk as the two fluids from which a human being is created (86: 5–7). The belief that milk creates the child's substance is supported by reference to the Koranic notion of a special relationship (*rida'a*) between a child and a woman, other than its own mother, who has nursed it, which creates a bar to marriage between those related through milk (4: 23). The effort to legitimise the customary rituals and their underlying notions by reference to Islamic tradition is pervasive. One *fakī* went as far as to suggest that men whose firstborn child is a girl are lucky because they are like the Prophet Mohamed, who also fathered a girl. The inclusion of the customary rituals within the mainstream of Islamic belief is even more strongly attested to by the fact that all speeches uttered during a ritual performance are addressed to God who alone may grant the well-being and safety which the rituals seek to bring about. In this respect, the Berti ethnography supports S. Ardener's observation that 'counterpart models are not generated independently of those of the dominant structure, but are to some extent shaped by them' (1975: xiii). Although not existing alongside Islam but within it, the customary rituals nevertheless seize on just some elements of the Islamic faith and tradition and elaborate them in their own way and in the process endow them with special significance and meaning. They do so through removing them from the context in thich they have originally been expressed and putting them into a new one. But this is common even with practices which the Berti see as properly Islamic. As I have explained before, the Koranic verses which are used in *hijbāt* and *mihāi* have been endowed by the *fugarā* with meaning that is quite different from that which they have in the context of the Koranic message. Such manipulation of meaning is thus certainly not the reason why the Berti differentiate the customary rituals (*'awāid*) conceptually from what they consider to be proper religion (*dīn*). When making the distinction between these two types of rituals, the Berti emphasise their respective means: religious rituals achieve their envisaged ends by following God's injunctions as revealed in the Koran. By showing their awareness of them and by showing their willingness to follow them, the performers of the ritual aim at predisposing God favourably towards themselves. In customary rituals, divine interference is also presupposed, but it brings about the desired state of affairs in conjunction with symbolic manipulation, through which the performers of the ritual affect their future state or that of others in much the same way as they affect their future state through their directly experienced power on the things they act upon.

While customary rituals are predominantly women's affairs, religion is predominantly, if not almost exclusively, the domain of men. Although both boys and girls may attend Koranic schools, only boys apprentice themselves to prominent religious leaders to continue their religious education and to learn the Koran by heart. As this is the necessary qualification for becoming a *fakī*, only men can achieve this status. Some religious rituals are performed exclusively by men, so only men perform sacrifices and *du'a*. During a funeral, only men carry the body to the grave irrespective of whether the deceased is a man or a woman, bury it and say prayers at the grave while women stay behind in the village assembled in the deceased's house. Even those religious actions whose performance is open to and ideally expected from both sexes, are mostly performed only by men. So only a few women pray regularly or at least attend the Friday noon prayers. They are certainly more lax than men about fasting during Ramadan, and they hardly ever go on pilgrimages to Mecca.

Although the Berti are aware of the differences between customary and religious rituals, they play them down in their conceptualisation. They see both classes of ritual as bringing about the well-being, safety, health, comfort and prosperity of specific individuals who undergo them or on whose behalf they are performed. This is clearly indicated by the fact that some of the more pious tend to give up customary rituals; in their eyes, these have been superseded, in the pursuit of well-being and prosperity, by Islamic practices. But only a few, even among the more pious ones, go as far as seeing customary rituals as *sanam* or *kanūz*, words which have the distinct connotation of 'superstition'. On the whole, customary rituals co-exist easily with the Islamic orthodoxy as it is locally perceived. However, the fact that the Berti have no difficulty in legitimising them and their underlying notions by reference to Islamic traditions, provides only a partial reason for this state of affairs. Before suggesting a fuller explanation, I shall deal briefly with a related but more straightforward problem: given that the message expressed through the symbolic structure of the customary rituals presents men as dependent on women, and thus implicitly puts forward a different view of gender relations from that which men emphatically express, why do men willingly participate in these rituals?

It may, of course, be possible that only women are fully aware of what is being dramatised in ritual performaces and that men are enticed into participation because they are unaware of the implications of what they are doing, but this is not my impression. The men I talked to seemed to be as much aware as women of the meaning of the ritual performances and the symbols employed in them. I believe that there are two rather different reasons for men's participation.

The first stems from the fact that, whatever the rituals' semantic components, they are aimed at achieving goals that benefit men as well as women. As men desire well-being, health and safety as much as women, most of them willingly participate, whenever appropriate, in rituals performed to bring about these goals.

The second reason becomes apparent once we appreciate the difference which Tambiah draws between the ritual's symbolic and pragmatic meanings (Tambiah 1979). I have so far been concerned solely with the former. In fact the Berti are equally well aware of the latter and they express this awareness when they stress that the customary rituals are important markers of their identity or, as they themselves express it, part of the Berti *sunna* (tradition). They are something that is uniquely theirs and that clearly distinguishes them from all their neighbours, with whom they otherwise share many elements of a common culture, including the Arabic language. As the main posts in the symbolic boundary of Berti society, the customary rituals contrast with Islam, which the Berti also share with all their neighbours and which, in consequence, rather erodes or threatens their identity. This aspect of customary rituals is another reason why the Berti distinguish them conceptually from religion (*dīn*) and also a reason why men not only do not resist them but willingly take part in them. While women may be participating primarily because they are women, men participate primarily because they are Berti.

The fact that the pragmatic meaning of customary rituals may be the most important thing about them for men also explains to some extent why men seem to be unconcerned with their symbolic meaning and why they are willing to let them portray creativity as largely feminine. But it is only a partial explanation.

As I have argued above, Berti customary rituals are predicated on the idea of the procreative power as the source of all creativity, and they stress the creative role of women through the instrumental symbols which they employ. By expressing the knowledge that creativity is essentially a feminine role, they elaborate, in their own way, a model of gender relations which depicts men as dependent on women. It is a model which coexists with the model of male dominance and female subordination. Ultimately, the two models complement one another. The model of male dominance, which the Berti see as substantiated by their Islamic beliefs, expresses the ways in which women depend on men for strength, authority and protection. The model put forward in customary rituals expresses the ways in which men depend on women for their physical existence, health and the formation of their characters. In their complementarity, the two models reflect the knowledge of the interdependence of the sexes to which both men and women tacitly subscribe. I would suggest that one of the main reasons why the customary rituals persist alongside the religious ones derives from the fact that what the Berti understand as Islamic orthodoxy does not alone adequately reflect their commonsense knowledge of the interdependence of men and women. There is probably yet another reason why the impact of Islam on Berti beliefs has not led to the abandoning of customary rituals and, in consequence, to the straightforward strengthening of the model of gender relations expressed through Islam. As I have explained earlier, the Berti do not emphasise the polluting aspect of female blood and, in consequence, they construe women's powers as exclusively beneficent.

Paradoxically, the persistence of these views is again facilitated through the adherence to Islam and through the existence of notions about what is and what is not proper Islam. It was mentioned before that although the customary rituals are conceptually differentiated from the Islamic religion, on the whole they are not seen as superstitions. However, what is generally dismissed by the pious as *sanam sākit* or *kanūz sākit* (sheer superstition) are the beliefs that certain events can spoil the country and detain the rain. To anticipate the accounts below I will just mention here that this view is supported by pointing out that no human action can affect the rain, for it is sent and can be withdrawn only by God. Among the events which spoil the country are the spilling of female blood in an abnormal birth: a birth outside the hut, a birth of twins and a miscarriage. As these events are polluting, it is through them that the procreative powers of women could be seen as both beneficent and malevolent. But any elaboration of beliefs about the malevolent aspect of women's natural powers is effectively precluded when beliefs about pollution through female blood are dismissed as superstitions. By considering them not to be in accordance with Islam, any possible construction of women as inherently ambivalent, and hence in need of subjugation to male control, is effectively precluded. The result is that the positive aspect of female creativity, clearly dramatised in other customary rituals, is left unchallenged.

However, the interdependence of religion and custom in Berti culture is not exhausted by the fact that customary rituals complement or modify in an important way the model of society which has its origin in Islam. To appreciate fully the nature of this interdependence, it is necessary to consider how the Berti themselves picture their conversion to Islam. This is described in a mythological story which is known by virtually every adult Berti and which is often told during the story-telling sessions. It is a variant of the 'Wise Stranger' myth told in many parts of the Sudanic Belt (see e.g. Trimingham 1968: 135; Holt 1963; 1973: 76–8; O'Fahey and Spaulding 1974: 112–126; O'Fahey 1980: 123, Hurreiz 1986). Here I give one version of it as it was told to me in 1961 by Amāra Ahmad Duggu.

During old times, the king of the Berti was a giant called Nāmadu or Hobay who had his house on one of the hills in the Tagabo Mountains. In his days, the Berti were not Muslims and had no religion. One day, a Fellātī[1] arrived and settled in Jebel Sakeni in Dar Hijir (an area in the Tagabo Mountains). He had two beautiful daughters who attracted Nāmadu's attention and aroused his desire for them. He sent his messengers to bring him the girls. When the messengers arrived in Jebel Sakeni, they abducted the girls and brought them to Nāmadu who kept them by force in his house.

The Fellātī was dismayed and left for Mecca to complain to the sultan there. The sultan dispatched a group of *ansār* (helpers) led by El Haj Mohamed Yambar on a *jihād* against Nāmadu. El Haj Mohamed Yambar was to return the girls to their father and to convert Nāmadu's people to Islam.

When El Haj Mohamed Yambar and his *ansār* arrived, they made their camp in Wādī Melik. Nāmadu was getting ready for a battle with them and he ordered his spies to observe them constantly and to report back to him all their movements. The spies kept telling him that the strangers in Wādī Melik were very powerful and that they would certainly kill him if he decided to fight them. Nāmadu started to be afraid and he eventually abandoned his war plan and decided to flee to Sanusia to save his life and to leave the girls behind. Before he left, he threw all the cows, camels, donkeys, horses, sheep and goats in his land

---

[1] The term Fellāta (sg. Fellātī) refers to peoples from the west of the frontier between the Sudan and Chad. A considerable number of Fellāta pass through the Sudan on their pilgrimage to Mecca and many of them have settled permanently in Darfur or elsewhere in the Sudan. O'Fahey estimates that the number of settlers of West African origin may comprise one third of the whole population of Darfur (1980: 4).

into the deep wells and he filled the well with huge rocks and boulders which only he was able to move. He left just one well open and he ordered his people also to fill it after they had drawn water from it. But people were afraid of El Haj Mohamed Yambar and his *ansār* and left the well open. This well is Mau in Jebel Tagabo and it is the oldest of all Berti wells. For his journey across the desert, Nāmadu took a *khuruj* (a pair of large water bags carried on the donkey's back) filled with water and *jurbān* (bags made of cow hides) filled with millet. The water dripped from the *khuruj* and millet grains from the *jurbān*, which were only hastily sewn together and, although it was the dry season of the year, the millet germinated, grew and ripened. There was a famine in the country and people followed Nāmadu's footsteps and found millet to eat.

When El Haj Mohamed Yambar arrived in Nāmadu's house, Nāmadu was gone and there was only his *wazīr* (deputy) left in the house. El Haj Mohamed Yambar befriended him and taught him to say *bism il-lāhi* ('in the name of God') before the start of a meal and to read short chapters from the Koran.

El Haj Mohamed Yambar's *ansār* spread all over the country to convert other people to faith. They established Koranic schools and mosques and they taught people how to marry properly by paying *sidag*[2] and saying *fātha*. They taught them the names of the days, the seven days of a week, the thirty days of a month and the names of months, and they taught them the Muslim names which they were to give to their children.

The people accepted the religion and they liked El Haj Mohamed Yambar. El Haj Mohamed Yambar married the *wazīr*'s daughter and he had a son by her whom he called Ismāīl. He asked people to give their daughters in marriage to his *ansār*.

El Haj Mohamed Yambar and the *wazīr* went to Farok (north of Kuttum) to see Shau Dorsīd, the Tunjur sultan. The *wazīr* told him that El Haj Mohamed Yambar was a good man, that he taught the people religion and that he taught them how to behave properly and how to live happily. He told the sultan that he was better than he (the *wazīr*) himself and he asked him to make El Haj Mohamed Yambar the king of the Berti. But El Haj Mohamed Yambar refused to become the king and suggested that his son Ismāīl should become the king. And so Ismāīl became the king of the Berti and El Haj Mohamed Yambar became the *imām* in the land.

---

[2] *Sidag* is the Berti equivalent of the Arabic *mahr*. It is the payment which legalises the marriage contract and which is transferred by the bridegroom's father or marriage guardian to the bride's guardian during the first stage of the wedding.

The myth about the origin of religion portrays, through the use of similar imagery the same dichotomy as that expressed in the myth about the origin of fire. In both myths, the autochthons are not fully human: Nāmadu is a giant and, in this respect, similar to the Farkh al-Ganān of the myth about the origin of fire, who are said to have been tall, big and strong with their bodies covered in hair. In both myths, the autochthons live up on hills whereas the incoming strangers appear in the plain below (El Haj Mohamed Yambar and his *ansār* made their camp in Wādī Melik). In both myths, the incoming strangers are men and the new era begins by them marrying daughters of the autochthonous inhabitants. In both myths, the new beginning is equated with the beginning of a truly cultural life which replaces the previous animal-like existence. In the myth about the origin of fire, the eating of raw meat is replaced by the consumption of cooked food. The myth about the origin of religion tells a similar story. As the result of El Haj Mohamed Yambar's teaching, people stopped simply feeding themselves and started to eat in a proper human way; they stopped simply mating and adopted proper marriages. The powerful message of the myth is that to be properly human means to follow the Islamic way. The myth is quite explicit about the the fact that only through the adoption of Islamic practices have people over-come their natural drives and impulses and learnt to gratify their natural needs in a proper human way. The myth is as much about the origin of religion as it is about the origin of cultural life and, in this respect, it can be seen as a 'charter' for opposing culture to nature.

In the customary rituals, this opposition is expressed through the concrete imagery of village and wilderness. In one of its aspects, the village is the place of well-being or mercy (*rahma*), whereas the wilderness, in which 'there is nothing', is a place of deprivation. The same opposition is also expressed in the myth about the origin of religion. The autochthonous people are portrayed in it as suffering before they adopted the customs which the strangers brought them. Before he fled, Nāmadu killed all the domestic animals. There was famine in the land and people had nothing to eat; to survive, they had to gather the millet which sprouted from the grain which Nāmadu took with him.

There exist numerous versions of the story about the arrival of El Haj Mohamed Yambar but the state of deprivation in which people lived before they accepted his teaching is stressed and elaborated, in one way or another, in all of them. One version of the story which I collected does not mention the *ansār* and represents El Haj Mohamed Yambar as having been sent alone from Mecca to convert the Berti pagans who were at that time ruled by the giant Nāmadu. Close to the borders of

Berti territory, El Haj Mohamed Yambar secluded himself for several years meditating in the desert. After he had successfully strengthened himself by seclusion, he resumed his journey to meet Nāmadu. His wisdom which he clearly demonstrated by introducing many new practices, eventually impressed Nāmadu to such an extent that he made him a king over all his subjects and offered him his daughter. El Haj Mohamed Yambar agreed to take her only after he persuaded Nāmadu and his people that a man and a woman living together should not be preceded only by the abduction of the woman by the man. They should start living together only after a proper marriage ceremony conducted according to the *sunna* of the Prophet. Among the good new practices which El Haj Mohamed Yambar introduced, the story dwells on the way in which he changed the existing practice of eating:

At meal times, the people used to assemble together and waited for the dishes to be brought from different houses of the village. Each time a dish was brought, the people rushed and consumed the food and then waited for the next dish to arrive. As a result, the meal was interrupted by periods of waiting, the food was not blessed and the villagers remained hungry. El Haj Mohamed Yambar did not like what he saw and decided to change the people's habit. He first asked everybody to wait until all the dishes were brought from the different houses. He then taught everybody to say *bism il-lāhi* before the meal started and to eat politely without hurrying. His advice made a lot of difference. For the first time, everybody finished the meal without feeling hungry any more and plenty of food was still left.

In other versions of the story, the origin of religion and Islamic practices is also seen as the origin of the truly cultural life which in itself is the source of people's well-being.

I have argued before that in the customary rituals, the village and the wilderness are employed as concrete images of the two realms whose distinctiveness is maintained through ritual action. The village is the concrete image of the realm of humans, who are God's animals and the only creatures who know God and follow his instructions. It is a concrete image of anything that is uniquely human and manifests itself in the awareness of God. Similarly, the wilderness is the concrete image of the non-human world of creatures and objects which merely exist without any awareness of God. This distinction is ultimately the distinction between the realm of the divine and its opposite. For the Berti, the *shētān* is the main anti-divine force in the universe and it is only logical that they see *khalā* as his abode. The opposition with which the customary rituals are concerned is thus more than the opposition between the village and *khalā*; it is also the opposition between God and *shētān*.

At the same time, the opposition underlying the customary rituals is also seen as an opposition between people and *shayātīn*. The Berti point out that the *shētān* lives either in tall trees, rocky outcrops and hills or in the antholes. He thus inhabits places either above or below the ground and in this respect is opposed to human beings who live on the ground. He is also opposed to human beings in that he moves around at the time when people are least active: after sunset when they have stopped their daily work and returned to their homes or in the heat of the early afternoon when they take their mid-day rest. All this is in line with conceptualising the *shētān*, not only as the enemy of God but also as the enemy of people. Purity derives from following God's instructions. As the *shētān* revels in anything that is impure (*nijis*), he perpetually tries to lead people astray from God's ways and he tries to corrupt them and to induce them into performing acts which are *harām* and polluting. People too are involved in the cosmic struggle between God and *shētān*, and their place in this struggle is unequivocally on God's side: they are his animals (*bahīma rabbina*). People protect themselves against the intrusion of the *shētān* into their domain, the village, by keeping it distinct from his domain, the *khalā*, and by ritually controlling the movement across the boundary which separates the two domains.

When the Berti explain that the purpose of the prohibitions on bringing various things from the *khalā* into the village is to prevent the *shētān* from entering the village, they do more than express, in concrete imagery, their basic cosmological beliefs or rationalise their non-Islamic beliefs in terms appropriate to the religious discourse. By seizing on the image of the cosmic struggle between God and *shētān*, in which they themselves are active participants, they construe their customary rituals as complementary to the religious rites. Such complementarity derives from the fact that both types of rituals express, in their own way, a cosmology which has its origin in Islam as the Berti understand it.

Although it would certainly be an exaggeration to say that the Berti proclaim their Muslim faith as much through the performance of customary rituals as they do through the performance of religious rites, we can perhaps see both custom and religion as a kind of discourse about the world. From these two discourses, religion is quite clearly dominant: whereas there are people who evaluate *'āda* negatively, *dīn* is never evaluated negatively by anyone, as that would amount to denying God, which no Berti would consider thinkable. The very fact that religion is fully shared makes the religious discourse clearly dominant, for an important implication of ideological dominance is precisely that the ideology is shared (Whyte 1981: 364). Women accept, support and share the dominant religious ideology as much as men. In spite of the greater involvement of men in religious rituals and women in customary rituals, the orientation towards customary rituals does not differ according to the divide between men and women, but according to the degree of piety among individual men and women.

It would certainly be too simplistic to try to explain customary rituals and their underlying beliefs as survivals from the pre-Islamic past. Whatever their possible historical origin, the cosmology in which they are grounded may be seen as being expressed through symbols which, even if possibly not of Islamic origin themselves, certainly relate to basic Islamic notions. Precisely because these symbols and concrete images do not represent any radical alternative to these notions, most Berti do not see the *'awāid* as challenging the dominant Islamic ideology. As I have explained before, it is true that the *'awāid* seize on particular elements of this ideology and elaborate them in their own way and, in the process, they endow them with different significance and meaning. But such removal of the Islamic notions from the context in which they have been originally expressed is certainly not the reason why *'awāid* are conceptually differentiated from *dīn*. I have already mentioned one of these reasons above. The other is that the Berti do not see the *'awāid* as having been prescribed, recommended or permitted in either the Koran or *ḥadīth*. For the pious, this very fact constitutes a deviance. They do not go as far as seeing them as superstitions, but they tend to see them as superfluous. In their eyes, they are not aimed at achieving different aims from the strictly religious rituals and, if that is the case, there is no need for their performance. The desired well-being, health and prosperity will be granted by God as long as people follow his ways and faithfully perform the actions stipulated in the Koran and in the Prophetic tradition, and this is all they ever need do.

However, those who are inclined to see the customary rituals as superfluous, constitute only a very small minority in Berti villages. Most people do not see any conflict between the *'awāid* and Islam. This is for three main reasons. The first is that the cosmological notions on which they are founded do not directly contradict or clash with Islamic ideas. On the contrary, in their own way they elaborate ideas – like those about divine and anti-divine forces – which can easily be seen as having Islamic origins. The second reason is that, in any case, the customary rituals incorporate overt Islamic elements, such as addressing the incantations during a ritual performance to God, which clearly indicates that they derive from Islam and hence are fully compatible with it. Finally, the customary rituals are seen as part of the Berti tradition. Even the pious admit that they are part of Berti *sunna* which they do not see as being in any way in conflict with the *sunna* of the Prophet. As part of the Berti tradition, the customary rituals cannot be challenged without challenging the very principles on which normal existence is founded.

6

Life cycle

Customary rituals accompany various stages of the agricultural cycle –
they are performed before water is first drawn from the well at the
beginning of the dry season, when a man returns to the village from his
first journey to the rock-salt deposits in the desert, and at various other
occasions to which I have already alluded. These situations are not
subject to any ritual elaboration in Islam. They are not mentioned in the
Koran and there are no records in *ḥadīth* that they were ever celebrated
in a particular way by the original Muslim community whose actions
should be emulated by contemporary believers. The life-crises situations
are different. There are numerous references in *ḥadīth* to the rituals
which should accompany the birth of a child and both the Koran and
ḥadīth are explicit about the way in which marriage should be concluded
and the death of a person dealt with. In consequence, the Berti see
births, marriages and funerals as religious events at which appropriate
Islamic rituals must be performed. Like other Muslims, they also
consider circumcision to be an important religious duty although there is
no mention of it in the Koran and *ḥadīth* mentions it as a pre-Islamic
custom. Because the customary rituals co-exist easily with the dominant
religious ideology, specific customary rituals also accompany these
major life crises and very often seem to be subject to greater elaboration
and appear to have greater importance than the religious rituals
themselves. I have already mentioned briefly some of the customs
associated with the major events of the life course. In this chapter, I
sketch more systematically the religious and customary rituals which
accompany birth, marriage and death and I devote the following chapter
to the discussion of circumcision.

Birth
A woman gives birth to her first child usually while she is still living in
her parents' household and her child is delivered in her mother's hut.

Even if she has her first child after she has already started living with her husband in their independent household, a few weeks before her baby is due, she moves to her parents' household to give birth in her mother's hut, as is generally the custom throughout Northern Sudan (see e.g. Barclay 1964: 214). Only her subsequent children are born in her own hut.

In every village, there is one woman who acts as a midwife (*dāya*). She has usually learned the skill from her mother or some other close kinswoman and apart from assisting with deliveries, she also performs female circumcisions. She is paid a little money immediately after a delivery. Services of a knowledgeable woman are required as the vagina, scarified as the result of circumcision, has to be cut open with a knife and then resewn again. The midwife stays with the mother for a few days attending to her needs, or she comes to check up on her a few times every day if she lives nearby. When a woman gives birth to her first baby, she is also always assisted by her mother, or by one of her close female relatives if her mother is dead; the mother usually also attends the births of her daughter's other children and often a few female kin and neighbours are also present in the hut during the delivery.

The woman gives birth squatting on the floor of the hut facing east and half suspended by a rope tied to the wooden frame of the roof which she holds with both her hands stretched above her head. This method of giving birth is common in the riverain Sudan (see Crowfoot 1918: 129; El Tayib 1955: 149–50). A report from the Fur suggests that it may be a recent practice among them (Beaton 1948: 14) and it is thus quite possible that it may have spread to Darfur from the east. The umbilical cord is cut off by a piece of string and the placenta is buried outside the hut beside the door. A few seeds of millet and water melons are planted on the spot[1] on which the rim of an old pot is then placed; a few ears of millet, a twig of the *hajlīd* tree and palm leaves are stuck inside the pot. The place at which the placenta is buried immediately indicates the sex of the baby to the visitors who come to 'greet' the mother during the next few days. The people of the village learn the sex of the newborn baby right at the moment of delivery. The birth of a boy is seen as *gisma kabīr* (a great gift from God), especially by men, because a son perpetuates the man's lineage. It is greeted by shouts of *izāna* (*Allāhu akbaru* – the call to prayer) and the father may fire a gun; when a girl has been born, women ululate.

The millet sown on the spot where the placenta is buried is watered

---

[1] For a similar custom in Omdurman see Hills-Young 1940: 333.

during the dry season and when it develops ears, these are covered by a piece of cloth to protect the grain from birds. Millet grown in this way is used as a medicine against stomach pain and diarrhoea. If there is only a little grain, this is fed directly to the sick person. If there is enough of it, *kajāna* (fermented millet dough normally filtered to make beer) is made from it and the sick person drinks it as a medicine.

Right after the delivery, the midwife smears her forehead and the mother's and baby's forehead with flour. All women who are present in the hut do likewise so as not to get blind from the sight of the 'blood of birth' (*dam wilāda*), and to protect themselves from *shayātīn* which are attracted by it. As will be obvious from the following description, this concern with protection against the dangers resulting from the polluting effect of the 'blood of birth' reappears all the time during the various customs and rituals following birth, and the smearing with flour, butter and milk and the use of white cloth, string and beads are a constantly recurring theme.

The mother and the baby are put on a *hasīr* – a bed on which women sleep and which consists of a mat made of the woody stalks of *tumām* grass (*Panicum turgidum*) spread on a low table-like wooden frame at the back of the hut. Locally grown tobacco and *kawal*[2] are ground into powder and together with a little bit of flour, they are mixed with water into a thin paste which is smeared on top of the baby's head to cover the fontanelle (*nafūkha*). This is done to prevent the wind from entering the baby's stomach through the *nafūkha*, so that it will not suffer from tummy ache.[3] The baby's head is covered with a piece of cloth and is kept covered all the time to protect it against *shayātīn* and wind. To protect the baby against wind entering it through the feet, its toes are smeared with butter and rock salt. The mother too is prone to wind and to protect her against it, her toes are also smeared with butter and rock salt; to protect herself against the wind entering her, she must wear shoes all the time. The rock salt is also put on the mother's and baby's head; rock salt is *murr* (bitter) and as such it repels *shayātīn* who are otherwise attracted by the 'blood of birth'. To protect the baby against *shayātīn*, a white cotton thread is tied round its wrists, ankles, neck and waist.

Sometimes the father slaughters a goat in sacrifice so that meat can be offered to the guests from neighbouring villages who come to greet the

---

[2] *Kawal* are the fermented leaves of the wild-growing Cassia plant. After they have been dried, they are pounded in a mortar and the resulting black powder is used for spicing the relish.

[3] In Omdurman, cooked animal fat is applied over the fontanelle to prevent the child developing a cold or cough as it is thought that the child breathes through this part of the skull (Hills-Young 1940: 335).

mother during the first few days following the birth when the news has reached them. Very often the father sacrifices a goat only for his firstborn child, particularly if it is a boy. If it is a girl, there is often no sacrifice, and it is not unusual that a man who has already several daughters slaughters a goat in sacrifice when his first son is born.

Following the delivery, the woman stops cooking and grinding flour. All the domestic work is done by her mother or by some other close kinswoman, if the woman's mother is dead. She prepares a special dish called *medīda* which the mother of the baby eats during the time she stays confined in the house. It is a thin gruel which, unlike the staple gruel, is not made from the flour of germ but of fresh millet boiled in water or milk to which some rock salt, oil or melted butter is added. In the case of a firstborn child, the cooking is done by the woman's mother who herself supplies the ingredients for the first two days. On the third day, the father's mother delivers the necessary ingredients: flour, additional millet, salt, rock salt and oil. To make sure that she will gather in time the necessary amount of flour, she usually distributes grain to all her neighbours to help her with grinding it.

For the first seven days, the mother stays with her baby on the *hasīr*. The baby must not be left alone lest a *shētān* would change it, or at least change its eyes, and if the mother has to leave the hut to relieve herself, her own mother sits next to the baby. When the mother goes out of the hut, she carries a knife and a stalk of millet, the substitute for a short stick which is used for driving donkeys and which young men, unless they have an axe or a throwing stick, always carry with them so that they can kill any snake they might come across. Before leaving the hut, she taps both doorposts with the knife and the millet stalk to chase away the *shētān* who always hovers on the threshold and she does the same before she re-enters the hut. If the mother goes to relieve herself at night, she carries glowing embers on a potsherd to repel the *shētān*. Sometimes a soft branch of *'ushar* shrub (*Calotropis procera*) is placed on the threshold after the baby has been born and all those who come to greet the mother step over it so as not to bring the *shētān* inside the hut with them. I was not able to elicit any opinions about why *'ushar* repels the *shētān*. But *'ushar* is clearly seen as wet and soft and it is also associated with femininity; in this respect it shares the auspicious connotations of all other instrumental symbols. When the Berti talk about men as hard and women as soft, they sometimes resort to the imagery of stone and *'ushar*. It is likely that the appropriateness of an *'ushar* branch as an instrumental symbol is grounded in this concrete metaphor.

When the child has been born, it may be given a temporary name, known as the 'navel name' (*isim surra*) by the midwife. This name usually does not survive and as a rule it is known only to the child's nearest relatives. However, it may sometimes be used, particularly by the child's maternal grandparents, even after the child has been given its proper name during the ceremony called *agūga* (*aqīqah* in classical Arabic). This is held on the seventh day after the birth in accordance with the Islamic *sunna*, and is attended by people from neighbouring villages and the child's relatives from farther away. *Agūga* for the firstborn child is organised by its maternal grandfather who slaughters a goat to provide meat for the guests; *agūga* for the subsequent children is their father's responsibility. Late in the afternoon, after the festive meal, the child's name is chosen from among the names appropriate for the day of the week on which it was born. The narrow range of people's names is quite striking and in a small village there may be several men and women of the same name who have to be differentiated by their nicknames. The names which the children should properly be given are referred to as *usum al-kitāb* (the names of the book), and the Berti see their system of naming as a religious practice. These names are mostly those of prophets and religious figures of importance in the Islamic tradition. At least some Berti know that the prophet Mohamed was born on a Monday and they state this as the reason why Mohamed is an appropriate name for a boy born on that day. Most Berti know a few common names appropriate for each day[4], but the knowledge of the full range of appropriate names is part of the *fugarā's* lore and a *fakī* is usually consulted. Two names are selected by the assembled men from the list which he suggests as appropriate and two rosaries, each one standing for one of the names, neither of which is known to the mother, are sent to her to pick one of them. The rosary which she has chosen is then brought back to the *fakī* who declares the child's name. This system is mostly adhered to, but sometimes a child may be named after one of its forebears, usually a grandfather or a grandmother, or a name may be chosen according to the circumstances of its birth. So a boy born when there were guests staying in the house may be called Dēfa ('guest') and a girl Um Dēfān; a child born during the time of sowing (*tērāb*) may be given the name Tērāb or Um Tērāb; a child born during the rainy season

---

[4] Saturday: 'Abdullāhi, 'Abd el-Rahmān, 'Abd el-Rahīm, 'Abdallah and other names starting with 'Abd for boys; Mariam, Mariōma for girls.
Sunday: Ibrahīm, Da'ūd; Halīma, Hallōm.
Monday: Ahmad, Mohamed, Hāmid, Mahmūd, Mohammadēn, Hammadōn, Hamad; Fātna, Fātnīa, Fattūma.
Tuesday: Sabīl, Sileimān, Salmān, Sālim, Ismā'īl, Ishāg, Ya'gūb; Khadīja.
Wednesday: 'Alī, 'Osmān, Yahya, Hārūn, Zakaria; 'Asha.
Thursday: Abbakar, 'Omar, Idrīs, 'Īsa, Mūsa; Kaltūma, Kaltum, Umkaltum, Umkhamīs.
Friday: Ādam, Yūsif, Yūnis; Hawa, Umjima.

(*kharīf*) may become Kharīf or Um Kharīf; a child born when it is raining may be called Matar ('rain'), or Mitēra if a girl; or a child may bear the name of the month in which it was born (Ramadan, Rajab), etc. The parents may not like the chosen name, but it is dangerous to change it. In the last few decades, the Berti have come into increasing contact with the outside world and this has led to a wave of new names which differ from the 'names of the book'. But they still assert that a name must not be chosen haphazardly for a person's 'star' is divined by a *fakī* from his or her own name and the name of his or her mother, as I have explained before. Should the *fakī* conduct the divination on the basis of a wrong name, it is bound to come out incorrectly and that may be disastrous, especially when a man wants to find out through divination whether a particular woman would make a suitable wife for him.

A child born after several of its older siblings have died has no *agūga*, and its head is not shaved on the fortieth day after its birth. Such a boy is given the name Sabīl and a girl Sabīla. If an *agūga* has been held for such a child and it was given a name appropriate for the day on which it was born, on the fortieth day after its *agūga*, it is taken by its grandmother or some other old woman to a pen in which a donkey is kept or to a place where a donkey is tethered (*tibin*). The pole (*ruksa*) to which the donkey is tied is smeared with milk and butter and the child is carried three times around it. A boy's name is then changed to Tibēn and a girl's name to Tibēna or Rikēsa.

On the day after an *agūga*, a mat is spread in front of the bed and the mother sits down on it facing east. Her mother and the midwife anoint her hair, forehead, nose, chin, abdomen and both wrists and ankles with milk and butter. The baby is also anointed in the same way with milk and butter and the cotton thread tied around its neck, wrists, ankles and waist is replaced with strings of white beads. If there are not enough beads to go round, they are tied only around the baby's right wrist and left ankle.

The midwife is exposed to the dangers of the 'blood of birth' more than any other woman, and to prevent her from getting blind from the sight of it and to protect her from *shayātīn*, she is given a bowl of flour so that she can smear her forehead with it.

Following the anointing of the baby, the mother is ritually brought into contact with the things associated with the hut. A small bowl with water is brought to her while she is seated on the mat and she dips her right hand three times into it. Then a small winnowing basket filled with grain is brought to her; she takes a little bit of grain from the basket three times with her right hand and pours it back into it again. Following that, a cooking pot is brought to her; she holds a lump of porridge and a bone of the goat killed in sacrifice in her right hand, which she puts three times inside the pot. She eats the meat left on the bone and then sucks the marrow; the bone is then stuck into the roof of the hut on the inside. Finally, a small grinding stone, which has been smeared with milk and butter, is brought to the mother who holds it together with her sister or another kinswoman. The two women jointly grind a little bit of millet which is then mixed with water and the resulting *dashīsha* is flavoured with salt and sugar. It is fed three times to the mother on the tip of a knife; the mother does not swallow it but spits it out three times onto the head of her baby. These ritual actions suggest that the woman and the baby polluted by the blood of birth are conceptualised as being outside the human community. As the hut is the concrete symbol of the human domain, the woman and the baby have to be reintroduced ritually into it. Physically, the woman and the baby have of course never left the hut but the symbolic re-entry into the hut is still ritually enacted.

The remaining *dashīsha* is offered as a sacrificial meal to the people who came to attend the *agūga* and are still assembled in the house. They too anoint themselves with butter: women anoint their foreheads and men their right wrists. Following this ritual, the mother can again start cooking and grinding flour and can leave the baby alone on the bed when she is leaving the hut. She can now move freely around the house and the yard but she can leave the homestead only later after her hair has been replaited and the baby's head shaved.[5] This again suggests that the woman and the baby polluted by the 'blood of birth', although physically inside the hut, are conceptualised as being outside the human community. They can re-enter it only after their impurity has finally been removed so that they are no longer dangerous to other people.

A woman who has given birth before usually starts cooking and grinding flour right after the *agūga*; a woman who has just had her first baby usually abstains from grinding flour for a few more days. About two weeks after the birth, the hearth is swept clean and all the ashes are thrown out.

In the case of a woman's first birth, the anointing of the baby (*jīr ŋaŋa*) on the day following the *agūga* is a more formal and elaborate occasion. The mother of the child's father brings to the maternal grandmother, in whose hut the birth took place, thirty-three baskets of

---

[5] The shaving of the hair, which grew on the head of the baby inside-the mother's womb, is of Islamic origin. The classical Arabic *'aqīqah* (derived from aggah: to cleave, split or cut) is used in *hadīth* to refer to a sacrifice of a sheep or goat for a child but it is also applied to the hair of the newly born baby. In the *hadīth*, its shaving off is seen as the removal of impurity.

grain if the baby is a boy, and twenty-two if it is a girl. All the paternal grandmother's female neighbours in the village contribute some grain, the amount of which depends on their relationship to her. If the grandmother does not collect enough grain for *jīr ŋaŋa* from her neighbours, she has herself to make up the right amount. A few grains of white sorghum are spread on top of the millet in each basket. The millet is part of various payments made by the bridegroom's kin to the bride's side. The baskets are displayed in the yard of the homestead and counted as prestations for specific purposes. Nine baskets are counted as the payment for the nine poles of the shelter (*sabābīr sha'ab rakūba*) built for the young couple in the bride's homestead. Others are counted as payment for plaiting the young mother's hair on the fortieth day after the birth of her baby (*sabābīr arba'īn* or *sabābīr mushāt*), and as contributions towards the expenses of her later move to her new homestead (*sabābīr rahūla*), of building the couple's future house (*sabābīr bani bēt*) and threshing floor (*khashm madak*), of providing them with their domestic utensils (*sabābīr burma*) and water bags (*sabābīr bīr*), etc. Some baskets count as 'greeting of the mother-in-law' (*salām bita' ama*). The number of baskets which are appropriate for each particular payment differs from village to village and it is usually a subject of much haggling among the women.

It is customary that people from the groom's village come to attend the *jīr ŋaŋa* for his firstborn child. The firstborn child, whether a boy or a girl, is always anointed by both its grandmothers. After the baby has been anointed, six twigs of a *hajlīd* tree are brought into the hut. They are smeared with milk and butter and the two grandmothers build from them a 'shelter' (*rakūba*) above the baby which lies on the floor of the hut, so that two twigs are stuck vertically into the ground on each side of the baby's body and the remaining two are placed horizontally on them. The baby is then rolled over so that the construction falls down on top of it. The stated purpose of placing the baby in the 'shelter' is to ensure an easy life for it; 'in the shade of the shelter' is a standard metaphor for an easy life. The purpose of pulling the shelter down is to ensure that the child will live longer than a shelter can last and the action is quite clearly a dramatic literalisation of a verbal metaphor (Dundes 1980: 229, n.3). Even if the homeopathic logic of the ritual appears to be quite transparent, however, it does not explain why the construction above the baby, which is explicitly likened to a flat-roofed shelter, is built from *hajlīd* twigs: *hajlīd* is not used for building huts or shelters. If *hajlīd* is taken to be the symbol of the village, an additional meaning is suggested for the practice. Until now, the baby has not left the hut in which it was born. From now on, it can be carried by its mother outside it. The pulling down of the *hajlīd* twigs thus precedes the moment when the baby will leave the safety of the hut and be exposed to the world outside it for the first time. For some time, this will only be the world within the village boundaries; before entering into it the child is first brought in a ritually controlled way into physical contact with what symbolically stands for this world. More specifically, the space which the baby is entering is the space within the boundary of the homestead where flat-roofed shelters stand. This may be an additional reason why the *hajlīd* twigs placed around the baby are positioned so as to resemble this structure.

If a woman has given birth while visiting, she stays confined in the hut in which the birth took place and *agūga* is held there. The mother is allowed to leave the homestead in which she gave birth after her hair has been replaited and the baby's head shaved. This is always done forty days after the birth of a first child, but can be done as early as two or three weeks after the birth of subsequent children. No animal is slaughtered for the occasion but a sacrificial meal of ordinary millet porridge is offered to neighbours and guests. The head of a firstborn child is shaved by its maternal grandfather, other children are shaved by their fathers. A few grains of boiled millet (*belīla*) are put on the razor blade with which the hair has been shaved and the blade is placed twice on the child's head; the boiled millet is then sprinkled on the child's head. A scull cap (*tagīya*) is then put on a boy's head so that he will live long; a girl's head is covered with a scarf.

After the child's head has been shaved, the mother can leave the house and she can move freely around the village with her baby. She may also go to the well or to the fields as long as she does not carry the baby with her. She may, however, take the baby outside the village after special rituals have been performed at the well and in the field. I have already described these rituals. After they have been performed, the midwife receives her final *bayād* (whiteness): a small basket of grain, a bottle of oil, a pound of sugar, soap, some perfume and *dilka*.[6]

When a woman miscarries, the Berti say that she 'throws' (*barmi*). This can happen up to about the sixth month of pregnancy when the foetus is not yet seen as human and is referred to as *rimāi*. From the sixth month, the foetus is considered to be a person (*zōl*) and a miscarriage is classified as a stillbirth. It is said that 'the woman gave birth but her child was dead' (*mara wildat lākin wilēdu mayit*).

In the case of a stillbirth, both the mother and the father of the child

---

[6] *Dilka* is made of millet porridge dried above the fire and pounded into powder which is then mixed with pounded sandal wood, commercial perfume and oil. This mixture is rubbed on the skin to clean it.

stay confined in the hut until a ritual visit to a *hajlīd* tree a week after the birth has proved that it is safe for them to leave the hut. I have already described this ritual. While staying in the hut, the father constantly wears his skull cap as a protection against *shayātīn* and he does not brew tea or touch the sacks or bins in which grain is stored inside the hut. Like his wife, he leaves the hut only at night to relieve himself and he carries glowing embers on a potsherd to repel *shayātīn*. Neither he, nor his wife may sit on the ground: he stays on his bed and his wife on the mat (*hasīr*) spread on the wooden construction on which women sleep.

A stone is put on the bed and a knife is placed next to it. When the woman goes to the latrine, somebody must sit next to the stone on the bed to protect the bed from the *shētān* who is attracted to it by the blood with which it is soiled. When the couple are free to leave the hut, the stone is thrown out or, if a grinding stone was used, it is returned to its proper place in the hut.

If the child was stillborn, all the customary rituals which concern the mother are performed on the seventh and fortieth day after the birth, but not the rituals which concern the new-born baby. So there is no *agūga*, but the mother's hand is put into the water, grain and inside the pot on the seventh day. She is, however, not fed any *dashīsha* as she has no baby and she does not suck the marrow as no animal has been killed in sacrifice. She is brought the grinding stone to grind some flour and a white string is tied round her neck, right wrist and left ankle. She is anointed with milk and the stone on the bed is also smeared with milk.

The mother stays confined to the house for forty days if it was her first birth or a shorter time if she has had children before. She leaves the house only after her hair has been replaited. However, as she has no baby, no ritual is performed at the well when she goes there for the first time after the birth and she also goes to the fields and starts gathering firewood without any ritual.

Marriage

A marriage is legalised when the groom's father or guardian (*wakīl*) hands over to the bride's guardian the first part of the bridewealth known as *sidag*. Traditionally this used to be a quarter of a dinar, but, with the introduction of the pound as the Sudanese currency, it changed to a quarter of a pound (25 piastres). In spite of the recent high inflation in the country, the *sidag* has remained fixed at this amount. Nowadays, 25 piastres is a negligible sum of money even for the poorest Berti villagers but the actual transfer of it is all important for, in line with established Islamic practice, it signifies the conclusion of a legitimate marriage. *Sidag* is transferred during a ceremony called *fātha*. It usually takes place in the guest shelter of the bride's parents' house. The bride and the groom are not present and they are both represented by their guardians. It is not uncommon that the bride has not even been informed that her marriage will be concluded and, as the choice of the spouse is the prerogative of the parents, she may sometimes even be ignorant of the identity of her husband. During the ceremony, both marriage guardians sit facing each other with the groom's guardian to the east as 'the man is in front and the woman behind'. The *fātha* is usually attended by the men and women from the village and by a few kin or friends of the bridegroom from his village. The men are assembled in the guest shelter, the women stay in the inner yard of the homestead or in the bride's mother's hut. A *fakī* is usually present. After the *sidag* has been handed over, he announces *al-fātha* and all the men present recite the opening sura of the Koran in the way described before. A few men from among those present announce the marriage by a cry (*kōrarak*) which is the men's equivalent of ululation, and women inside the house join in with their ululation. The Berti see *fātha* as one of their religious rituals. It is, however, a very simple ritual which does not require any specialised religious knowledge and if no *fakī* is present, it can easily be performed by the illiterate men themselves.

All the men are entertained after the *fātha* in the guest shelter or in front of the house; the women eat inside it later. Food and millet beer are provided by the bride's parents and the bridegroom's father contributes tea and sugar. In the evening, young people from the bride's village and the bridegroom's kin who are present dance in the open space in the middle of the village. The next day, visitors and neighbours may still be treated to food and millet beer in both houses. The second day after *fātha* the village elders are especially invited by the bride-groom's father while his mother usually invites all her female neigh-bours.

The spouses continue to live in their respective households after the *fātha* and their marriage is consummated only during the second stage of the wedding called *'irs, jīza* or *dukhla*, which is usually held about six months after the *fātha*. As a rule, it takes place after the harvest when there is enough grain and money to pay for the ceremonial feast.

Apart from circumcisions and funerals of prominent men, weddings are the largest social occasions in Berti villages. Three days before the *'irs* a celebration called *'azūma* starts in the bridegroom's village. It is attended by young people from all the neighbouring villages and lasts three days, during which there is dancing and the participants are given plenty to eat and drink. The ceremony is associated with *lamīn dagīg* (the collection of flour) after which it is sometimes called. Each woman brings flour and oil to the bridegroom's mother. Non-related women bring a *mukmāt* of flour and a bottle of oil, kinswomen bring a *shēla*[7] of flour and a bottle of oil. Men who participate in the ceremony give money to the bridegroom's father, the amount depending on their degree of closeness. The *'azūma* reaches its climax on the third day, when hundreds of people have assembled in the bridegroom's village. In the late afternoon, shortly before sunset, the bridegroom is taken to a *hajlīd* tree and the next morning before sunrise, he is taken to the house of his bride.

I have already described the customary rituals performed on this occasion. The bridegroom's first contact with the bride also has a religious aspect. When the bride has been brought to the groom, the *fuqarā* who are present chant the Yā Sīn sura. After the chanting, all present pronounce *fātha* which marks the end of the religious part of the occasion.

The final part of the wedding (*rahūla*) is not accompanied by any religious ritual at all. The bride's entry into her new house and the construction of her own hearth are occasions which are accompanied only by customary rituals which I have also previously described. The construction of the couple's new house which precedes the *rahūla* has, nevertheless, a certain religious aspect, as indeed has the construction of any new house for that matter. After the roof has been lifted on its supporting poles and before women start building the straw wall, all men sit down under the roof facing east. A *fakī* stands in front of them and chants a few Koranic verses, usually from the Yā Sīn sura. Afterwards all men say *fātha* in the usual way.

Death

The observer of Berti life and culture is struck by the people's precise orientation in space in relation to the four cardinal points, the frequency with which the four points are used in directional reference (where we would simply use expressions such as 'left', 'right', 'further on', etc.) and the regularity with which the performers of various ritual and secular activities position themselves in relation to them. This perpetual awareness of one's orientation in space derives from the symbolic significance of various directions and directional oppositions.

The Berti do not conceptualise the four cardinal points as two simple pairs of opposites as though, for example, east was to west as south is to north. In the Berti classification, a whole series of oppositions can be established in which the cardinal points are opposed to one another in

---

[7] *Mukmāt* and *shēla* are wicker baskets for flour. *Mukmāt* contains about 12 lb of flour, *shēla* about 30 lb.

several different ways. I have discussed these oppositions elsewhere (Holy 1983). Let me here just summarise a few points which are relevant to the present discussion.

In certain contexts, east and south are jointly opposed to west and north. This opposition is semantically expressed by west and south being referred to as *jīha* (direction) and east and south as *gibla* (from *yigābil*, to face). For the Berti, east is the direction of Mecca and, consequently, they face east when praying. They also face east, however, in all other ritual activities, irrespective of whether they are of a religious or a customary nature. While east and south are both *gibla* they are also mutually opposed to each other in that east is referred to as *giblat as-sala* (the direction of prayer) or *giblat an-nās* (the direction of the people) and south as *giblat al-mayit* (the direction of the dead). The opposition between east and south thus parallels another basic opposition, that between the living and the dead or between life and death.

The basic spatial orientation of activities which are concerned with engendering life or promotion of growth or health is along the east-west axis. So millet seeds are always planted in rows which run from east to west irrespective of the shape and location of the field. Weeding, which is semantically connected with death by reference to it as 'killing' the grass, is always done in the north-south direction. The basic spatial orientation of the living along the east–west axis is also observed in other contexts. The correct position for a person to sleep in is on his or her right (auspicious) side. It is proper to place the bed at the rear of the house opposite the door which always faces the auspicious south. People fall asleep lying on their right side with their head towards the west and thus facing south. When they get up in the morning, they rise from the bed again facing south.

When a person is about to die, or is so ill that he or she is expected to die, the body is put on a mat or on the bed with the head pointing towards the south; this is the proper position in which to die. As soon as the person has died, young men are dispatched to all nearby villages to spread the news; people immediately abandon their work to attend the funeral, and if they are not able to reach the village of the deceased in time for that, they arrive as soon as they possibly can, and certainly in time for the main sacrifice which is arranged on the third day after the death.

Unlike birth and marriage which are accompanied by certain religious rituals but are, on the whole, dominated by the performance of numerous customary practices, funerals and mournings are occasions which the Berti see as being performed in strict accordance with the Koran and the prophetic tradition. According to Islamic practice, a body is buried on the day of death, often within no more than the three or four hours which it takes to dig the grave. Only those who die in the evening or at night are buried the next morning, although sometimes the funeral is held that night.

If the deceased is a man, his body is washed by old men in the village; the ritual washing of the corpse is often supervised by the village *fakī* who may sometimes do it himself. A female corpse is washed by old women. Lumps of cotton are placed into the ears, on the face, genitals, anus, palms and feet of the deceased. The cotton is sprinkled with perfume and sometimes with the powdered aromatic leaves of the *nabag* tree (*Ziziphus mauritiana*). The corpse is then sewn into a sack (*kafan*) of white cloth in which it will be buried.

Meanwhile the younger men from the village are digging the grave. It is always oriented from north to south and, like anywhere else in the Sudan, it is shallow, rectangular, with a narrow trench at the bottom for the corpse. The corpse has been measured with millet stalk to make sure that the trench is as tight as possible. The earth dug out from the wider upper section of the grave is heaped to the east and west of it, the earth from the trench at the bottom of the grave is piled first beside the southern and then the northern side of the grave.

Immediately after the grave has been dug, the corpse is put on a bed which is then carried to the cemetery by the men, taking turns by sixes. All men take a turn because everybody who helps to carry the corpse obtains *ajr* (a reward from God for a good deed). Two rules inform the way in which the body is carried to the cemetery. It should not be carried feet first and the head should point towards the south. Most villages have their cemeteries to the south as both rules can easily be satisfied if the body is carried southward. If the ground south of the village is too rocky for the digging of graves, the cemetery is located either to the east or west of the village, as the body can still be carried to the grave with the head pointing towards the south and without going feet first. The rule that the body should not be carried feet first has to be violated if the cemetery is located to the north; when this is the case, it is always because the ground on the other three sides is too rocky.

In the cemetery the corpse is placed to the west of the grave and parallel to it with the head towards the south. Only men attend the internment, even if the deceased is a woman. They stand behind the corpse facing east and the *fakī* who leads the prayer stands in front of them. The prayer, which is standardised throughout the Maliki Muslim world, is a short one and, immediately after it, the corpse is placed by four men into the trench at the bottom of the grave. It lies on its right side with the head to the south and facing east. The trench is sealed with logs and all the men take part in filling the grave. With their bare hands they scoop into it first the soil heaped on the eastern and western side and then the soil which was excavated from the trench and piled on the northern and southern side. Both ends of the grave are marked with a short upright stake and thorny branches are placed between them to prevent the grave from being disturbed by animals. The grave is not attended thereafter, and nothing marks it. The thorny branches and stakes soon disintegrate and the soil heaped on the grave sinks with the passage of time. The men have to remember precisely where each grave was dug so that they do not disturb an old grave when they dig a new one. Each internment ends with the saying of *al-fātha* in the usual way and this may sometimes be followed by an incantation by the *fakī*, like: 'Let God bless him and forgive him his sins. Let Him take him to paradise, bless his children and help them through their grief. We have given the *fātha* to the deceased.'

After the internment, men return to the house of the deceased where the women are gathered. Before the departure for the cemetery a goat or sheep will have been killed in the dead person's house. The women of the deceased's household, helped by other women from the village, prepare the meat and cook millet gruel as *karāma*. After the return from the cemetery this is consumed by the men while the women have their own *karāma* at the same time.

The first three days after the funeral are called *mētam* and they are the main period of mourning. During this time kin from distant villages and many people from neighbouring villages, who have not managed to come in time for the funeral, visit the dead person's house. Every time a newcomer meets one of the deceased's close kin, he or she says *al-fātha* whereupon both of them, and all the other people around them, raise their hands and quickly recite the words of the opening sura of the Koran and end them by saying 'we grant it to the deceased'. The newcomer then shakes hands with the kin of the deceased and joins the other mourners. *Fātha* is said any time somebody meets a relative of a deceased person for the first time after the death. When people return to the village after a prolonged absence, very often they suggest *al-fātha* before they start the usual greetings, simply on the assumption that somebody must have died in the village during the long time they have been away.

Every afternoon during the *mētam*, a *karāma* of meat, millet gruel and *kisra* (thin wafer-like pancakes made of millet flour) is prepared by the members of the deceased's household. Everyone who happens to be present in the village participates.

The main day for visits by people from neighbouring villages is the third after the funeral, when a large *karāma* takes place. Most of the mourners arrive around midday and are offered tea and perhaps a small meal. The main sacrificial meal is served in the late afternoon, when all the visitors have assembled in the village. This *karāma* is usually attended by several hundred people: all adults from the village, the deceased's kin from other villages and most of the inhabitants of neighbouring villages. Only those who have to look for stray animals or care for sick animals do not attend, but at least one member of each family tries to be present. If none of a family can take part, its members attend the *karāma* held on the seventh or fortieth days.

The men take their meal in the village mosque, the women eat apart behind or near the dead person's homestead. One or more bulls from the deceased's herd, or a few goats or sheep if there are no cattle, are sacrificed. If a wealthy or well-known man has died, a large number of bulls or cows may be slaughtered, sometimes completely decimating the herd so that hardly any animals are left to be inherited. The slaughter of the sacrificial animals is done by the men of the dead person's household or others of his near kinsmen, who also cook the meat. The millet gruel is prepared by the women of the household assisted by other women from the village. Neighbours help in entertaining the guests. The neighbouring households also lend dishes, pots and glasses for tea, which are required in great number. Women from neighbouring villages bring flour or oil and spice with them and give it to the women of the deceased's household. Men pay their contributions in cash after the *karāma* is over.

The *fugarā* who have come to attend the *karāma* gather in the guest shelter of the deceased's house to read the Koran. A few leaves from a loose-leaf hand-written book are distributed to each *fakī* who keeps them in sequential order and chants his text loudly together with all the other *fugarā* who chant simultaneously their alloted parts of the Koran. After each *fakī* has recited the part of the Koran which he was given to read, he puts it aside and asks for more pages. This goes on until the whole Koran has been read. When an important or widely known man has died, sometimes as many as fifteen or twenty *fugarā* may attend the *karāma* and they may read the Koran more than once: on the other hand, if the number of *fugarā* present is small, they may not succeed in reading the whole of it.

The illiterate men are assembled in the village mosque and perform *du'a* (sometimes also referred to as *subhaniya*, the counting of rosary beads) while the *fugarā* read the Koran. The *du'a* has the usual form. One of God's names is agreed upon and repeated by all the men as many times as possible. The men count their utterances by the beads of their rosaries and whenever a man completes a full round, he announces: *salām* (peace). The man who keeps the total count on his own rosary acknowledges this by saying *marhab as-salām* (welcome the peace). Seven thousand utterances are called *jāria*. This word means 'she slave' in classical Arabic but does not carry this meaning in Berti Arabic; it is never used outside the *du'a* ritual. The purpose of the *du'a* is to offset the deceased's sins and to enhance his or her blessings. To be effective, at least seven *jāria* have to be achieved, which means that the chosen name of God has to be repeated 49,000 times. If there are not enough men to perform the *du'a*, the target of seven *jāria* is still kept but the value of each *jāria* is reduced to four or even three thousand utterances.

Smaller sacrifices are arranged on the seventh and fortieth day after the funeral. They are attended by the people from the deceased's village, his kin from remote villages or those who were unable to attend the main funeral *karāma* on the third day. A final sacrifice may also be arranged on the day of the first anniversary of the death.

For the village inhabitants who are not immediate kin of the dead, the *mētam* is the period of strict mourning when only the most important activities, such as drawing water and care of livestock, are performed. No work which can be deferred is done in the fields or elsewhere. The close kin of the dead person mourn for a period of six or seven months, and the members of his immediate family for about a year. During this period they do not wear festive dress. The women wear no ornaments, use no perfumes and have their hair done in coarse braids. They do not take part in any dancing feasts (*subu'*) and they do not marry. The village inhabitants who are not immediate kin to the dead person mourn for a period of about two months. There are no dances in their village during this time and they take no part in dances in neighbouring villages.

In accordance with the standard Islamic practice, a widow stays secluded in her homestead for four months and ten days following the death of her husband. This period is called *hizin*. No men except her nearest kin who live with her in the same household may come into contact with her during this time and only the old women from among the people outside her own household may visit her. The widow is secluded so that if she is pregnant by her dead husband, the proper paternity of her child will not be in doubt.

Directional oppositions and people and animals

Although no *'awāid* accompany the death and funeral, certain customary practices accompany the transfer of rights of disposal over a field to the surviving members of a household after the death of its head in whom these rights were vested. The cultivating season following his death begins with a part of his field being sown in the south – north instead of the usual east–west direction. This area is subsequently weeded in the east–west direction, though the remainder of the field is sown and weeded in the normal way. The ritual sowing is called *tērāb mina'ash* (sowing revived). The millet harvested from the area sown in this way is ground into flour from which gruel is cooked and offered as *karāma* to all the residents in the village. People partaking in this sacrificial meal are said to 'taste the new for [or, on behalf of] the dead' (*yidōkhu jadīd lel mayit*). Only after this ritual has been performed can the members of the deceased's household eat the produce from his field. The reversal of the directions of sowing and weeding, when part of the field is sown for its deceased owner, again expresses the opposition between the living and the dead by opposing east to south.

The opposition between the east–west and south–north direction coupled with the opposition between right and left are also seized upon symbolically to express the opposition between people and animals, which may be seen as one particular aspect of the basic conceptual opposition in Berti cosmology described before. When an animal is being slaughtered, it rests on its left side with its head to the north and a man, facing east, kills it by cutting its throat. The prescription that the slaughterer face east would be equally well satisfied if the animal rested on its right side with its head pointing to the south. But then it would die in the same position in which people die. That a symbolic motivation expressing the opposition between people and animals motivates the animal's position is also suggested by other practices. Some informants maintained that when a horse or donkey is tied to a pole, it should be given fodder to the south or west of the pole. They argued that it would be wrong to give it fodder to the east of the pole as it would then be eating facing east, which is the *gibla* of people. It would be equally wrong to give it fodder to the north of the pole, as it would then be eating facing north, which is a bad or unlucky direction.

A hut should always be constructed with the door towards the south and I have never come across one oriented otherwise. The entrance to the homestead must not be from the north. This again is a prescription which is fully observed, though there is no rule stipulating one specific direction for the entrance. Generally it faces the middle of the village. Thus, homesteads at the northern end of the village have their entrances facing south; those at the western edge face east and those at the eastern edge face west. However, although it would be the most convenient direction from the practical point of view, entrances to homesteads on the southern edge of the village never face north. Homesteads in the southwestern corner of the village have entrances oriented towards the east and those in the southeastern corner, towards the west.

When asked why the entrance of the hut should be oriented towards the south, the Berti offer in the main two types of reasons: the first may be called ecological. It is pointed out, for example, that it is not practical to orient the doors towards the east or west, as the rising and setting sun would shine into the hut and make it hot. Orienting the doors towards the north is also impractical, as the cold northerly wind would blow into the hut in winter. The south is thus the only alternative. The second type may be called conscious symbolic reasons. Here the local exegesis relates the positioning of huts and entrances to the fact that north is the direction in which there appears, every few years, an unlucky red star. The doors of huts and homesteads face away from it so that people are not exposed to its malevolent influence and can stay healthy and prosper.[8]

This exegesis still leaves unanswered the question why the unlucky star is placed in the north. An answer to the question of why north is ascribed a negative and south a positive value could be provided by connecting the south–north opposition with another opposition discernible in Berti dual symbolic classification: that between right and left. The right (*yamīn*) is clearly the auspicious side, the left (*shimāl*) the inauspicious one. Berti lateral symbolism exhibits in its own cultural idiom a general contrast of values associated with right and left which seems to have a worldwide distribution (cf. Needham 1973).

Many actions which are considered polite and good can be performed only with the right hand and many of those considered unclean or bad must be performed with the left. The association of right with good and left with bad is quite consciously and explicitly made, and small children will immediately be corrected if they use the wrong hand. All gifts and food must be handed over and accepted with the right hand and food must be eaten only with the right hand even by left-handed people; when washing the mouth after a meal only the right hand may be used. It is the right hand which is used in greeting. When serving food and drink, the host proceeds from the guest sitting on his right side, provided that all the guests are of equal status. As I have mentioned earlier, people lie on their right side with their hands folded under their head to go to sleep and corpses are buried lying on the right side. When

---

[8] This custom of orienting a hut so that its entrance does not face north is probably widespread in Northern Sudan. Aglen (1936: 344) reports from Kordofan that it is considered unlucky to build a hut with the door facing the north star.

mounting donkeys, camels and horses, one stands on the left side of the animal and starts by lifting one's right leg; this ensures that no danger will arise during the journey. The left hand is the proper one for unclean tasks: it is used for cleaning the anus and for touching the genitalia. Many Berti omens are also associated with the opposition of right and left. It is, for example, an auspicious omen if a certain bird crosses one's path flying from right to left.

All this is general in Arabic cultures but, unlike classical Arabic, Berti Arabic shows no semantic connection between north and left (north: *rīh*, left: *shimāl*). An association between north and left and south and right can be derived rather from the fact that the east provides the primary ritual orientation for the Berti, as I have explained before. When facing east in various ritual activities, people automatically position themselves in accordance with the cardinal points: the right (auspicious) side of the body points to the south and the left (inauspicious) side to the north. The auspicious character of the south and the inauspicious character of the north can thus be derived from the primary ritual orientation of the human body in space.

The Berti stress emphatically that cattle enclosures should be situated south of the homestead and, again, I have never seen an exception to this rule, although this positioning sometimes causes practical problems for households at the northern edge of the village whose cattle have increased considerably in number since the original homestead and enclosure were built; as they have to build their cattle enclosures inside the village, they can find themselves severely restricted in space. The cattle enclosures are situated to the south of the homesteads so that the cattle will not be exposed to the malevolent influence of the unlucky star in the north and will stay healthy and prosper.

There is, however, no unanimous agreement on how the entrance to the cattle enclosure should be oriented. In general, it was stated that, like the entrance of the homestead, it should not face north. Some Berti also maintained that it should not face north or east. Of the few whom I observed to have constructed their cattle enclosures with north-facing entrances, most admitted that it was done for practical reasons but that it was wrong, while others argued that the prohibition on entrances facing north applies only to homesteads. This ambiguity may be related to the fact that two oppositions may be motivating the practice simultaneously: the opposition between south and north (which informs the rule that the entrance should be to the south) and the opposition between men and animals (which generates the contrary rule that the entrance should not face in the same direction as the entrance to the homestead). At a general level, this ambiguity bears on an important theoretical problem which concerns the question of cultural integration assumed in most anthropological analyses.

Cultural integration

Whether the analysis of culture proceeds on the analogy between culture and language or the analogy between culture and a literary text, one of its central assumptions is that culture, like language or literary text, has the properties of a closed system, in that its elements (usually conceptualised as symbols and meanings) are arranged in a patterned, structured or logically articulated way. Any given culture is then explained when its underlying logic, pattern or structure is described and clearly formulated. This idea of cultural integration or global thematic consistency has been assumed since Ruth Benedict's *Patterns of Culture*. This in itself is ironic as Ruth Benedict herself (1934) emphasised that cultural integration is variable and that she had selected for description some highly integrated cases.

If cultural integration is indeed variable, it can be argued that the systemic property of culture or its perceived order cannot be assumed to exist outside the description but is solely the result of that description and is constructed through the very process of the description itself.

The systematic character of culture is hence not something that can be deduced through the study and analysis of culture; on the contrary, it is something that is axiomatically assumed to exist so that symbols and meanings can be described. This assumption is necessary before any interpretation of symbols and meanings can even begin, for we cannot comprehend and explain chaos, we can only comprehend and explain order. In other words, we have to perceive order to be able to explain anything and, in consequence, the presupposition of order is a precondition for the possibility of explanation. This, of course, means that even if symbols and meanings used and preceived by a certain group of people were a haphazard collection, a hotch-potch, mutually non-integrated and unrelated, and possibly even contradictory, they still would have to be treated in analysis as a system. And, it also means that the order which we perceive in culture (the *system* of symbols and meanings) is solely the product of our effort to comprehend and explain it. Brunton poses the same problem when, referring to 'the unity and consistency of the . . . world picture', he asks whether 'this unity and consistency [is] more than just an inference from a model constructed on the assumption that the inference is correct' (Brunton 1980: 118). Unless this question can be unambiguously answered in the negative (and as it is a question about the validity of a fundamental assumption, it obviously cannot) there remains a strong possibility that the notion of culture as a system is the function of our *theoretical* interest in it and that people whose interest in their culture is practical are not under pressure to perceive it as orderly, structured or systematic.

In considering the existing ethnographic literature on Melanesian religion, Brunton detects in it 'a general tendency towards overstructured presentations' (1980: 122). Taking the existing reports of some of the Melanesian people's inarticulateness and uncertainty about the supernatural as accurate reports of ethnographic fact, he suggests that the order perceived by the analyst in the religious systems of many Melanesian societies may be simply misconstrued.

Of course, if we allow for the possibility that the postulated cultural order is an artefact of the observer's analysis, we also have to allow for the possibility that the reported lack of cultural order may be a product of his analytical failing. The concrete cases of a reported lack of order cannot then be taken at face value and seen as proof of people's ability 'to tolerate a considerable level of cognitive chaos' (Brunton 1980: 122). This also applies to studies which attempt to show empirically the lack of cognitive consistency among different individuals (Fernandez 1965; Maddi 1968: 267–8). As they had, of necessity, to show the degree of cultural understanding of specific individuals on the basis of their explicit verbal statements, it can be argued that the reported cognitive inconsistency may be only apparent: cognition can still be highly integrated at the level of tacit or non-conscious understanding.

However, if it cannot be demonstrated empirically that the systematic integration of its elements is not necessarily an ontological property of culture, it can nevertheless be argued on logical grounds. If cultures were at all times perfectly integrated systems, no cultural change would be possible. A change in the system of symbols and meanings presupposes that new ideas will get a hold in the system and that they will get expressed through symbols that have not hitherto been part of the symbolic system in question; or, alternatively, the existing symbols will be endowed with new meanings to express new ideas. Whatever the situation, the total array of symbols and meanings has to be out of balance to a lesser or greater degree, depending on how radical the change is, and we may reasonably assume that at least at certain times in their development, cultures cannot be coherent systems of perfectly integrated parts. I would suggest that present-day Berti culture needs to be seen like this, for there is good evidence that it has undergone a dramatic and rapid change within the last two centuries or less. As I have suggested before, it is unlikely that Islam had taken any significant hold in Berti villages earlier than in the eighteenth, and possibly only during the last century, and that the Islamisation was accompanied or followed by language change which must have been rather rapid.

Adoption of a new religion and language must have a profound effect on the whole culture. It is hence probably not surprising to find that some of its elements are not fully integrated. I would suggest that the ambiguity about the opposition between men and animals is a case in point. Another one may be the fact that, in the ritual contexts, women are associated with auspicious symbols and men with inauspicious ones, while at the same time men are associated with the auspicious right and women with the inauspicious left, as well as the fact that not all customary practices, although they express the same cosmological scheme, are seen in a positive light. But here I am anticipating the final chapter.

7

Circumcision

Circumcision, regarded by Muslims and non-Muslims alike as a cardinal religious duty in Islam, is not mentioned in the Koran. References exist to it in the *ḥadīth* in which it is presented as a pre-Islamic custom. Certain differences exist between the major 'schools' of Islamic law but, on the whole, legal texts give no greater prominence to circumcision than to numerous other practices which the Muslims are adjured to follow. In popular opinion, however, circumcision has come to be seen as an indispensable mark of adherence to Islam.

Anthropologists studying Islamic societies have, for the most part, followed this popular view. In most cases, they have been content to note that their subjects, being Muslims, practise circumcision as part of their adherence to Islamic precepts and, if they have paid any specific attention to it, they have usually concentrated on analysing the sociological aspects of circumcision rituals, celebrations and feasts (e.g. Marx 1973). The emerging impression is that the cultural aspects of these events have not been seen as problematic, and that the cultural meaning of circumcision has been seen as exhausted by its signification of 'essentially a man's induction into the religious congregation' (Marx 1973: 414). Yet, the age at which children are circumcised in different societies and communities varies from the seventh day after birth to the mid or even late teens and the degree of ritual elaboration which accompanies the operation also varies. This clearly suggests a considerable variation in the meaning and significance of circumcision in the overall systems of notions of the societies in which it is practised. Certain recurrent themes can be gleaned from the brief remarks scattered in the existing anthropological writings.

Among the Kabyle, circumcision is regarded as a second birth through which a boy is transferred from the world of women to the world of men. Circumcision gives him a magical protection which enables him to confront women and, appropriately, he is presented to his mother's male kinsmen by a delegation of men from his sub-clan in the same rite which takes place before marriage (Bourdieu 1977: 127, 135, 143, 227, n. 75). In nineteenth-century Cairo, a boy to be circumcised was dressed like a girl and paraded in a procession similar to the bridal one. Similarly, in the riverain Sudan, the circumcised boy was dressed like a girl and the circumcision ritual took the form of 'a miniature celebration of the wedding ceremony' in which the circumcised boy was treated like a bridegroom (El Tayib 1964: 19). Lane interprets the boy's donning of female dress as a protection against the evil eye but it is more likely that what was actually symbolised was the boy's removal from female company (Lane 1978: 64). In Sidi Amneur village in Tunisia, the mother of a circumcised boy is treated like a bride and certain details of the circumcision celebration again parallel the customs performed on the wedding night (Abu Zahra 1982: 88, 93, n. 12, 138). The symbolic separation of the boy from the world of women is suggested by the fact that the circumcised boy's song is exclusively devoted to honouring his mother and her sister (ibid.:91) and that 'before the circumcision takes place, a woman client of the boy's family, or if the family is poor, the boy himself . . . goes with his mother and other children to invite the friends of their *dar* to the circumcision ceremony' (ibid. 137). In the Meknes area of Morocco, a mother leads her son to the house where he will be circumcised while his father usually disappears for the occasion (Crapanzano 1973: 229, n. 18). The details of the circumcision ritual among the Negev Bedouin similarly suggest 'that the boys are, by the circumcision, removed from women's society and admitted into male society' (Marx 1973: 424). Circumcision 'fulfils a precondition of his marriage later on, for an uncut man . . . is not adult, is ritually unclean and not fit to enter matrimony' (ibid.: 425). Among the Rubatab in the Sudan, the circumcised boy 'with his member in his left hand and a sword or spear in his right hand . . . goes first to the row of women and shakes the weapon at them, smiling as if nothing had happened or as if he were happier than usual, and the women reply by trilling: and next he comes over to the men strutting with a sort of goosestep, and often pretends to jump forward as if to wrestle with an opponent' (Crowfoot 1918: 132).

Such examples could be added to. Two recurrent themes emerge from them: the relation between circumcision, birth and marriage, and the transition of a boy from the world of women to that of men. The same themes are also elaborated in a culturally specific way in Berti circumcision ritual.

The Berti circumcise boys as well as girls and, as for other Muslims, circumcision is for them a major religious duty. It signifies a person's entry into the *sunna* (religious community).[1] There is some ambiguity about the ritual status of uncircumcised children. Some men and women maintain that they are *nijis* (ritually unclean). This view is supported by the belief that *shētān* is attracted by anything unclean. A woman after childbirth, and a new-born baby, who are *nijis* because of the blood with which they are stained, are particularly prone to attacks by *shayātīn*. So are people who have not cleansed themselves from the pollution of the sexual act. Children are, on the whole, more vulnerable to attacks by *shayātīn* than adults and, to some people, this indicates that they must be *nijis*, for otherwise the *shayātīn* would not be attracted to them. Their view is also supported by the very name of circumcision – *tahār* (from *tahhar* – to clean), which indicates its aspect of ritual purification; they point out that only something that has not been pure before can be purified. Others, however, deny this interpretation, for they see the imputation of ritual uncleanliness to children as the denial of their humanity which, in their view, is wrong. They point out that children start attending the Koranic school long before their circumcision. There they learn the Koran and are taught the basic Islamic duties. Surely they cannot be *nijis* when they have already learnt the rudiments of Islam, they argue. Whatever the expressed opinion, the actual conduct of children nevertheless suggests that they are not considered to be members of the *sunna* prior to their circumcision. They are not expected to fast during Ramadan and, if they attempted to pray, it would be seen as pretentious and inappropriate. These two aspects of their behaviour change after circumcision. From then on they keep the fast like any other adult and they are expected to pray, although they usually fail in this duty, as do most adults for that matter. On top of this, boys acquire the right to slaughter animals which accrues only to the male members of the *sunna*, and this right is always emphasised when the Berti talk about circumcision as the children's induction into the community of believers.

Boys and girls are normally circumcised when they are about seven or eight years old, but circumcision is an expensive ceremony which requires a lengthy preparation and, for this reason, it is frequently postponed. It is not unusual for a child to get circumcised in his or her early teens and, particularly in the case of girls, even later when the girl is approaching marriageable age. Then her circumcision cannot be

---

[1] The Berti never use the common Arabic word *umma* to refer to the Islamic community. They use the word *sunna* to refer both to the Islamic tradition and the Islamic community. They refer to their own traditions, which differ from those of the Islamic community at large, as *sunna* Berti.

postponed any longer as it is unthinkable to be married without having been circumcised. The Berti are emphatic on this point and in their view the marriage of an uncircumcised man or woman is *harām* and as such it is invalid. Should such a marriage take place, the partner who has been circumcised is free to remarry without any need to dissolve the union through formal divorce. In the sense of the distinction made by Allen (1967) between puberty and initiation rites, circumcision is a puberty ritual but, in that it is seen as a precondition of marriage, it also has distinct connotations of initiation. It is this connotation that fosters the view that a girl should be circumcised before she starts menstruating. She has become capable of bearing children after the onset of the menses, and there is always the danger that she might misbehave and become pregnant. Should that happen, she would be circumcised when she gives birth. Although this possibility was often mentioned, I have no evidence of any such case. However, it is not unusual for an unmarried girl to become pregnant. As a rule, the Berti avoid the scandal by arranging a marriage to her lover as quickly as possible. As circumcision often gets postponed for years, it also sometimes happens that an uncircumcised girl becomes pregnant and has to be married quickly to avoid the shame. In this case, her circumcision will be speedily arranged and the girl married soon thereafter; although such an arrangement provokes much gossip, her marriage is legally valid.

The meaning of circumcision as the ritual entry into the Muslim *sunna* and as a precondition of marriage are two ideas which the Berti emphasise in their verbal statements. They are also symbolically elaborated during various stages of the circumcision ritual. But they certainly do not exhaust all that the ritual represents. When it comes to its other meanings, the Berti are silent about them; these meanings are, nevertheless, quite clearly apparent from the ritual actions themselves.

The circumcision ritual
Circumcisions are usually held in winter when all the work in the fields has ceased, the grain has been threshed and stored in January and February and there is enough food for a large-scale entertainment. If a man, for some reason, does not manage to have his children circumcised in winter, it can take place during the slack period of the year in the dry season preceding the onset of rains in June.

A circumcision is not held together for boys and girls of the community and neighbourhood, but each family organises it separately for its children. It is, however, unusual that one child alone is circumcised and, as a rule, several children go through the ritual together. This is also the reason why their age may vary quite considerably, for a man usually waits until several of his children are ready for the operation. Occasionally two brothers or otherwise closely related men who live in the same village decide to hold jointly the circumcision ceremonies of their children. This is particularly the case when one of them has only one child of the appropriate age and finds it more convenient to pool resources than to stage the event alone.

The date of a circumcision is announced well in advance to all the neighbours in the village as well as to the people in neighbouring villages and to kinsmen who live far away. Such an announcement amounts to an open invitation and all people from the neighbouring villages and kins-men from further afield are expected to, and usually do, attend. A few days before the circumcision, a flat-roofed rectangular shelter built of poles and straw is constructed adjacent to the homestead so that the straw fence of the homestead forms its back wall. The shelter faces east and its front is left open and merely covered with blankets and other suitable pieces of cloth to provide shade inside. As it will be abandoned after the circumcision or dismantled so that its material can be used for building some more permanent structures, it is often a rather flimsy affair. If girls are to be circumcised, a straw enclosure in which the operation will be performed is built next to the shelter. This enclosure is sometimes built only of blankets and other pieces of cloth hung on poles.

The operation

On the night preceding the circumcision, a feast called *sahar* is held. It is attended by all the people from the village and by the guests who have already arrived from other villages. The latter are usually few in number. Some guests arrive the next morning but most, particularly the young men and women, only in the afternoon or evening after the circumcision to attend the feast with dancing (*subu'*). This starts in the evening and usually last for three days. The family of the children provides millet beer and food for those who came to attend the *sahar*. Boys and girls and the younger men and women dance the whole night in the open space in front of the house. Older men sit in the outer yard of the house, drink millet beer and chat while the older women are gathered together with the children to be circumcised in the woman's hut and in one of the shelters in the inner yard. During the night, they sing to the children to encourage them to be brave and to tire them out so that they will fall asleep immediately after the operation and will not feel the worst pain.

The circumcision is performed the next morning. If boys and girls are circumcised together, the boys are circumcised first and the girls later in the morning because 'the man is in front and the woman behind'.

In the past a boy was circumcised in the shelter where he stood facing east attired only in a new shirt rather clumsily sewn by hand. The hair on the sides and back of his head is shaved off and his head is wrapped in a turban or white cloth. In every village, there was one man who acted as a circumciser. He was not a ritual expert but simply a specialist (*usta*) who had learned his craft from his father or other kinsman. He was assisted by one of the boy's paternal kinsmen, usually his father's brother. A short piece of the soft core of a millet stem was inserted inside the prepuce which was then tied to the core by two pieces of string and cut off in between them. The cut-off prepuce tied to the core was put on a flat winnowing basket and, later, after the people had departed from the shelter, the boy's maternal grandmother, her sister, or any other close maternal kinswoman, untied it and put it onto a potsherd into which she poured water and sprinkled *garad* (the crushed fruit of *Acacia scorpioides* used for tanning leather) to preserve it. Originally, an ordinary knife was used for the operation but it was later replaced by a razor blade when blades became readily obtainable from the market. Traditionally, the wound was treated with a pounded root (*irg an nār*, the root of the fire) and powdered goat dung; nowadays it is treated with sulphathiazol powder obtainable from local clinics. The blood was allowed to drip on *mushuk* (the flour left after filtering of millet beer) spread on the ground which was then buried inside the shelter immediately after the wound had stopped bleeding. Nowadays, the boys are usually circumcised on a bed inside the house by a medical attendant who uses a local anaesthetic. After the operation, the boy is taken into the shelter where he rests on a bed but the cut-off prepuce is still treated in the manner described above.

Girls are circumcised by a midwife (*dāya*). There is usually one woman in every village who plays this role. She has learned the craft from her mother, grandmother or another close kinswoman and, in consequence, the position tends to be hereditary in the female line. Again, she is not a ritual expert but simply a specialist who has learned the necessary skill. The circumcision of girls is of the pharaonic type and consists of the removal of the clitoris, labia minora and labia majora. Traditionally, the cut was made with a knife, but nowadays a razor blade is used. To help the wound to heal, it used to be sprinkled with salt, pounded roots and crushed goat dung; nowadays sulphathiazol powder is used instead. The operation is performed in the enclosure adjacent to the shelter. The girl sits on an upturned watering trough facing east. One woman holds her head and other two women hold her outstretched legs while the midwife performs the operation under the cover of a sheet of cloth spread over her and the girl. Only these four women are inside the enclosure during the operation, for human blood is hot (*harr*) and people avoid the sight of it for fear of going blind. However, many women are assembled in front of the enclosure. Some of them beat earthen drums and others dance. Whenever a girl inside cries with pain, they ululate loudly to drown her cry. After the operation, the girl's legs are bound together by a piece of cloth at the ankle, above the knees and round her thighs to allow the healing of the wound by limiting movement, and the girl is carried into the shelter.

The cut-off parts of the genitalia are buried in a hole dug out in front of the trough on which the girls sat during the operation. When all the girls have been circumcised, the women who are inside the enclosure and who have been soiled with blood, wash their legs and arms thoroughly with water and soap; the trough is also thoroughly washed and all the blood is carefully covered with sand. White ashes are then spread on the spot where the blood is buried with white palm leaves, a twig of a *hajlīd* tree and an ear of millet are stuck into the ground. A few seeds of millet and water melons are planted on the spot. All the women, including those who were dancing outside the enclosure, mark their foreheads with flour, anoint their hands and arms with melted butter and sprinkle themselves with perfume. Traditionally, before commercial perfume became widely available, they sprinkled themselves with water.

There is widespread propaganda against pharaonic circumcision in the Sudan, and the Berti have recently become aware of it during their occasional labour migration to the more developed areas, their visits to El Fasher and other market centres in Darfur and, to a lesser extent, through listening to the radio. As the arguments are couched not only in medical but also in religious terms, the more pious among the Berti, in particular, find them acceptable. Many of them maintain nowadays that pharaonic circumcision is not part of proper Islamic religion but 'the work of the devil' (*shughul shētān*), as they put it, and that it is bad for the woman who can encounter difficulties in urinating and who has to suffer unnecessarily during childbirth when her scarified vagina has to be cut open with a knife to enable delivery. According to the view held by the pious, only the tip of the prepuce of the clitoris should be removed; this type of circumcision is believed to be in accordance with *sunna* (the prophetic tradition). Ironically, it is mostly men rather than women who hold these views. As only men are medical attendants and as it is unthinkable for a man to circumcise a girl, most girls, unlike boys, have not yet benefited from having the operation performed in a relatively hygienic and painless way. The *sunna* circumcision is gradually replacing the pharaonic one only in larger villages where at least a few midwives have had some basic medical training. In remote Berti villages, midwives continue to perform the pharaonic circumcision, arguing that this is how the operation has always been done.

The circumcised children spend three days in the shelter. The boys either rest on a frame bed (*'angarēb*) on which men usually sleep or, if there is none in the household, on a mat and blanket spread on the ground, as do the girls. If boys and girls stay together in the shelter, the girls always lie to the left of the boys, as the right and auspicious side is associated with men and the left with women. The children lay down with their heads to the west so that they face the auspicious easterly direction when getting up. A hole is dug in the shelter and dried goat dung set alight in it. From time to time, the boys and girls lay down on their stomachs on the ground with their genitalia above the hole. The smoke from the smouldering dung is said to help their wounds to dry up. For the same reason, the girls also sit from time to time on a stool with incense burning in a censer put under their skirts.

A *shētān* is attracted by anything that is *harām*, and as human blood has this quality, it is particularly attracted by it, and children who have shed it during circumcision are particularly vulnerable to its attacks. For this reason, the boys have one or two swords placed under their heads as a protection. A few dishes with flour and melted butter are placed in the shelter so that the children can anoint themselves for protection from time to time and particularly before they leave the shelter to relieve themselves.

Each child has an attendant (*wazīr, wazīra*) – a small uncircumcised child, usually chosen from among close relatives or neighbours. The attendant stays all the time in the shelter, fetches food and drink from the house and accompanies the circumcised child to the latrine in the yard of the homestead. The circumcised children never leave the shelter during the heat of the day nor during the first hours of darkness when the *shayātīn* are believed to be particularly active. During the day they urinate inside the shelter and they go to relieve themselves on the latrine only in the morning and in the evening before sunset when the *shayātīn* are less active. The attendant walks in front of the child pushing ahead of him or her a spear on the tip of which is stuck the dry core of a gourd (*gudu-gudu*). The spear and the gourd's core both repel the *shayātīn*.

Sharp iron objects are used for this purpose generally. So, for example, after a married couple have established their new household, a sword is left lying on the bed for forty days to protect the house from a *shētān* and, similarly, a circumcised boy protects himself by having a sword on the bed on which he rests in the shelter; a woman carries either a knife or a spear point when she has to relieve herself and leave the hut in which she is confined after childbirth. My informants did not agree as to why the core of a gourd repels *shayāṭīn*. Some maintained that this is because it is white and hence auspicious while others were of the opinion that it is because it is bitter.

The circumcised children are visited during the day by many others from the village who chat with them in the shelter, which gets very crowded at times. On the day of the operation, the young people who have come to attend the circumcision dance in front of the house while older men sit drinking beer and older women are assembled in the house, drinking beer and helping with cooking and with brewing more beer for the feast which takes place on the third day. Some women occasionally pick up their earthen drums and beat them in front of the shelter. In the evening, when more people have arrived, the dancing intensifies and continues throughout the whole night. On the next day, things quieten down. Only small children from the village stay in the shelter with the circumcised, and women occasionally drum in front of it.

The third day
The children leave the shelter on the third day following the operation. This part of the ritual is attended by many people from all the neighbouring villages and the presence of several hundred people is not

Figure 10 Circumcision. A circumcised boy returns from the latrine to the
        shelter

unusual even in a small village consisting of less than a dozen households. The guests start arriving during the morning. Women bring flour
as their contribution to the entertainment expenses and their arrival is
greeted with ululation. Women from the village contribute large pots of
beer and they assist with cooking together with many women from other
villages. Men give money to the father of the circumcised children, the
amount of their contribution depending upon their degree of kinship.

In the afternoon, depending on the father's means, either a bull or a
couple of sheep or goats are slaughtered as a *karāma*. Apart from meat,
the assembled guests are fed with millet gruel, *kisra*, tea and millet beer
prepared in the house of the circumcised.

In the afternoon, the girls are taken from the shelter into the
enclosure in which they were circumcised. Each girl in turn takes off her
dress, sits down on the trough and the midwife washes her face, arms,
legs, abdomen and genitalia. A new dress is then put on her, her hair is
anointed with melted butter and her head covered with a white scarf.
The boys wash themselves in the shelter, put on new clothes and also
have their hair anointed with melted butter. Their heads are then also
covered with white scarfs. The people waiting outside the shelter
sprinkle themselves with perfume; women anoint their hair and men
their right forearms with butter. Young men race their camels towards
the assembled people. The women ululate, men brandish whips and
sticks above their heads and the riders are greeted with shouts of *absher*.
Shortly before sunset, the circumcised children are taken to the nearest
hajlīd tree growing east of the village. They are accompanied by a large
procession of all the people who came to attend this ritual. Each
circumcised boy walks with his head covered with a white scarf and he
carries a drawn sword in his right hand. His attendant walks beside him
also with a drawn sword in his hand and behind him walks one of his
adult paternal kinsmen also carrying a sword. The circumcised girls walk
behind the boys carrying white palm leaves and with their heads covered
with white scarfs. Their attendants and close paternal kinswomen walk
beside them. Behind them walk a few women who beat earthen drums,
two women who carry on their heads winnowing baskets filled with
grain, a pot of beer and bowls containing water and melted butter, and a
woman who carries a rolled mat under her arm. They are followed by
women who dance and sing. Some of them carry empty winnowing
baskets and cooking sticks. From time to time, they put either a
winnowing basket or a corner of their wraps on the heads of the
circumcised children. This is to provide 'shade' (*dull*) for the child so
that it will grow up and stay in the shade, a metaphor for a comfortable
life. The men walk in front of the procession singing and brandishing

whips and sticks above their heads; they stop frequently, turn back towards the circumcised children and greet them with shouts of *absher*. Some men occasionally fire their rifles into the air.

The procession moves forward at a very slow pace and it takes about half an hour to reach a tree growing some 100 metres outside the village. After the procession has walked round the tree three times, two women, one of whom is *um binei* and the other *um wilēd*, squat on the western side of the tree and, facing east, sprinkle it with water and smear its trunk with butter. They dig a shallow hole on the western side of the trunk into which they sprinkle some grain and pour water and beer. The mat is then spread west of the tree. The circumcised boy stands on it facing east. His paternal kinsman who accompanies him, holds the wrist of his right hand, in which the boy holds a sword. They move the sword twice in the air and, with the third downward movement, cut off a small branch of the tree. The branch is put on the grain in the basket which a woman then carries back to the village when the procession returns there in the same fashion in which it left. The circumcised girls also

Figure 11 Circumcision. A circumcised boy standing at the *hajlīd* tree

stand to the west of the tree on a mat facing east and wave the palm leaves above their heads.

When the procession returns to the house of the circumcised children, the women dance for a while in front of the entrance holding flat winnowing baskets in their left hands, and cooking sticks, with which they fence in the air, in their right hands. No exegesis was offered for this performance and all informants stressed that it is merely a dance (*li'ib* – play). The circumcised children are then brought inside the house. The circumciser puts their right hands into a storage jar with water and, in the case of girls, also into a vessel in which grain is stored or into grain poured onto a basket, and into a cooking pot in which some porridge has been left. The children are then given a drink of beer and all present inside the house also have a sip of beer. A circumcised boy's father, seated outside the hut, announces which animal from his herd he is giving to the boy. It depends on his wealth whether it is a cow, sheep or goat. In addition to an animal, a wealthy man may give his son a gun.

Figure 12 Return from the *hajlīd* tree on the third day after circumcision. A woman carries back to the village the branch of the *hajlīd* tree which the circumcised boy cut off

The father's brother and paternal grandfather as well as close paternal kinswomen also usually give some animals to a circumcised boy. Girls also receive animals from their kinsmen, although usually not as many as boys. The children then return to the shelter, in which they spend four more days.

After the children have returned to the shelter, the guests start dancing. Many more young people from the neighbouring villages arrive specifically to take part in the dance which lasts until sunrise, and usually resumes after a few hours break in the morning and continues until late afternoon. Most guests start departing during the day but the young people from the village and neighbouring settlements may continue dancing the following night.

A small peg is cut by a paternal kinsman from the *hajlīd* branch which the circumcised boy cut off. The peg is tied to a piece of string made from the baobab tree bark to resemble a hobble (*ugāl*) tied round the front knee of a camel to prevent it from standing up and running away. The prepuce is slipped on the string of the hobble. The mother of a circumcised boy visits him in the shelter in the morning following the procession to the tree. She kneels down facing east and the boy ties her right knee with the hobble. He tells her which animal he is giving to her, unties her knee and slips the hobble with the prepuce round her neck. The mother wears it round her neck for seven days following her son's circumcision, during which she stays confined to the house. Before leaving the house, she sticks the hobble into the roof inside her hut where it stays as a memento of her son's circumcision. If two or more brothers are circumcised at the same time, other hobbles are put on the knees of their mother's sister or maternal grandmother who also receive animals from the circumcised boys and wear the hobbles round their necks. The mother of a circumcised boy also ties onto a plait on the right side of her head an ornament consisting of seven pellets of dry camel dung strung on a piece of string to which is also attached a short peg cut from the branch of the *hajlīd* tree, a short peg of sandal wood, and three dried dates. She wears this ornament either for seven days or until the boy's head is shaved forty days after his circumcision. She then hangs the ornament in the roof inside her hut. Sometimes, instead of wearing the *ugāl* round her neck, the mother wears the prepuce slipped on a piece of string in between two pellets of dry camel dung. Later, this necklace is also tied to the roof inside her hut.

After the children have been introduced into the hut, their attendants do not have to stay with them in the shelter all the time. The children can go alone to the latrine, themselves pushing in front of them the spear with the dry gourd core.

When a mother stays confined to the house until her son himself has left the shelter on the seventh day after his circumcision, she is subject to the same restrictions as a woman after childbirth, who also stays confined to her hut for seven days. In both situations, she leaves her hut only to go to the latrine in the yard of the homestead, and she does it only in the morning or in the late afternoon when the *shayātīn* are least active. She carries with her a knife or a stick with which she taps the doorposts before leaving and entering the hut to chase them away. If she has to go out at night, she carries glowing embers on a potsherd as a protection. Before she finally leaves the homestead, her plaits are undone and she places a few grains of boiled millet (*belīla*) on the razor with which the boy was circumcised and puts it three times on his head. The confinement of the mother is rationalised by saying that she would attract a *shētān* to the boy if she left the house. Some people are less strict in the observance of the mother's confinement; according to them she can move around the village but must not leave it. She must especially avoid the watercourses for the *shayātīn* congregate in tall trees which grow on their banks. The father of either a boy or a girl is not subject to similar restrictions and he is free to go wherever he pleases.

Unlike the mother of a circumcised boy, the mother of a circumcised girl does not stay confined in the house, although the girl is as much vulnerable to attacks by *shayātīn* as a boy. I would suggest that the difference in the behaviour of the boy's and girl's mothers derives from the fact that the idea of a new birth, which is the symbolically elaborated metaphor of the entry into adulthood, is much more important in the case of a boy than a girl. For a boy, his new 'birth' represents the severing of his ties with his mother and establishing of ties with his father and other men. A girl's circumcision does not have these connotations for it does not mean an interruption of her previous relations. In this respect, at least, circumcision does not mean a new 'birth' for her to the same extent as it does for a boy.

The seventh and fortieth days

In the late afternoon on the seventh day after circumcision or on the following morning, the boys accompanied by their attendants go round all the households in the village collecting *'āda* (customary dues). The circumcised boys are attired in new clothes, they carry swords hung on their shoulders, as adult men do on festive occasions, and many amulets, collected from among their kin, are hung round their necks, arms and across their chests to protect them. They ask for the *'āda* by saying *Addīna 'āda wala naktul jidāda* ('Give us the customary dues or we shall kill a chicken'). They receive a small amount of money from each household or delicacies like dried dates, sweets or biscuits. Should they be refused *'āda*, or, more likely, if there is nobody at home to pay them, they have the right to kill a chicken from the household which they then cook and eat together with other circumcised children from the village. This is the first time a boy can himself slaughter an animal, and the boys are eager to kill chickens, if they can, to exercise their newly acquired right. As mentioned before, the Berti put great emphasis on the fact that only a circumcised man may slaughter animals, and the killing of chickens clearly symbolises the boys' new status as members of the Muslim community. The girls too leave the shelter on the seventh day after circumcision but in their case this event is not ritualised.

After they have left the shelter, the circumcised children can move freely around the village. They may not go outside the village, however, before the boys have their heads shaved and the girls their hair plaited on the fortieth day after circumcision. That day the children are also taken to the well at the head of a procession of women from the village, some of whom beat earthen drums. A few men, particularly the close kinsmen of the children, may also join the procession. The children's mother or one of her close kinswomen carries a pot with fermented millet flour (*kajāna*) from which beer is made, a small basket with boiled millet (*belīla*) and a plate with butter. The circumcised children walk round the well three times anticlockwise and then sit down on its western side facing east. Any man whose firstbegotten child is a daughter (*abu binei*) and who happens to be present, lifts water from a bag (*dalu*) made of the skin of a female goat and places it three times on the head of each child, letting the water pour down on his or her face. He then anoints the children's foreheads with *belīla* mixed with butter and, with the same mixture, smears the four corners of the wooden frame at the mouth of the well. The water which he lifted from the well is poured into the *kajāna* to make beer which the women then filter into one of the watering troughs. All those present at the well are then invited to have a drink. The purpose of the ritual is to make the well a safe place for the children to visit in future and particularly to protect them from the *shayātīn* who tend to congregate there.

After visiting the well the circumcised girls are taken to collect firewood. They walk out from the village at the head of a procession of young women who sing and dance and some of whom beat drums. The procession walks three times around a *kitr* shrub. A woman who is *sabbar* and whose firstborn child is a daughter (*um binei*) and another woman whose firstborn child is a boy (*um wilēd*) sit down west of the tree facing east and smear its trunk three times with *belīla* mixed with butter. They then dig a shallow hole close to the western side of the trunk and pour into it a few grains of millet, water and millet beer. They anoint the girls' hair with butter and all women who are present also anoint their hair. A piece of bark is peeled off from the tree with a sharp stone. The bark is torn into thin strips which are then tied together in a small tassel and fastened to a plait on the right side of the girl's head which she wears for seven days. All women who accompany the circumcised girls also tie such tassels into their hair. The women collect some firewood and put it on the head of each girl who then carries it back to her house. After this ritual, the girls are safe to go and collect firewood, to work in the fields, to attend the animals or to leave the village for any other reason.

The meaning of the ritual
The interpretation of the meaning of the circumcision ritual has to start from considering its expressly stated purpose. This is to introduce the boys and girls into the Muslim *sunna* and to make them marriageable. As both marriage and full membership of the Muslim community are the prerogative of adulthood, the circumcision is, at a more general level, a rite of passage formally marking the beginning of adult life for the boys and girls. Like all rites of passage, the circumcision ritual displays the three characteristic phases of separation, liminality and aggregation, but it is particularly the second and third phase that are symbolically emphasised.

The separation of the boys and girls from their family homestead and from the village community at large is marked by their stay in the special shelter. This is built outside the homestead and thus clearly separated from it spatially. The children's entry into the shelter is preceded by the nocturnal party during which they are physically placed in the domain of women, the inner (female) part of the homestead, where they stay in exclusive female company. Their move into the shelter the next morning may thus be seen not only as symbolising their separation from the village community but, more specifically, their removal from female company. In fact, it is their removal from the women which is literally enacted when they are brought into the shelter in ceremonial procession. But, apart from this, their move into the shelter lacks any special ritual elaboration.

The main theme dramatised during the liminal phase is the children's state of ritual pollution. Although there is a certain ambiguity about whether they are *nijis* before their circumcision, there is no doubt at all that they are *nijis* by virtue of the blood they shed when they are circumcised. They become *nijis* by virtue of what happens to them during the ritual itself. In consequence, the ritual is not concerned with the children's movement away from the state of original pollution which has to be removed as a bar to their entry into the Muslim *sunna*. The whole sequence is not predicated on the existence of pollution but, on the contrary, the ritual itself creates pollution only to overcome it again on the way to a higher state of being. To achieve its stated purposes, the circumcision creates at the same time a new problem which it has to resolve and, indeed, much of the ritual action concentrates on this resolution. The problem is that in order to achieve the two stated purposes of circumcision, the Berti have to shed human blood and thus to commit an act which is otherwise *harām*. The very act of moving a person into the *sunna* of Islam thus exposes the person to danger from what Islam otherwise forbids. As the Berti see it, the children's pollution makes them vulnerable to attacks by *shayātīn* who are particularly attracted to human blood and the protection against such attacks motivates all the precautions the children take during their stay in the shelter: the boys' heads are perpetually covered by white turbans and the girls' heads by white scarfs, the swords are placed on the boys' beds and all those in the shelter smear themselves regularly with butter and flour. The circumcised children must not leave the shelter during the heat of the day and during the first hours of darkness when the *shayātīn* are most active and when they go to the latrine at the time of the least danger in the early morning or late afternoon, a spear and the dry, white and bitter core of a gourd, which repels the *shayātīn*, provides additional protection.

The liminal phase starts suddenly with the entry of the children into the shelter immediately prior to the operation but it ends only gradually and the phase of aggregation extends over a month. This phase itself consists of three stages: the re-entry of the children into the homestead on the third day after the circumcision, their re-entry into the village on the seventh day and their re-entry into full social life and unrestricted movement both inside and outside the village on the fortieth day. The phase of aggregation is ritually the most elaborate of all; in particular, the re-entry into the house on the third day is accompanied by a ritual and celebration which is seen as the highlight of the circumcision and attended by many more people than any other part of the whole ritual sequence.

The noticeable absence of specific rituals marking the phase of segregation and the ritual elaboration of the phase of aggregation clearly suggest that the circumcision ritual is less concerned with marking the end of childhood than the beginning of adulthood. Its emphasis on the beginning of the new phase in life is suggested, not only by the difference in the degree of ritualisation of the opening and final phases, but also in the heavy reliance on the symbolism of birth. The Berti acknowledge verbally the similarity between childbirth and the circumcision of girls, pointing out that in both cases the midwife cuts the woman or girl with a knife. Although not acknowledged explicitly, the similarity between childbirth and the circumcision of both boys and girls is attested to by the fact that the expression *dam wilāda* (the blood of childbirth) refers to the blood shed during circumcision as well as during childbirth.

In the case of the girls, the similarity between childbirth and circumcision is further suggested by the fact that the cut-off labia are buried in the same way as the placenta. This particular action may be seen as symbolically expressing the girl's future role for which her circumcision is a precondition and other ritual actions may be seen in the same way. So a girl's hair is plaited on the fortieth day after her circumcision, like the hair of a woman who has given birth, and when she is taken to collect firewood that day, the ritual is the same as when a mother goes to collect firewood for the first time with her baby forty days after its birth. In these instances, however, the girl could be seen as representing symbolically either a woman who has given birth or the new-born child. That the latter interpretation is probably more accurate is suggested by the fact that the boy's head is shaved forty days after circumcision in the same way as a baby's head is shaved forty days after its birth. The plaiting of the hair of a circumcised girl may be seen as a substitute for shaving. The idea of the circumcised children's own birth is further suggested by the fact that the ritual at the well is the same as that performed for a baby forty days after its birth. That it is indeed the baby and not the mother for whom the ritual is done is clearly indicated by the fact that the ritual does not take place in the case of miscarriage or stillbirth, or if the baby has died before it was old enough to be taken to the well.

The ambivalence about what precisely the girls stand for symbolically in the rituals of circumcision does not derive solely from the fact that women get born and give birth whereas men only get born, but also from the fact that the entry into adulthood which is symbolically expressed as a new birth, has different connotations for a boy than for a girl. For a boy its most important aspect is the severing of his relations with his mother and the establishing of close relations with his father and other men. For him the transition is much more significant than for a girl, for whom circumcision does not mean a change in association with other people. This, I would suggest, is also the reason why only the mother of a circumcised boy stays confined in her house like a woman after childbirth and observes the same precautions as she does when she has to leave it to relieve herself. That it is again the boy's birth that is symbolised through the conduct of his mother is suggested by specific details of her actions: before she leaves the homestead, her plaits are undone and her hair is replaited on the fortieth day in the same way in which this is done for a woman after childbirth; before she leaves her house, she places a few grains of boiled millet on the razor with which the boy was circumcised and puts it three times on his head in exactly the same way in which boiled millet is placed on a razor blade and put three times on the head of a newborn baby when its hair is shaved forty days after its birth.

A psychoanalytically informed interpretation could also postulate the boy's tying and untying of his mother's knee as a symbolic enactment of birth. The symbolic equation of legs and genitals is widely recognised in psychoanalytical literature (Bunker and Lewis 1965: 364; Freeman 1968: 383–84), and mythological stories of various African peoples about children born from their mothers' or fathers' knees or legs (see Jackson 1982: 298–99, n.4) might indeed support such an interpretation. But the Berti never hinted even obliquely at any association between the knee and the womb or genitals, and I doubt that the act of tying and untying the mother's knee connotes to them the idea of birth in any way. The main theme of this particular action seems to be rather the severance of the boy's relations with his mother. All my informants were clear that the string which the boy puts round the knee of his mother and then removes again is *ugāl*, a hobble used to tie down a camel. Even in the absence of any exegesis, the meaning of the removal of the hobble which ties the mother down seems to be quite transparent: the boy unties the mother on which he has hitherto depended and thus frees her from any obligation which she has, until now, had towards him. By freeing her of her obligations, he makes himself free and independent of her. As he was tied to her and depended on her while he was uncircumcised, it is only appropriate that his prepuce is taken by her and stays with her for, just as he has got rid of it physically, he has also got rid of what it can be seen as symbolically standing for: his dependence on his mother. If it belongs to anybody, it clearly belongs to her. The animal which he gives her at this time can be seen as his parting gift to her and as his reward for her care. A circumcised girl is not interrupting her relations with her mother and so she does not give her anything. The tying and untying of the mother, her retaining the prepuce and the boy's payment to her all seem to be logically connected.

They are actions symbolically appropriate to express the boy's severance of his relations with his mother.

The symbolic significance of this particular ritual may not be exhausted at this point. The mother is tied in the same way as a camel, and she puts an ornament made of camel dung into her hair or round her neck. All my informants insisted that it must be the dung of a male camel but I was unable to obtain any explanation of the significance of either the camel dung or the image of a camel that appears to be portrayed quite distinctly in the ritual. My informants stressed that the camel dung is used because it is *samih* (nice, a word which has for the Berti a distinct connotation of 'lucky' or 'auspicious') but were unable to say why it is so. I was also told that camel dung is used because a camel is strong and powerful: 'it is the strongest animal there is and no burden is too heavy for it'. Because of their strength, the Berti associate camels with men: *jamal rājil* ('camel is a man'), they say. Some people suggested that the mother is tied with *ugāl* because she is like a female camel. These remarks suggest that what is symbolically elaborated again in this particular detail of the ritual is one of its stated purposes, namely to make a marriageable man out of a boy hitherto dependent on his mother. If a man is metaphorically a camel, the strongest of all the animals which the Berti know, his mother is appropriately a female camel. If then the prepuce which has been separated from him belongs to her, so does the dung which has been separated from the camel, metaphorically a man. It appears that the metaphor 'a man is a camel' is again literalised here in the detail of the ritual, just as the metaphor, 'an easy life is a life in the shade of a shelter' is literalised in a detail of the ritual of the anointing of the baby. Through portraying his mother as a female camel a boy is made into a strong man (camel) to whom she gave birth. Although unconscious to the Berti, the boy's tying and untying of his mother's knee as a symbolic enactment of new birth (itself a metaphor for the beginning of a new phase of life – that of adulthood) would logically fit into the man/camel imagery.

As the children are in a state of severe ritual pollution during the liminal phase following the operation, the rituals of aggregation are understandably concerned with their purification as a precondition of their safe re-entry into ordinary social life in which no special precautions will any longer be taken against the threatening dangers. Thus, before leaving the shelter on the third day, the children are thoroughly washed to remove any traces of blood from their bodies, anointed with butter and attired in new clothes. The clothes in which they stayed in the shelter and which are likely to be soiled with blood, are either thrown away or thoroughly washed to be used later as working clothes. The shaving of the boys' heads and plaiting of the girls' hair on the fortieth day are also acts of purification. As water is seen by the Berti as a purifying element, the putting of the bag of water on the children's heads at the well can also be seen as having the same significance. This meaning is corroborated by the emphasis put on the fact that the water from the bag must be left to drip over their faces.

The procession to the *hajlīd* tree is not only part of the circumcision ritual but it also precedes the bridegroom's first entry into the house of the bride and his first cohabitation with her during the second stage of the wedding, called *'irs* or *jīza*. This is again the most ritualised stage of the whole wedding process and the lavishness with which it is celebrated suggests that it is seen as its highlight. In the context of the circumcision ritual, the rationale of the procession to a *hajlīd* tree can be seen as deriving from the expressly acknowledged aspect of circumcision as a precondition of marriage. On this interpretation, the circumcised children perform the ritual which precedes the bride's and bridegroom's first cohabitation to express symbolically their newly acquired status as marriageable adults.

The visit of the circumcised children to the *hajlīd* tree seems, however, to be concerned with yet a different aspect of their situation. The fact that the ritual performed at the tree is virtually identical with the ritual performed for a bridegroom before he first cohabits with his wife, clearly suggests the identity of its purpose in both situations.

There is no doubt that the three days after circumcision are the time of heightened danger for the circumcised children. When they leave the relative safety of the shelter on the third day, they become fully exposed to the danger that faces them outside. That this is the moment of heightened danger for them is attested by the fact that their heads are covered with white scarfs and the boys carry swords for protection. The white palm leaves of the girls may also have a primarily protective function. Given the protective and generally beneficent qualities of a *hajlīd* tree, a visit to it appears appropriate at this particular moment to secure additional protection for the children in the potentially dangerous world which they are now entering. A bridegroom also faces a dangerous situation when first approaching his wife. He is supposed not to have had sexual intercourse before as all sex outside marriage is considered *harām*, and the bride is certainly supposed to be a virgin. The sexual act itself is polluting and puts the couple in a state of ritual impurity which, like any other impurity, attracts *shayātīn*. In the case of the bride's defloration, which is expected to occur during the second stage of the wedding, the danger is compounded by the spilling of her blood with which the couple will be soiled and which, like all human blood, particularly attracts a *shētān*. Like the circumcised children who leave the safety of the shelter for the first time, the bridegroom too is entering a potentially dangerous situation when he goes to cohabit with his wife for the first time. The ritual visit to the *hajlīd* tree is to provide protection to those who are going to face danger in both situations and the similarity of the situations accounts for the identity of the ritual action which precedes them.

This particular aspect of the ritual visit to the *hajlīd* tree does not, however, exhaust all its possible meanings. Another meaning would suggest itself due to the fact that the Berti associate *hajlīd* closely with the village. Given this association, the ritual performed at it after a circumcision can be understood, not only as being concerned with the re-entry of the circumcised children into the hut, but also with their re-entry into the village from which they have been secluded in their shelter. The ritual visit of the bridegroom to the *hajlīd* tree prior to his first entry into his bride's house can also be made sense of in similar terms. No pollution by blood is involved in his case and he cannot be seen as dangerous to the community for this reason; although his re-entry into the community from which he has been excluded because of his ritual pollution cannot hence be seen as the object of ritualisation, a transition in the form of an entry into a community is still involved. When talking about marriages in general terms, the Berti always present them as inter-village affairs, although in practice this is by far not the case. The ritual then precedes what is ideally conceptualised as the bridegroom's move from one village to another, and his entry into a community of which he has not been a part till now.

In all cases, the ritual visit to a *hajlīd* tree precedes a boundary crossing: either a physical entry into a new community or a conceptual re-entry into one's community following a state of temporary exclusion.

Another aspect of the *hajlīd* tree is that it shares the symbolic attributes of women: like them, it is seen as soft and it is explicitly associated with the village as women are. Given this symbolic equivalence, the *hajlīd* tree can be understood not only as standing for the village but also as standing for women or femininity, as I have already suggested. If it is understood as having this symbolic signifi-cance, meaning can be ascribed to one specific detail of the visit to the *hajlīd* tree both during the circumcision and the second stage of the wedding process: the cutting of its branch by the sword. I was not able to obtain any exegesis of the meaning or significance of this particular action. None of my informants was able to go beyond saying that it is an old Berti *'āda*.

The bridegroom and the circumcised boy cut the branch of the *hajlīd* tree in such a way that they swing the sword twice in the air and then chop off the branch with the third blow. A circumcised girl does not touch the tree; she stands under it, waves her palm leaf above her head and ululates as a sign of joy. A sword is, of course, a typically male object. If it is seen as a symbol of maleness and masculinity in this particular context and the *hajlīd* tree as a symbol of womanness or femininity, what the act dramatises is the coming together of the man and a woman for which the circumcision is a precondition and towards which it may be seen as the first step. More specifically, the act may be seen as dramatising sexual intercourse and aiming at ensuring the boy's successful penetration of his future wife which, of course, immediately follows the visit to the *hajlīd* during the wedding. Because of the pharaonic circumcision performed on girls, penetration, as a rule, is difficult and it often takes weeks before it is successfully accomplished. Sometimes a midwife is asked to deinfibulate the wife by splitting the scar to widen the aperture when the wife 'has no passage' (*mā 'indu tarig*; the operation is called *tashim* or *masih*, easing). Seen against this background, swinging the sword twice in the air before cutting off the branch, can justifiably be seen as a symbolic enactment of successful penetration; a circumcised girl appropriately rejoices by waving the palm leaf and ululating. Alternatively, what the boy's action may dramatise is the deinfibulation done by a midwife before delivery.[2] In any case, the visit to the *hajlīd* tree following circumcision seems to carry an additional meaning of symbolically expressing concern with future fecundity as a specific aspect of the general well-being at whose attainment all customary rituals are explicitly aimed.

There may be yet another meaning of this particular action. It precedes the man's involvement in the shedding of human blood, which is, of course, polluting. The bridegroom is brought into contact with blood in the act of the defloration of his wife which follows soon after his visit to the *hajlīd* tree. Following his circumcision, the boy will shed only animal blood which is not polluting, but the circumcision makes him ready for entering marriage and thus ready for his future involvement in the shedding of human blood. If we recall the *hajlīd*'s ability to turn blood into water, which I have mentioned before, we may possibly see the cutting of its branch as an act concerned with the man's protection against the pollution by human blood; through this act he may invoke

---

[2] To make delivery possible, the circumcision scar must be incised along its length. Sometimes more than one cut is necessary to ease the delivery. The wound is usually left to heal itself but sometimes it is restitched after delivery to resemble the original state of circumcision.

the *hajlīd*'s potency for turning the polluting blood into water, the agent of purification.

My interpretation of this particular detail of the visit to the *hajlīd* tree has gone beyond any understanding conveyed by the local exegesis. Moreover, when I offered it to my informants, it was rejected by them although no alternative interpretation was offered. The interpretation has been arrived at by considering specific Berti notions invoked in other contexts and by assuming their relevance in the context in which they have not specifically been invoked by the actors.

Such a procedure is widely resorted to in the interpretation of symbols (see, for example, Werbner 1984), but it is also a procedure widely open to doubt. Usually, it cannot be corroborated by strong evidence which would rule out any alternative interpretation or the possibility that the practice may be completely meaningless to its performers (even at the level of their unconscious) and in the absence of such evidence, it is difficult to disregard the possibility that the interpretation springs solely from the fertile imagination of the analyst. The comparative evidence which we have also fails to dispel this doubt as it may again be interpreted in one way or another. In 1874, Nachtigal witnessed in El Fasher the installation ceremony of a *wazīr* of the sultan of Darfur. After the new *wazīr* had been presented with his official robe, he walked three times around a *hajlīd* tree which stood in front of the sultan's palace after which his own *wazīr* cut off one of the branches with his sword (Nachtigal 1971: 370–1). We do not know the possible meaning of the cutting off of a *hajlīd* branch, which Nachtigal interprets as symbolising the *wazīr*'s entry into office (ibid.: 371), but it is highly improbable that in this particular case the *hajlīd* tree could be seen as symbolising femininity or possibly even settlement in opposition to wilderness.

The equivalence of the form of the ritual action in both contexts is, however, undeniable and it is improbable that it is purely accidental. It is, of course, possible that the Berti may have adopted a ritual action performed at the sultan's court and endowed it with their own meaning different from that which it might have had in El Fasher. In this case the interpretation of the meaning of the Berti ritual which I have offered would have to be seen as suspect. Assumption of a man's new status is quite clearly common to both situations, but the question of why it should be marked by cutting off a *hajlīd* branch remains unanswered, and any answer is difficult to suggest in view of the fact that the assumption of numerous other statuses is not so marked by the Berti. But, it is equally possible that both actions have not only the same form but also the same underlying meaning, and equally possible that the Berti did not adopt for their own purposes a ritual performed at the sultan's court but that, as in Madagascar (Bloch 1986), the state co-opted a domestic ritual practice for royal purposes. The *wazīr* could also be seen as a potential blood shedder, in the exercise of his office, for whom the *hajlīd* tree provides a protective moral transformation in its ability to turn blood into water. In that case, the cutting of a *hajlīd* branch would be an appropriate action to perform both upon entry into political office and upon re-entry into the community after circumcision.

For the Berti, the *hajlīd* is clearly a multi-vocal symbol, perhaps the most multi-vocal of all symbols employed in their rituals. It is precisely its multivocality which makes it possible for it to be endowed with different meanings in different contexts. At the same time, it makes it possible to leave its precise meaning in any particular context undefined and open to different understanding by different people. If its multi-vocality and the vagueness of its connotations (its truly mysterious quality) is its strength and the source of its efficacy, its true meaning in Berti culture would be drastically altered by any interpretation that would circumscribe it more specifically than do those who employ it in their ritual actions. For this reason I have suggested possible interpretations without committing myself to any particular one. After all, an anthropologist's interpretation and understanding can never be a substitute for those of the actors. If they are uncertain themselves, he or she cannot but remain uncertain with them.

8

Blood and rain

Customary rituals express the separation of the unique world of human beings, whose lives are regulated by divine prescriptions, from the forces of the world which lack human reason and knowledge of God. Such separation can, of course, never be total since, for their sustenance, people depend on things that originate in or come from outside human society. Although the boundary between these two domains has to be maintained to protect human life from corruption by outside forces, it also has to be perpetually crossed so that human life can continue. All the rituals which I have discussed are preventive in character, in that their aim is to ensure that no adverse consequences will result from the necessary but inevitable crossing of the boundary.

In this chapter, I describe rituals which are retributive rather than preventive in character. They have to be performed when the boundary separating the two domains has been blurred, not as a result of people or things moving across it deliberately, but as a result of an uncontrolled intrusion of one domain into the other. Such an intrusion can occur in different ways and it leads not only to adverse consequences for specific people whose well-being then has to be restored through the performance of an appropriate ritual, but also, in many situations, it results in the disruption of the proper cosmological order which affects the well-being of the whole community. One such situation is the occurrence of a miscarriage, a birth outside the hut or the birth of twins.

Abnormal birth
The 'normal' human birth has to fulfil three conditions: one child is born, it is born after nine months' gestation and it is delivered in the proper place, i.e. inside the hut. The Berti see the birth of twins as an abnormal occurrence which triggers off a whole range of ritual actions. They describe the twins as *shēn* ('ugly', a word which has the conno-

tation of 'inauspicious') or *jelīd* (unlucky). Twins are said often to kill their mother or father, but the main reason for seeing them as inauspicious is the belief that they may cause their kin to go blind and that they prevent rainfall and bring strong dry winds.

When twins are born, the rituals ordinarily following a birth are modified. The *agūga* is held two weeks after the birth and the twins are given special names. As is generally the case in the Northern Sudan (see Hills-Young 1940: 334; El Tayib 1955: 158), the boys are called Hasan and Hisēn after the grandsons of the Prophet, who are believed to have been twins, and the girls Um al-Hasan and Um al-Hisēn. Alternative names are 'Īsa and Mūsa for boys and Tōma and Tōmīya for girls. The pairs of names appropriate for twin brother and sister are Hasan or Hisēn and Um al-Hasan, Um al–Hisēn or Hasania; an alternative pair is Tōm and Tōma or Tōmīya.

Two male goats or rams have to be sacrificed during the *agūga* lest one of the twins should die. Their blood is not allowed to pour onto the ground as in ordinary sacrifice but is collected in two gourd vessels, each of which has to be a *kās murr* (bitter, i.e. fresh gourd vessel) that has not yet been used for anything else. Two young men sprinkle the blood around the village with a bundle of grass, a green twig or a feather. When doing so, they walk out from the village towards the west and after a while one of them turns southwards and the other one northwards until they eventually both turn towards the east. If they meet anyone, they do not greet or speak to them. They both finish the sprinkling of the blood east of the village where they leave the empty vessels in the branches of a green tree or shrub before they return together to the village which they re-enter from the east. This ritual is performed so that the birth of twins does not spoil the earth (*bakharib al-wata*), the rainy season (*bakharib al-kharīf*) or water (*bakharib al-mōya*). If it were not performed, there would be no rainfall but only dry wind in the rainy season. Before this ritual has been performed, those who were present in the hut during the birth may not leave it lest they too would spoil the rainy season.

A mother of twins may leave the house in which she gave birth after her hair has been replaited on the forty-sixth day following the birth, when the heads of the babies are also shaved. A little hair is left at the back of the head of each child and a white bead is tied to it to repel the *shayātīn*. The mother is now free to leave the village and to go to the fields, to the well or to the market as long as she does not carry the twins with her. However, her movements are still restricted as she has to be able to return home from time to time to nurse them.

If a woman gives birth to twins while she is still living in her parent's household, a house is built for her immediately after her confinement is over and she moves into her own household irrespective of whether her husband has or has not transferred the full bridewealth. Her house is built in the same way as any other *bēt 'āda* except that the top of its conical roof is not beaten flat in the usual way but a few millet stalks are left protruding like two horns at the edges of the flat top.[1]

Irrespective of when they were born, the twins stay confined to the house until the harvest following their birth. By then, the rainy season is over and there is no longer any danger that they might spoil it by being allowed to leave the house. When the first ears of millet are to be cut, they are taken to the field. One is carried by its mother, the other by another woman, usually its maternal grandmother. A strong and well-growing millet plant in the middle of the field is smeared with milk and butter and the mother and the twins are also anointed. The mother cuts off two ears of millet while two women grasp the wrist of her right hand in which she holds the knife. These ears are the first ones to be put on a flat winnowing basket. Then all the women who accompanied the mother start harvesting the ripe ears and carry them to the threshing floor. The women are accompanied by at least two men, neither of whom needs to be the children's father. Before the harvesting begins, one of them slaughters two goats or rams in the field and their blood is again sprinkled around the fields and the village in the same way as during the *agūga*. The meat of the sacrificed animals is cooked in the field and eaten by everybody present. After this ritual has been performed, the mother is free to take the twins with her anywhere she goes.

If a woman gives birth to twins while on a visit to a different village from her own, she stays confined in the house in which she gave birth as in the case of an ordinary birth. However, when the twins are brought back to her own village for the first time, a goat again has to be sacrificed and its blood sprinkled along the whole way between the two villages.

The rituals performed after the birth are not only modified when twins are born but additional restrictions have to be observed and additional rituals performed.

The closest relatives of the twins, even if they live in other villages than that in which the twins were born, refrain from eating salt for two

---

[1] The grave of a twin or of the father and the mother of twins is similarly marked by having two poles, instead of the usual one, stuck vertically into the ground at both ends of the grave. Sometimes straw is placed horizontally on the poles and a flimsy flat-roofed shelter thus constructed above the grave.

Alternatively, the grave may be marked by two crossed stalks of *marhabēb* grass stuck into the ground at both ends. This again is done to ensure that rain rather than dry wind will come in the rainy season.

weeks following the birth to ensure that they will not go blind. As ordinary relish prepared without salt is considered tasteless, they usually eat the staple millet porridge with milk instead of the usual relish made of oil, onion, dried tomatoes, dried meat, okra and powdered red peppers. As far as I am aware, the prohibition on eating salt does not apply on any other occasion and I was not able to elicit any exegesis why salt must not be eaten.

As a rule, a woman is not alone in the hut when she gives birth. A midwife normally assists if she can be summoned in time, or else she comes soon after the child is born; the woman's mother is also usually present and there are often other people in the house, mostly women, but occasionally also men, who come to greet the expectant mother. When the woman gives birth to twins, all those who are present in the house during their birth, have to stay in it until the *agūga*. To relieve themselves, they leave the hut only at night carrying glowing embers on a potsherd to protect themselves against the *shayātīn* who are especially attracted by the birth of twins because more blood has been spilled than in a normal birth. As a further protection, the men wear their skull caps and women keep their heads covered with white scarfs or wear a piece of white cloth tied round their heads all the time they stay in the house, and for another seven days following the *agūga*. Before they leave the house, their foreheads are smeared with the blood of the goats or sheep slaughtered for the *agūga*.

When it becomes obvious that, after one child has been delivered, another is about to be born, those present leave the mother's house in a hurry for fear of being confined in it for two weeks. However, it sometimes happens that some people remain present during the birth of the second child and that they leave the house thereafter to avoid confinement. In such a case, a goat has to be sacrificed early in the morning before anybody leaves or enters the village, and its blood sprinkled all around it so that the pollution will not spread. There is no restriction on people coming to the house after the birth, and women come to greet the mother as they would any other, but they bring two baskets of grain instead of the customary one. If people who come to greet the mother pay money, as men usually do, they put one coin on one flat winnowing basket and one coin on another basket.

During their life, the twins are not treated differently from anybody else, and when they die they are buried like anybody else, except when they die in a different village from that in which they were born. In that case, irrespective of whether the deceased twin was a child, an adult or an old person, a goat has to be sacrificed and its blood sprinkled the whole way from the village in which he or she has died to the village in which he or she was born. If there is not enough blood to last the whole way, it is diluted with water to last longer. This again is done to ensure that proper rainfall will arrive in the rainy season.

The belief in the twins' ability to cause wind appears in various other contexts. So it is said that a wind rises when a twin is circumcised or gets married. When women winnow the threshed grain, a mother of twins is summoned to the threshing floor, if there is such a woman in the village. She is made to stand on the edge of the threshing floor facing east and the winnowed grain is poured on her feet.[2] This is done to make the grain 'heavy' (*tagīl*), i.e. to last long and not to be blown away by the wind. When grain is winnowed, wind is essential, and when there is none, various actions are performed to bring it about. One of them is to burn incense called *um at-timān* (the mother of twins); it is quite possible that the only reason why incense is seen as appropriate is its semantic association with twins.

The next child to be born to a woman who has had twins is called *tōr farid* (a single bull). It also stays in the house until the harvest following its birth lest it 'spoils the rainy season'. Water is believed to be dangerous to *tōr farid*, who must avoid the watercourses and certainly not enter them when the water is running lest it would kill him or her.

A birth outside the hut or a miscarriage 'spoil the rainy season' in the same way as the birth of twins, and their adverse effect on the weather has again to be averted through ritual action. The Berti are particular to make sure that the woman is in the house when her baby is due. If a pregnant woman stays in the cattle camp, she moves back to the village a few weeks before the expected delivery. If the baby is premature and the woman gives birth in the cattle camp, at the well or in the fields, she and her baby are carried to the village and thereafter they stay in the hut as in the case of a normal birth. However, immediately after they are brought home, a male goat has to be sacrificed and its blood sprinkled all the way to where the baby was delivered, lest the rainy season be spoiled and the people who cross or walk along the path by which the woman was carried home spread the pollution to their own villages. If there is not enough blood, it is diluted with water to last the whole way. The *kās murr* from which the blood was sprinkled is left in a green shrub or tree near the place where the woman gave birth.

If a woman miscarries, she is again brought immediately to the village and a male goat is again sacrificed and its blood sprinkled along the way by which she was brought home to ensure that the rain will not be adversely affected. If she has a miscarriage in the village, the blood is

[2] Aglen (1936: 344) reported the same custom from among the Beja in Kordofan.

immediately sprinkled all around it so that the people from other villages who will come to greet her do not spread the pollution. The woman stays confined in her hut, as in the case of an ordinary birth. Her toes are smeared with butter and rock salt and she wears shoes all the time. A week after the miscarriage, her hand is put into a bowl with water, into the grain and into the cooking pot and she can start cooking and grinding flour again; however, no animal is sacrificed, as there is no *agūga*. The woman stays confined in her house until her hair has been replaited on the fortieth day in the case of her first pregnancy, and after three or four weeks if she has given birth before.

The local exegesis provides no answer to the question of why the birth of twins, a birth outside the hut and a miscarriage affect adversely the weather and hence trigger off a ritual action. All those I asked said that they did not know and I have not met anyone prepared to speculate. But even in the absence of local exegesis it is not that difficult for an anthropologist to comprehend why these types of births should trigger off a ritual action. Any such event is abnormal or anomalous and, following Mary Douglas' insight, it is easily understandable why it should be seen as a sign of danger that requires ritual propitiation.

When considered in isolation, the rituals which follow abnormal births would seem to be predicated on the beliefs in the dangerous property of the 'blood of birth'. The ritual performed to alleviate the dangerous effects of shedding the blood of birth brings to view both the similarities and differences in the symbolic relationship between the blood of birth and the blood of the sacrificial animal. In the case of human beings, the shedding of blood leads both to life (a desirable relationship) and to danger (an undesirable relationship). In the case of sacrifice, the shedding of the animal's blood leads to its death (an undesirable relationship) but also to the desired prosperity and well-being (a desirable relationship):

Humans	*Animals*
Shedding of blood : life (desirable)	Shedding of blood : death (undesirable)
Shedding of blood : danger (undesirable)	Shedding of blood : prosperity (desirable)

In the ritual, this comparison proceeds to use the animal blood as a vehicle or agent of life, the meaning being: may the danger disappear and prosperity appear, just as the shedding of the animal blood stimulates prosperity. The ritual may be seen as expressing the wish that one relationship that is undesirable (shedding of blood : danger) is replaced by another desirable one (shedding of blood : prosperity) (see Tambiah 1973).

This analysis would be able to explain why, in the Berti view, the blood shed in creating life should be dangerous. If the shedding of the blood that leads to the death of the sacrificial animal is valued positively, in terms of binary oppositions it makes sense that the shedding of the human blood that leads to the creation of new life is valued negatively. In terms of this simple binary opposition that endows human and animal blood with their respective meanings, it also makes sense that menstrual blood, blood drawn in fights or 'blood of birth' shed during circumcision do not have the same consequences as the 'blood of birth' shed in a birth of twins or a birth outside the hut: no giving of life is involved in its spilling. On the other hand, this analysis is unable to explain why the blood shed during an ordinary birth, which is also dangerous in the same way as the blood shed in an abnormal birth or, for that matter, human blood generally, does not have an adverse effect on the rain and its shedding does not trigger off the particular ritual action which is aimed at protecting the rainy season. Even more importantly, this analysis becomes clearly inadequate in explaining numerous other events which also 'spoil the rainy season' but in which no shedding of human blood is involved.

At the beginning of the rainy season when the fields are sown, shallow holes are dug with a long-handled hoe and a few seeds are sprinkled into them and covered with the foot. The sowing lasts several days but at the end of each day the hoe must be brought home to be carried again to the field the next morning, when the sowing resumes. If the hoe were left in the field overnight, no more rain would arrive. As people find it inconvenient to carry the hoe back and forth every evening and morning, when they finish the day's work, they remove the iron blade of the hoe from its wooden handle. The blade is buried in the sand so that it will not get stolen and the handle is left lying on the ground. When this is done, the rain is not adversely affected; the apparent reason is that a dismantled hoe is no longer a hoe. If a dutch hoe, normally used for weeding, is used in sowing, it has to be treated likewise. The rule applies to the sowing of any crop anywhere.

There are other actions which can be safely performed for the rest of the year but which stop the rain and bring about only a strong and dry wind when performed during the rainy season. Thus the wicker door (*sidāda*) which closes the hut or the fence around the homestead must not be moved in or out of the village after the onset of the rains. People often make new wicker doors in cattle camps, which are as a rule located near the watercourses on the banks of which grow the sticks from which the doors are made. People who are not needed for sowing move from the camp to the village only when the rainy season is well in progress and the clay depressions around the village have filled with water from which the cattle can drink. When dismantling the camp, they have to leave the doors behind and bring them into the village only after the rainy season has run its course.

Another item which must not be brought in or out of the village after the onset of the rains are the wicker bins (*sarganiya*) which are made by women from the rigid stalks of the *tumām* grass (*Panicum turgidum*) and in which grain and melon seeds are usually stored in the man's hut.

Chickens may also not be moved in or out of the village during the rainy season; if they are to be taken to the market during this time, the ill effect on the rain is prevented if one of them is killed and its blood is allowed to drop on the ground during the journey.

When a flat-roofed shelter is built in the fields or in the cattle camps during the rainy season, the rains will also stop. People rest in these shelters when weeding the fields but they must be built in advance either in the dry hot season (*sēf*) of else their construction must be completed at the latest during the time of sowing right after the onset of the first rains in the period of the year called *rushāsh* which immediately precedes the rainy season (*kharīf*) proper.

The events which 'spoil the rainy season', other than those involving the shedding of human blood in an abnormal birth, concern the movement of things which are products of human creativity (the hoe, the wicker door, the grain bin) or which are closely associated with the village (the chickens, the wicker door, the grain bin) across the village – *khalā* boundary. The construction in the *khalā* of the flat-roofed shelter, which ordinarily forms part of the homesteads within the village, may also be seen as a case of such boundary crossing. For the Berti, all these events represent a conceptually unitary class, together with the birth of twins, miscarriage and a birth outside the hut, because they are all seen as having the same effect and because this effect can be nullified by the performance of the same ritual. The selection of the events which form part of this class is thus obviously determined by more general notions than those involving the belief in the ill effects of the shedding of blood in an abnormal birth. These notions again concern the separation of the domain of humans, the only creatures who know God, from the domain of the world outside human society. Events which blur the boundary between the two domains destroy or upset the world order, of which regular rainfall is the most important for Berti agriculturalists. The boundary between the two domains can be disturbed either by the non-human intruding into the human or by the human intruding into that outside human society. The birth of twins, miscarriage or the birth of a human being outside the hut, which is the symbol, *par excellence*, of the domain resulting from the creative efforts of human beings, are instances of the non-human domain intruding into the human. Although the selection of these events may appear haphazard, they are all in fact clearly motivated. I have already explained that the village, which is a result of the creativity which only humans possess, is the concrete symbol of everything that is uniquely human. In it, people can preserve their *sutra* through living in the houses which they have themselves constructed and which enable them to hide what others are not supposed to see, and to do in private what other creatures do in public. The wicker door which encloses the hut and the homestead from the outside world is an appropriate material symbol for this uniquely human quality. *Rahma* is another quality which the Berti associate with the village and which they see as lacking in the world outside it. Just as the wicker door can be seen as a symbolic token of *sutra*, the wicker grain bin can be seen as a material symbol of *rahma*. The flat-roofed shelter which provides the desirable shade has already appeared in various other contexts as the material symbol of comfort and ease (*rāha*) which the Berti value highly, and which again is a quality associated with the village and lacking in the world outside it. Of all the domestic animals, chickens are the ones most closely associated with the village. While all other domestic animals are either kept outside the village (camels, sheep), move in and out of it (goats, cattle, riding and pack camels, donkeys, horses) or are seen as animals of the *khalā* despite living in the village (dogs), chickens stay in the village all the time. Moreover, they live closest to the humans as the chickens coops lean towards the fences of the homesteads. When pointing out the association of women with the village, the Berti often say that women are like chickens in that, unlike men and other animals, they do not travel anywhere.

The hoe appears to be motivated by another quality which the Berti see as uniquely human: the ability to produce which distinguishes people from all other creatures, which simply depend on the food found in the wild. There are, of course, many other tools which could have been selected as symbolic tokens of this uniquely human ability but a hoe came to be seen as appropriate probably because it is the tool used in sowing, the first task in the pursuit of agriculture which the Berti see as the most important of all their economic activities and as the source of all wealth (see Holy 1988). I have mentioned that both people and things have to move across the village – *khalā* boundary for life to be possible but that this traffic should take place only during the day if it is not to have adverse consequences. In the case of the prohibition on leaving the hoe in the field overnight, the opposition between day and night again impinges on the opposition between the village, the symbol of all that which is uniquely human, and the *khalā*, the symbol of that part of the world that does not know God and is not governed by human morality and values. If things from the *khalā* can enter the village only during the day, it is logical that things from the village should also re-enter it only during the day and that a hoe has to be brought back to where it conceptually belongs before the end of the day; if it is left in the field overnight, it violates the ordered relationship between the two main conceptual domains. Conceptually it becomes matter out of place and as such it disturbs the categorical order.

The rituals which I discussed previously dramatise the crossing of the village – *khalā* boundary, which is both physical and conceptual. This crossing occurs in two ways which are both regulated by ritual. Firstly, people move in and out across the boundary and, secondly, the material from which the village is made and the food that sustains people in it has to be brought in across the boundary. The ritual discussed in this chapter is concerned with yet a third kind of boundary crossing. Such a crossing is either the result of the intrusion of the non-human domain into the life of humans or of the uncontrolled infringement of the non-human world by the things which symbolise the morality and values of the uniquely human domain. Unlike the first two kinds of boundary crossing, the third one is unintentional. It just happens either by itself (miscarriage, the birth of twins or a birth outside the hut) or through people's mistakes.

The conceptual separation of the world of humans, who know God and whose life is governed by morality and values which have divine origin, from that part of the world in which this morality and these values do not apply, also underlies the ritual concerned with propitiating a mystical being called *habbōba* which afflicts children with measles. The illness is also referred to as *habbōba* by the Berti.

Habbōba

For the Berti, the knowledge of God implies conduct towards other people which is based on generosity and honesty. When people do not live up to the divine prescriptions which regulate their lives, the cosmological order, in which the lives of humans are kept separate from the lives of non-human creatures which do not know God, is disrupted. One specific manifestation of such disruption is the 'visit' of the *habbōba*.

Habbōba is a term denoting female kin of the second and higher ascending generation on both the father's and mother's side. Its male counterpart is the term *jidd* which is also often used in the sense of 'ancestor'; analogically, the term *habbōba*, used to denote the mystical being afflicting children with measles, could probably best be glossed as 'ancestress'. *Habbōba* is invisible and the Berti have no views on her appearance; the term *habbōba* is, however, also applied to a hedgehog (*ab ganfūt*) which is also sometimes described as *habbōba's* child. It is an auspicious sign if a hedgehog appears in a house and it must never be killed on pain of children dying of measles; when children bring home a hedgehog to play with, they are always urged not to kill it. The Berti do not contemplate any specific genealogical relationship between the *habbōba* and the afflicted children. She is certainly not thought of as any particular named *habbōba* of the child. On the other hand, they are clear about her coming into the village from the outside, as the hedgehog does, and they think of measles as the manifestation of her visit, which occurs usually at the time of the harvest. *Habbōba*, however, does not come regularly every year; her visit is particularly likely to occur if the moral order of the village has been violated by neighbours fighting, quarrelling or harbouring grudges against one another, or by neglecting the performance of communal sacrifices.

Present here is clearly the notion that *habbōba* is a creature of the *khalā* penetrating into the village and afflicting children when the boundary between the world of humans, which is regulated by divine prescriptions, and the world of non-human creatures which do not know God, has been blurred through the violation of the moral order on which the lives of humans are based. Also clearly expressed is the notion that *habbōba* will withdraw, and the affliction will be alleviated, when the boundary is again restored by people reverting to proper moral behaviour. It is emphasised that during *habbōba's* visit, neighbours, and particularly members of a household where a child or children have been afflicted, should show forgiveness, stop harbouring ill-feelings towards one another and not be rude to one another. Hospitality is an aspect of general morality which the Berti particularly emphasise and, appropriately, *habbōba* is treated with respect and deference due to distinguished visitors.[3] Rashes that appear on the body of the afflicted children, and also the spots of light on the floor of the hut caused by the sun shining through the holes in the straw roof and wall, are spoken of as *habbōba's* children. They must not be trodden on and anybody entering the hut must take off their shoes so as not to harm them and thus entice *habbōba* to kill the child. As an apology for incidentally stepping on them and harming them, people utter *habbōba, arētu bārid* ('*habbōba*, let it be cold') before entering the hut. The visitors to the homestead address their greetings to the *habbōba*. *Habbōba's* children get irritated by noise, dust and strong smell. In consequence, people in the house speak in low voices, the house and the

---

[3] For a parallel among the Fur see Beaton. 1948: 38–9.

yard are not swept, no onion is fried and no perfumes are used. No flour must be ground in the house at night and, when pounding grain, women from all households take their stamp-mills outside the village. Other prescriptions and prohibitions have to be observed. People should visit the house only in the morning or in the evening but not during the day when it is hot; there must be no fire in the house at night and all cooking has to be done only in the morning; no *kisra* must be cooked; no houses or shelters in the village can be built for no holes must be dug in the red ground and no thorny branches must be brought into the village. All animals have to be slaughtered only outside the village and no goat or gazelle meat must be eaten or goat milk drunk in the house visited by the *habbōba*. The afflicted children themselves may eat only camel meat.

That *habbōba* is seen as a visitor is expressed in the often uttered incantation *malik zāir, mā ghāir* ('a visiting king, not a trespasser'), and in eventually bidding her farewell from the house by saying: 'you came to us with goodness and we likewise part with you in goodness'. At the same time, the affliction is clearly seen as resulting from the crossing of the village boundary by a mystical being appropriately belonging to the *khalā*. I have suggested that the customary rituals are clearly concerned with controlling such crossing to avert its dangers. Although the *habbōba* ritual differs from them in that it is retributive rather than preventive, it employs, nevertheless, similar instrumental symbols. As already mentioned, the rashes which appear after the child has been afflicted are talked about as *habbōba's* children. Their appearance is welcome as they are necessary for the child's recovery. To induce their appearance, the sick child is smeared with milk, which is believed to whiten *habbōba's* heart. The sick child may wear only white clothes, stays on the mat used in childbirth and is given millet beer to drink, into which onion, sorghum grains and seeds of a thorny grass called *marār* are added. All these substances are apparently used because of their whitish colour. The child is forbidden to drink water and his or her food is prepared without oil, butter and dried meat. The inflammation of the throat is treated with liquid prepared from resin (*luban*) and the child is also fed fermented hibiscus seeds or given water to drink in which cattle dung has been diluted to stop diarrhoea.

In the morning and evening, the child's mother sprinkles water and scatters white sorghum grain or cucumber seeds on the floor of the hut and in the yard of the homestead uttering *arētu bārid* ('let it be cold'), and other incantations indicating that *habbōba* is treated as a visitor. The dried cucumbers from which the seed has been scattered are hung on the roof poles inside the hut.

After seven days, water is brought into the house in an untied small leather bag into which some *kajāna* (millet dough used for making beer) has been put. The water must not be scooped from a surface pool but must be lifted from a well; it must not be transported to the village on a donkey as usual, but must either be carried on the head or by hand if the well is not too far, or otherwise it must be brought on a camel. The person bringing the water must not greet anyone or talk to anyone on the way to the well and back. The child is seated on a log cut from a *gafal* tree (*Balsamodendron africanum*) which has no thorns, and his or her body is washed with the water to which red lime and bark of a comifora tree may be added. After the child has been washed, *habbōba* is bidden farewell out of the house: a woman seeing the *habbōba* out sprinkles water and scatters sorghum on the ground the whole way from the hut to the entrance to the homestead, uttering incantations expressing the *habbōba*'s goodwill and people's goodwill towards her. For some time following *habbōba*'s departure, the child must abstain from eating meat other than camel, from riding donkeys, climbing trees and leaving the house after sunset.

The retributive rituals which I have described in this chapter express the same cosmological order as the preventive rituals described earlier. As I have already explained, the Berti see this cosmological order as being of Islamic origin, and certainly as compatible with Islamic teaching and, in consequence, they do not see the *'awāid* as challenging the dominant Islamic ideology. This is true also of the *habbōba* rituals. The pious may doubt the efficacy of such actions as the scattering of sorghum and cucumber seeds or the efficacy of the prohibition on fire in the house and other restrictions which are imposed during the *habbōba*'s visit. But on the other hand, they value positively people's heightened awareness of the moral rules which should govern their conduct, and they see the point of the imposed dietary restrictions and do not doubt the medical value of the various actions aimed at treating the symptoms of the illness. On the whole, they do not see *habbōba* rituals as threatening, in any way, the Islamic orthodoxy as they understand it. This view is, to a great extent, facilitated by the fact that *habbōba* rituals are performed exclusively by women. In the view of the men, women are lesser creatures anyway, and it is not in their nature to be as deeply religious as men.

The attitude to the other retributive rituals is, however, substantially different. The pious see them as *sanam* or *kanūz*. These expressions connote a belief that is irrational or unfounded in relation to the accepted religious doctrine and which is ultimately parasitic on it, and they clearly refer to a practice in which good Muslims should not indulge. In the remaining chapter, I discuss reasons for this attitude.

9

Custom and superstition

The major assumption which underlies much of the anthropological analysis of culture is that culture is first of all a cognitive device. On analysis, it is not seen as practically but as cognitively functional. If it is seen as an instrumental device at all, it is seen as such, not for achieving practical goals, but for imposing meaning on experience and for expressing that meaning.

In the past three decades or so, this concern with meaning has generated a number of influential studies and ideas. It has not, however, generated a unified methodological approach to the study of cultural forms, perceived as symbolic forms, and their meaning. There exists a wide range of approaches to the study of culture in anthropology. These can probably best be sorted out in terms of the respective models used to conceptualise culture.

It was undoubtedly language which provided the most influential model for the analysis of culture. This model was seized upon by structuralists, who have employed a methodology developed in linguistics, and who carry out the analysis of culture in taxonomic terms. In their view, culture can be seen to operate as a linguistic system and, in consequence, they see meaning as resulting from relations between signs and not as being placed by ourselves on and through the objects and acts we see and experience (Parkin 1982: xiii). As Parkin has observed, this concept of meaning converted 'society into nothing more than a metaphor for the socially decontextualised language of grammarians and certain theoretical linguists' (ibid.: xvii).

In my view, it was the emphasis on the cognitive function of culture and the neglect of its pragmatic functions which led to the choice of language as the model of culture. But I would seriously question that the right model was seized upon in this case. The generally accepted assumption underlying linguistic semantics is that the central function of language is the communication of meaning and that the illocutionary and perlocutionary force of utterances is parasitic on their locutionary meaning. Put in developmental terms, an utterance has first to have a locutionary meaning before it can acquire an illocutionary or perlocutionary force. I would seriously question that the same is true for culture. I would rather suspect that language and culture are in a sense opposites: while language has to mean before it can do, cultural forms have to do before they can mean.

Be it as it may, this was not the reason why language has been found to be an inappropriate model of culture. It was rather a dissatisfaction with the too formalistic conceptualisation of meaning in structuralism which led to the emergence of different models of culture than language. Once it had been generally accepted that meaning does not lie in culturally produced messages of various sorts, but in the minds of the people who interpret these messages, culture came to be seen not as language but rather as text. The most influential advocate of this view is Clifford Geertz. In his seminal paper on the Balinese cockfight, he proposed that the understanding of cultural forms is analogous to penetrating a literary text: 'The culture of people is an ensemble of texts, themselves ensembles, which the anthropologist strains to read over the shoulders of those to whom they properly belong' (Geertz 1971: 29). He admits that this is not the only way that symbolic forms can be sociologically handled, but he maintains that 'to regard such forms as "saying something of something", and saying it to somebody, is at least to open up the possibility of an analysis which attends to their substance rather than to reductive formulas professing to account for them' (ibid.).

Geertz is here clearly referring to the structuralists' conceptualisation of culture as language, which can be analysed in formal taxonomic terms, when he refers to reductive formulas professing to account for the meaning of cultural forms. But he still shares with structuralists the basic assumption about culture, namely that culture is primarily cognitively functional. On this point he is explicit when he says: 'to treat the cockfight as a text is to bring out a feature of it . . . that treating it as a rite or a pastime, the two most obvious alternatives, would tend to obscure: its use of emotion for cognitive ends'; or when he suggests that 'attending cockfights and participating in them is, for the Balinese, a kind of sentimental education' (ibid.).

He argues convincingly that, for the Balinese, cockfights are more than a blood sport, and that more is at stake in them than material gain or loss through heavy gambling. What is at stake is esteem, honour, dignity or respect; in brief, status. In what he calls deep cockfights –

where bets are high, odds even, cocks equally matched and the match is between near-status equals (or personal enemies) and between high-status individuals – the owner of the cock and his collaborators and their backers on the outside put their money where their status is. Although it is ostensibly the cocks which are fighting one another, actually it is the men. The cockfight, and especially the deep cockfight, is fundamentally a dramatisation of status concerns. It activates village and kin-group rivalries and hostilities in 'play' form. In this sense, the cockfight is a means of expression. What it talks about most forcibly is status relationships, and what it says about them is that they are matters of life and death. As Geertz puts it: 'its function is neither to assuage social positions or to heighten them . . . but, in a medium of feathers, blood, crowds, and money, to display them' (Geertz 1971: 23). 'It is a Balinese reading of Balinese experience; a story they tell themselves about themselves' (ibid.: 26).

I do not want to question whether to some Balinese, this is what the cockfight is all about, or what the proper cockfight should be all about. Geertz is explicit about who these Balinese are: they are 'the really substantial members of the community, the solid citizenry around whom local life revolves, who fight in the larger fights and bet on them around the side. The focussing element in these focussed gatherings, these men generally dominate and define the sport as they dominate and define the society. When a Balinese male talks in that almost venerative way, about "the true cockfigher", it is this sort of person . . . that they [sic] mean. For such a man, what is really going on in a match is something rather closer to an *affair d'honneur* . . . than to the stupid, mechanical crank of a slot machine' (ibid.: 17).

But about half of all cockfights are relatively trivial matches in which economic considerations seem to be more important than the 'status' view of gaming. Those involved in them are addict-type gamblers who, it seems, are in it mainly for the money. They may, of course, be men who have not properly internalised their culture, who do not understand what this culture is all about – Balinese equivalents of those who shovel peas into their mouths with knives. This is certainly the view of the 'true cockfighters', with which Geertz quite clearly concurs. The 'true cock-fighters' see these men 'as fools who do not understand what the sport is all about, vulgarians who simply miss the point of it all' (ibid.). But, in my view, it is greatly unsatisfactory to leave the explanation at that and thus to imply that if these men have missed the point of it all, they are passionately involved in an activity which must be for them without any significance or meaning. Or if it has any significance or meaning for them, it is an idiosyncratic one which does not enter into the meaning of the cockfight in Balinese culture. Whatever view we take, we end up with a highly elitist view of culture according to which the privileged individuals define it and arbitrate on it, whereas the others, although passionately involved in the same cultural forms as the privileged elite, remain basically uncultured. To me, this is a highly unsatisfactory view, particularly if it is the majority of men who appear to be totally oblivious to the significance and meaning of cultural forms which they quite effectively operate, as indeed seems to be the case in Bali. The men who participate in the lesser cockfights are not only the personally idiosyn-cratic and the socially despised, but also the poor men and those who lack the status to join in the large matches. Geertz mentions that the most prominent addict-gambler on his cockfight circuit 'was actually a very high caste satria who sold most of his considerable lands to support his habit. Though everybody privately regarded him as a fool and worse . . . he was publicly treated with the elaborate deference and politeness due to his rank' (ibid.: 34, n.28). It seems that even the true cockfighters join in the trivial matches. At least Geertz mentions that the addicts are 'regarded as fair game for the genuine enthusiasts, those who do understand, to take a little money away from, something that is easy enough to do by luring them, through the force of their greed, into irrational bets on mismatched cocks' (ibid.: 17). 'Most of the fights are . . . organised and sponsored by small combines of petty rural merchants under the general premise, very strongly held by them and indeed by all Balinese, that cockfights are good for trade because "they get money out of the house, they make it circulate"' (ibid.: 32, n.18).

All this would seem to indicate that the meaning of most cockfights for most men cannot lie in their dramatisation of status relationships. If it did, these men would obviously not be doing what they do. If we accept that, for the elite, for the 'true cockfighters', cockfighting is an expressive or symbolic activity through which status relationships are dramatised and their true nature is cognitively apprehended, we are also forced to recognise that for most Balinese men, cockfighting is not an activity with these connotations. Purely as a cultural form, cockfighting is something in which both the 'true cockfighters' and all other men are passionately involved; what is significant, however, is that these two categories of men must obviously impose quite different meanings on the same cultural form.

This situation has an important bearing, not only on Geertz's view about the motivation of the cockfight, but on the general assumption about the motivation of cultural forms which underlies all symbolic analyses of culture. The remarkable thing about cockfights in Bali is that they flourish in spite of the fact that they have been declared illegal by the Indonesian government and that those who participate in them face prosecution and imprisonment. Geertz sees the reason for their remarkable resilience in the cognitive function which they fulfil. If, however, this function is lost on most men who in fact keep cockfights going, the general assumption of symbolic analysis to which he subscribes, namely that cultural forms are cognitively motivated, appears to be rather doubtful.

I shall return to the problem of the motivation of cultural forms in a moment. Before I do that, I want to consider briefly the method which symbolic anthropologists habitually employ in their formulation of the meaning of the observable cultural forms. In my view, the formulation of such meaning is a product of the conceptual generalisation and decontextualisation to which they resort. This generalisation and decontextualisation takes two forms: firstly, the explicitly formulated folk concepts are assumed to apply in areas in which they are not expressly invoked by the actors themselves and, secondly, their range of reference is extended by raising them to ever increasing levels of abstraction. This is, of course, fairly common in structuralism, but it also applies to other styles of symbolic analysis. In the Balinese case we have just considered, the expressed village and kin-group rivalries have been seen as applying to cockfights and subsequently generalised as concerns with status. Goody argues that decontextualisation is in its turn made possible by the recourse to writing which has a profound influence on cognition by enabling the concepts to be inspected, manipulated and re-ordered in a variety of ways. 'The result is often to freeze a contextual statement into a system of permanent oppositions' (Goody 1977: 72–3). It is also the process of writing which makes over-generalisation possible:

In an oral discourse it is perfectly possible to treat 'dew' as a thing of the earth in one context and a thing of sky in another. But when faced with its assignment to a specific sub-grouping in a list, or a particular column in a table, one has to make a binary choice, it has to be placed either up or down in rows, in the left column or in the right. The very fact that it is placed in a list which is abstracted from the context of ordinary speech gives the result of this choice a generality which it would not otherwise have had; the possibility of choice is now radically reduced . . . Through a series of forced choices, binary choices, literacy established the victory of the overgeneralised schema. (Goody 1977: 106)

This systematisation of notions which can be seen by the analyst as giving meaning to the observable cultural forms, leads to a very specific conceptualisation of native thought or native-thought processes as objects of contemporary anthropological interest. If, as I have so far tried to argue, the anthropologist's thought does not duplicate the actors' thought, to what extent can it be seen as shedding light on the latter? To answer this question, it is best to look again at how the anthropologists arrive at their conceptual understanding. In most cases, and certainly in those where virtually no local exegesis exists, they formulate the conceptual schema which gives meaning to the cultural forms they have observed, through their analysis of myths and other verbal utterances, ritual practices and customs, in brief, through their analysis of the very same cultural forms which they, through their analysis, see as being ordered by a coherent conceptual schema, i.e. by a coherent system of underlying notions. Geertz can again be singled out as an example. He has reached his conclusion that the Balinese cockfight is a dramatisation of status concerns, not because this is what the Balinese men told him. He arrived at it through the analysis of the cockfights themselves: through his analysis of the social relations among the cock owners and their principal collaborators and supporters, the size of the bets and the odds eventually accepted, the pattern of betting and of borrowing money for betting, the efforts to ensure the equal match of the cocks, etc.

In general, the system of notions which the anthropologists formulate through their analysis of the cultural forms themselves, has not been formulated by anyone else prior to their analysis. In a very real sense it is their product. But they are, of course, not satisfied to treat it merely as such. After all, anthropology is not an exercise in the analyst's ability to formulate cultures or to 'invent' cultures. It is about other people's cultures, about other people creating their cultures. So the notions the anthropologists have formulated have to be attributed to the people from whose myths, utterances, ritual practices and customs they have been formulated. As they have never been formulated by any specific informant, they cannot be attributed to any specific individuals. They can only be attributed to an undifferentiated collectivity: they are seen as 'collective representations', 'collective thought' (Needham 1973: xxi), 'collective consciousness', or even 'collective unconscious' (Lévi-Strauss). Like Zande beliefs, the symbolic analysis of culture is effectively protected by secondary elaborations of which the postulation of the actors' understanding, other than that which they can explicitly state verbally, is the most important one. There now exists a whole range of such specialised forms of comprehension: tacit, unconscious, taken-for-granted or prereflexive knowledge, inarticulate reference (Bateson 1958), implicit meaning (Douglas 1975), doxic experience (Bourdieu 1977), etc. are the most commonly used labels for the kind of knowledge we assume the actors possess but are not able to formulate verbally.

All these expressions are at best metaphors to which we resort to cope with phenomena we have constructed as objects of our interest, but which, so constructed, are too vague and illusive to be ascribed an unambiguous ontological status. They are our own metaphors which become reified and have the status of objects only through this reification. At worst, they are metaphysical categories created by the anthropologist whose presumed ontological status cannot withstand close scrutiny. Ontologically, mind cannot be anything else than the property of an individual human organism, and thought cannot be anything else than the product of such an individual mind. The notion of a collective thought or collective representation can have real meaning only in the sense of a thought or representation of specific concrete individuals intersubjectively shared with specific others. But the shared cultural notions have not been formulated from the notions expressed by the individual members of the culture: they have been read directly from the cultural forms (myths, rites, customs). Their intersubjective sharing is not empirically deduced. It is presupposed and this presupposition derives directly from the presupposition that the cultural forms express the shared notions. The thinking subject has been eliminated effectively from consideration; on the anthropologist's view the culture thinks itself in a very real, and not merely a metaphorical, sense.

Keesing (1982) has aptly characterised the anthropologists' formulation of cultural notions from their analysis of myths, rites, customs, etc. as 'cultural cryptography'. By being engaged in it, anthropology does not face the danger of degenerating into 'metaphysical speculation disguised as an empirical science' as Fabian (1983: 143) warns. It has already become the art of metaphysical contemplation.

Admittedly, to some anthropologists this may appear not to be a fair characterisation of their own endeavours. After all, in their formulation of cultural notions they have been guided by the explicit exegesis and interpretation of a few informants of an exceptional philosophical bent, like Turner's Muchona (the hermit) or Griaule's blind Ogotemeli. They became the anthropologist's main informants because they showed a theoretical interest in their culture. In this respect their view of it is more like the view of the anthropologist whose interest is also theoretical. Their understanding is in consequence more akin to that of the anthropologist (even if it may differ in detail or even in substance) than to that of other members of the culture, whose interest in it is practical. They may thus be imposing meaning on their culture which is in no way shared by anyone else, and which may be quite different from the meaning imposed on it by others. No doubt, being themselves members of the culture studied, the meaning which they impose on the cultural forms has to be treated in analysis as their cultural meaning. But this in itself does not justify treating it as *the* meaning which these forms have in the culture studied, and it justifies even less the assumption that a meaning which some actors impose on the cultural forms is a meaning of which all of them are aware, albeit only tacitly or unconsciously.

Moreover, there is another problem here: if the cultural notions formulated by the analysts, on the basis of the statements of their gifted informants, are conceptualised as collective representations which must not be confused with the conceptual apprehension of individuals (Needham 1973: xix–xx; 1979: 58) because not all of them have a clear or comprehensive view of them (Needham 1973: xxxi), the notions which clearly exist at the level of the actors' individual consciousness are summarily relegated onto the level of unconscious representations, or indiscriminately fused with it.

It is obvious that the symbolic analysis of culture has clearly parted company with the sociology of knowledge and its notion of the social distribution of knowledge. For the symbolic anthropologist, the distribution of knowledge among the members of the culture studied is at best unproblematic: even if there are informants who know more than others or have better interpretative ability than others, the difference between them and others, who have not that ability, is seen merely as a difference in degree and not in kind. The knowledgeable are able to provide the anthropologist with information about collective representations or collective thought that is assumed to be shared by all and sundry, albeit unconsciously. The difference between the conscious and the unconscious, tacit and explicit knowledge, is irrelevant. In the best Durkheimian tradition, knowledge and thought are studied as objects with total disregard for who thinks the thought and who it is that actually knows.

To obviate the difficulties into which the symbolic analysis of culture has run requires a radical rethinking of the tacit and explicit assumptions which generate them. An alternative conceptualisation of culture has to reject language, text, discourse or whatever, as appropriate models of culture and has to start with recognising a culture for what it is to those whose culture it is. This can probably best be done by recognising two important facts about culture.

The first is that culture is not an object independent of the activities into which it enters and through which it manifests itself. If it is not an object, it cannot be analysed as one. Culture is a mental phenomenon sustained in existence by those who use and manipulate it. In order that, in the process of its comprehension and interpretation by the analyst, it does not change from what it is for the actors into something that it can be only for the analyst, his or her own mental processes and knowledge must not replace in analysis the comprehension and interpretation of the actors.

But what are we to do when faced with the common problem that the actors themselves are not able to provide us with any statements of their understanding of cultural forms? When asked why they perform a certain ritual, for example, they reply that they do it because it is their custom, or when asked about the meaning of the paraphernalia of the ritual, they say that they do not know. As I have mentioned before, concern with meanings that the actors cannot verbalise is the main concern of symbolic anthropology in which culture is seen as sending coded messages. The actors receive them and apprehend them somehow but are unable to verbalise them. Only the anthropologist is able, through his or her method of analysis, to decode the messages and to say what they are. Lewis rightly observes that

if we claim to understand a coded message and are then asked what it says, we should be able to say. This feature does not seem to fit well with the experience of those who perform ritual or the evidence of anthropologists who observe it. (Lewis 1980: 35)

My answer to this problem is simple: instead of assuming the existence of specialised categories of the actors' comprehension which only a sophisticated analysis of the cultural forms themselves can reveal, let us assume the obvious: if understanding a coded message does not seem to fit well with the experience of those who, for example, perform ritual, why could it not simply be that there is no coded message to be transmitted? In other words, when the actors say that they do not know or understand, let us believe them and assume that they indeed do not know or understand.

Such an assumption is perfectly feasible if we take seriously the second important fact about culture, namely that culture fulfils not only a cognitive but also a pragmatic or practical function; it is sustained in existence not only because it is cognitively motivated, not only because it imposes meaning on experience, but also because it makes possible or facilitates practical interaction. The ability of actors to use and manipulate cultural forms in the course of their practical behaviour does not require them to understand their symbolic meanings.

As I mentioned before, considering culture exclusively in terms of its cognitive function is linked to viewing culture as communication. This view need not to be abandoned once it is realised that it can be used, not only in the communication of the meaning, but also in what Malinowski called 'phatic communication', i.e. communication in which 'words are used rather to fulfil a social function . . . this is their principal aim but they are neither the result of intellectual reflection nor do they necessarily arouse reflection in the listener . . . each sentence is an act serving a direct aim of binding hearer and speaker by a tie of some social sentiment or other' (Malinowski 1923: 315). Cultural forms are also used in phatic communication: they also have the direct aim of facilitating the purposive interaction.

At the same time, considering culture as something more than merely a cognitive device does not rule out the possibility that the primary motivation for the use of specific cultural forms can lie in their semiotic rather than in their purely pragmatic functions (in their rational-technical sense).

When I put on a jacket, I do it only partly because I want to keep reasonably warm (if we take this to be a purely pragmatic function of my dressing). I do it also because I want to achieve another goal: to avoid being snubbed for being inappropriately dressed or, under specific circumstances, to avoid being refused entry. I do it to be able to get on with what I want to do or, to facilitate interaction. But I do it also to indicate, in the culturally appropriate way (that is the way we have agreed upon), my awareness of the solemnity of the occasion, and my dress is 'read' by others as an indication of this awareness on my part.

Because cultural forms are read in this way to communicate awareness, intentions, understanding, agreement or disagreement, etc., and are understood by others as indices in the complex communicative system that constitutes cultural behaviour, they are not necessarily symbols, if symbol is understood as linked by a metaphorical relationship to that which it stands for. Most of them are used and understood as signs, which are linked by metonymical relationships to activities and situations which they themselves constitute and of which they are a part. They give direction and orientation to the interaction, permitting the coordination and co-existence of various participants (Fernandez 1965: 913). They clearly facilitate the orientation of actions towards one another by being simply seen by the actors as 'situation-referential'; that is, in so far as they are singled out for attention, they refer back to the activity from which they sprang rather than to meaning beyond that activity (ibid.: 911). Any effective interaction rests upon the acceptance of a set of signs and an agreement about their significance, in the sense that there is acceptance of the appropriateness of these signs as orienters of interaction in a specific social situation, and a commonality of response to them (ibid.: 917). The signs are matter-of-factly experienced as the necessary paraphernalia of a given activity, without which that activity could not go on (ibid.: 912) or would become an activity of a different kind. In this respect, cultural forms are not particularly meaningful in the cognitive sense, that is, as having special meanings in and of themselves. Although they have no meaning, they have significance but they have their significance only in relation to the specific context in which they function.

What I am suggesting is not that cultural forms should be seen as signs rather than symbols which possess meanings that are not simply a function of the particular social situation in which they appear, but refer to something beyond that activity. I am simply suggesting that they can be either and that it depends solely on how they are perceived by the actors who use and interpret them, whether they are signs or symbols.

Stuchlik and I have previously suggested that the dichotomy between representational and operational models is one of the most important aspects of the organisation of actors' knowledge (Holy and Stuchlik 1983). If we accept that symbols are cognitively motivated (good to think with or to represent with) and signs pragmatically motivated (good to do with), it follows that both these facets of the actors' knowledge are involved in their comprehension of cultural forms. The analyses of culture which have paid specific attention to the actors' meanings and to their understanding of symbols have all come up with a dichotomy which in some way parallels the dichotomy between representational and operational models.

Thus Fernandez makes a distinction between cultural and social consensus. The first is an agreement on the meaning of symbols, the second an agreement with respect to the interaction requirements of signals and signs. He argues that a high degree of social consensus, in the sense of agreement about signals and signs, and smooth coordination of interaction does not necessarily imply a high degree of cultural consensus (Fernandez 1965: 922).

Lewis, in his sensitive study of the rituals of the Gnau people in the West Sepik Province of Papua New Guinea, in which he patiently determines the meaning of ritual forms for the Gnau themselves, makes a distinction between a meaning, which may be indeterminate, private, various and individual, and a ruling, which is public, clear and social (Lewis 1980: 19).

In his study of Kwaio religion, Keesing (1982) distinguishes the representational knowledge of the actors from their operative knowledge.

Spiro, in his discussion of religious beliefs, makes a distinction between 'religion-as-a-doctrinal-structure' and 'religion-in-use'. 'Religion-as-a-doctrinal-structure' refers 'to the organization of religious doctrines taken as a cognitive system, that is a system of propositions together with their constituent meanings'. 'Religion-in-use' refers to the 'purposes to which the religious actor puts his beliefs' (Spiro 1982: 58):

To say that religious actors are primarily concerned with religion-in-use is to say that although religious systems are cognitive systems, they persist not only because of the cognitive basis for the belief in the reality of the mythico-religious world, not only because its symbols are good to think, but because the belief in its reality satisfies some powerful human needs (Spiro 1982: 58).

This kind of duality in the actors' comprehension of cultural forms is characteristic of the way in which the Berti understand their own customs and rituals. It manifests itself both in the difference in the comprehension and understanding of the objects, relations and qualities which are manipulated and played upon in the performance of the various *'awāid*, and in the differences of the conceptualisation and interpretation of the various *'awāid* by specific individuals.

Let me sketch the differences in people's insight into what I have treated in analysis as the symbols to which the customary rituals resort. I made a distinction between instrumental symbols, which are employed to bring about the rituals' envisaged goals (described in Chapter 3) and symbols which express the cosmological notions which the rituals reflect (described in Chapter 4). This is, of course, an analytical distinction but it parallels closely the observable differences in the Berti comprehension and understanding.

There is a much higher degree of what Fernandez calls 'cultural consensus' with regard to the expressive symbols than to the instrumental ones. My efforts at eliciting the exegesis of the instrumental symbols were mostly unsuccessful, and I received very little of it even from otherwise excellent informants. There was never any exegesis spontaneously offered during the performance of the various ritual actions which I observed on numerous occasions. This does not mean that no advice was ever given to the performers. On the contrary, in most performances I witnessed, people were advised on the sequence of actions, how to perform them properly, and on who should perform them. Specific women who wanted to join in were often turned away because they had been divorced, their child had died, or their firstborn child was a boy. They were told that the ritual must be performed by those who are *sabbar*, or that it has to be performed jointly by two women one of whom is *um wilēd* and the other one *um binei*, but I have never heard it spontaneously explained why the ritual would be ineffective if it was performed by those without appropriate qualifications, or why these qualifications are what they are. I have also never heard anybody asking for these reasons.

Similarly, I witnessed women being reminded that they must cover their hair when they are performing a ritual action, or that they must say *bism il-lāhi* before they start it, or being reminded that they should not smear a shrub with oil and being asked if they had not brought any butter with them. These are just a few examples from my fieldnotes which could be multiplied. But again, I have never heard any reasons being given or anybody asking for them. As a result, a great deal of social consensus on how the rituals should properly be performed has been fostered, but there is very little cultural consensus about their symbolic meaning.

This lack of cultural consensus is not a hindrance to the persistence of the *'awāid* in Berti culture for they simply work when the right actions are performed on the right occasions by the right people. Achievement of the ritual's goal is not jeopardised if the performers do not know why they are the right people and their actions the right actions. The ritual, as it were, works on its own without the people being necessarily aware of how it does so. The operational knowledge of the ritual's procedure is all one needs to possess in order to perform the ritual successfully; no representational knowledge is necessary. The ritual practices are perfectly capable of persisting as part of Berti cultural tradition in spite of their lack of cognitive function; it is the persistence of their pragmatic or instrumental function which keeps them alive in the cultural repertoire.

This is not to say that there are no Berti who have any representational knowledge of the instrumental symbols or, in other words, any insights into their meaning or motivation. There are a few such women and men in almost every village. But the exegesis they gave me was often very opaque and fragmentary, frequently resorting to explaining one metaphor in terms of another. I tried, nevertheless, to follow its leads as faithfully as I possibly could when offering my own interpretation in Chapter 3.

The degree of cultural consensus is much higher when it comes to the expressive symbols which figure prominently in the customary rituals and which I discussed in Chapter 4. Virtually everybody is aware and is able to express verbally that the village is the place and the day the time of safety, and that *khalā* and night are the dangerous place and time. Most people have no difficulties in stating the other qualities with which the village is associated in its opposition to *khalā*. The association between the village, women and *hajlīd* is clearly conscious. Even if the exegesis often resorts to concrete symbols or images, the awareness in Berti consciousness of the basic dichotomy between the divinely ordered life of humans and the world which lacks human morality, reason and the knowledge of God is indisputable.

The degree of awareness between the cosmological scheme expressed through the opposition of various concrete images like village and *khalā*, day and night, or through the opposition of such qualities as safety and danger, mercy and deprivation, differs considerably from the awareness of the meaning and motivation of the various instrumental symbols employed in the customary rituals. This difference derives from the different relation of the instrumental and expressive symbols to the dominant Islamic ideology. The cosmological scheme reflected in the expressive symbols does not conflict in any way with this ideology; on the contrary, it is seen as deriving from it and as expressing the same notions which are basic to Islam. As I explained before, there is also an all-pervasive tendency to legitimise the instrumental symbols in terms of the Koranic notions. But the instrumental symbols still challenge the Islamic ideology, in that they express a different picture of personality, procreation and the relations between men and women from that which has its origin in Islam. Whereas the customary rituals do not construct, by means of their expressive symbols, a different cosmology from that which is embedded in the religious beliefs and practices, they do so, at least to some extent, by means of their instrumental symbols. In other words, it is primarily through the instrumental symbols that customary rituals can be construed as deviating from, challenging or contradicting the dominant Islamic ideology. Such contradiction has, of course, to be cognitively resolved, accommodated or managed. And this, I would suggest, is done by denying them the potency of symbols, by not seeing them as standing for anything other than themselves, by denying their efficacy, in short, by seeing them as signs metonymically linked to the action of which they are a part, but not as symbols metaphorically linked to anything beyond that action. This cognitive defence against what could be construed as non-Islamic should become clearer after I have discussed the Berti notion of superstition.

The retributive ritual which I described in the previous chapter clearly expresses the same cosmology as the preventive rituals described before. Given that this cosmology is not seen as conflicting with the Islamic belief but as grounded in it, why are the preventive rituals valued positively by virtually all the Berti, whereas the retributive ritual is dismissed by at least some of them as a superstition? The Berti resemble many other Muslim societies in that women are much more distinctly concerned with customary rituals than men while religious rituals are predominantly the concern of men. It is also true that those who tend to see the retributive ritual as a superstition are mostly men. They are first of all the *fugarā* and young men with at least some school education. There is a great emphasis on religious instruction in all Sudanese schools; in the first grade of the elementary school the reading and learning of the Koran takes almost a third of the whole syllabus and it is done in a way which does not differ substantially from the way in which the Koran is learnt in the traditional Koranic schools. The number of Berti who have spent at least a few years at school has been slowly but steadily increasing during the past decade or two. They have a different knowledge from most illiterate villagers, and even some of the *fugarā*, of what is recognised as proper Islamic beliefs and practices in the Sudan, and they are in the forefront of those who see the customary practices with suspicion and some of them as clearly incompatible with Islam. But also a few illiterate men as well as some women – partly the young ones who have been to school, but also some older illiterate ones – belong to this category. These are the people to whom I have referred as the pious. They all have in common a higher degree of religious piety than their less-sophisticated neighbours and a more extensive knowledge of the basic tenets of Islamic beliefs and practices.

The ritual which the pious dismiss as a superstition differs in several ways from most other customary rituals. Not only is it retributive rather than preventive, but its aim is to restore the natural order disturbed by the accidental and unintentional violation of category boundaries, whereas the aim of other customary rituals is to prevent misfortune befalling human beings as a result of their necessary and intentional crossing of the boundary between the two conceptual domains of the world. It differs from them also in that it involves a sacrifice, an act which the Berti see clearly as part of the Islamic religion. It is thus a ritual that transcends the conceptual distinction which the Berti make between religion (*dīn*), as it is stipulated in the Koran and the prophetic tradition, and custom (*'āda*), which is part of the Berti tradition (*sunna*) and has no Koranic basis. But it is unlikely that the pious see the practice as *sanam* or *kanūz* because of the religious element involved in it. The opening of the well at the beginning of the dry season, which is an act classified as *'āda*, is also accompanied by a sacrifice. It could thus also be seen as a ritual that transcends the distinction between religion and custom, but I have never heard anybody expressing any objection to it or resisting it on the grounds that it was *sanam* or *kanūz*.

Whereas in an ordinary sacrifice, which is an important part of Berti religion, the blood of the sacrificial animal is left to sink to the ground, in the ritual aimed at preventing the 'spoiling of the rainy season', it is collected and sprinkled over a wide area to achieve the desired effect. This is clearly understood by the pious as a practice that does not have a Koranic origin and hence as something that is akin to custom rather than religion. But again, this is by far not the only situation in which the blood of the sacrificial animal is treated as a protective agent, or an agent of purification or healing. Such treatment of blood has been reported from elsewhere in the Muslim world (El-Zein 1977: 250) and, in fact, is quite common throughout the Sudan. In a suburban village of Khartoum, a pilgrim sacrifices a sheep five or seven days after his return from Mecca. Sometimes he puts a drop of the blood on his forehead, or he places his hand in the blood and imprints the blooded hand on the door of his house (Barclay 1964: 154). The Rubatab and other Sudanese Arabs dip a hand in the blood of a sacrificial animal and imprint it on a camel or other beast to protect it from being harmed or stolen (Jackson 1926: 15). In many urban areas of the country, people who have acquired a new car or built a new house, dip the palms of their hands in the blood of an animal which has been sacrificed on this occasion and imprint them on the car or the wall of the new house to protect them against the evil eye (*'ēn*). Part of the *zar* ceremony is a sacrifice of a sheep or goat of the appropriate colour provided by the patient. The cult leader or her assistant dips her finger into its blood and marks the patient's forehead with it as part of the treatment (Barclay 1964: 200). When the blood of the sacrificial animal is allowed to pour into the well during its opening, this can be seen as a variant of the widespread Sudanese belief in the protective, healing or purifying property of the blood, which is an integral part of the local Islam. Even the Berti *fugarā*, who dismiss the retributive ritual as a superstition, use the blood of a sacrificial animal as a healing agent when they smear with it the forehead of a person 'grasped' by *'ārid*.

The sprinkling of the blood of the sacrificial animal to restore the natural order is a major non-religious ritual that is performed by men. Among the Berti, as in all Muslim societies, men too are provided with major ritual roles in Islam and, in consequence, they become concerned with religion to a much greater extent than women. The Berti certainly hold the view that it is in the nature of women to be less religious than men. Because women's active participation in customary rituals can be seen as compensation for their merely passive participation in religious rituals, it can easily be tolerated. Moreover, as the rituals in which women are involved do not need to be construed as being in competition with religious rituals, they do not in any way pose a threat to religion, which is primarily the men's concern.

Men, being entrusted with the leading role in all religious rituals, do not have the same need as women to engage in any rituals which do not have a strictly Islamic origin. If they then perform such rituals, these become inevitably conceptualised as competing with and alternatives to those actions which they have been entrusted to perform in the name of Islam. Being alternatives, the non-Islamic ritual actions subvert the Islamic beliefs; they become mere superstitions which should not be tolerated (see Strange 1984: 137). Although this explanation may hold for many Muslim societies, it is too simplistic to account satisfactorily for the fact that it is only the ritual aimed at restoring the natural order which is seen by some people as a superstition. It is by far not the only customary ritual which men perform. Men open the well, inaugurate ritually the weeding, threshing and thatching of a new house and, together with women, participate in many other rituals which are not seen as contradicting or even questioning their religious beliefs.

None of the above factors can explain why the retributive ritual is seen as different from all other customary rituals, although of course all of them may add some additional weight to this view. However, those who see the beliefs that certain events can spoil the country and detain the rain as *sanam sākit* or *kanūz sākit* (sheer superstition), argue that no human action can affect the rain, for it is sent and can be withdrawn only by God. At face value, such an argument might again appear unconvincing as it can equally well be argued that the health, well-being and prosperity which all other customary rituals aim to achieve, can also be granted or withdrawn only by God, and no manipulation of objects or substances by humans can possibly alter this fact. But we can appreciate the strength of the Berti's own argument if we recall the distinction between the social and cultural consensus with regard to the objects and substances employed in customary rituals. In the view of most Berti, they bring about the desired health, well-being and prosperity because of their auspicious qualities or the auspiciousness which they represent in their material form. For these people they are true symbols, and it is the 'sympathetic' thought which endows them with the power to create for people the same qualities which these symbols represent or themselves possess. By denying them this 'meaning', the pious deny their efficacy. They see them not as symbols but as signs, or simply as empty forms without any meaning beyond the activities in which they are employed. As cultural forms, they are, of course, part of the Berti tradition, but in that respect they are not different from the traditional Berti dress, house-style or other innumerable secular objects and activities which are also part of the Berti tradition or custom. As such, they are, of course, not without significance but they are not seen as endowed with any specific meaning. They are not really all that important. Because the *'awāid* can be denied any efficacy and need not be seen as acts which aim at achieving in their own way the same objectives as prayers, fasts or sacrifices, they need not be seen as conflicting with or contradicting the religious beliefs. They do not have to be branded as superstitions for they can be seen in the same light as the festive dress, dancing or special meals which, like the *'awāid*, are also part and parcel of numerous special occasions. Perhaps most importantly, they can be tolerated by the pious because they can be ignored by them. Many pious men disassociate themselves from the customary rituals by claiming that they are women's affairs which only women know about. There is no pressure on anyone to participate in them or even to take a special note of them. You can perform the customs if you wish, just as you can take part in a dance if you are so inclined, or listen to a story when it is being told, but you do not have to if you do not want to. Or you can even take pride in them for they are part of your tradition and part of what gives you your identity as a Berti. With regard to your being a good Muslim it makes no difference. But it makes all the difference whether you pray, fast or partake in a *karāma* or not, and whether you drink or do not drink beer, and eat or do not eat the meat of animals which have died without being properly slaughtered, or were slaughtered by women or uncircumcised men. And it also makes a difference whether or not you believe that carrying certain things in and out of the village during the rainy season, or occurrence of abnormal births will stop rain.

Even the pious among the Berti display a great deal of tolerance of actions which Islam prohibits. As I have mentioned, all sex outside marriage is considered *harām*. But sexual liaisons before marriage are not uncommon and they sometimes result in pregnancy. If the girl's marriage to her lover cannot be arranged for some reason, her child is brought up by her parents as their own, and its illegitimate status is soon forgotten. The girl has usually no difficulties in marrying later when her motherhood has become overshadowed by some new scandal and ceased to be a main object of village gossip. The pious, and particularly the *fugarā*, abstain from drinking millet beer which they see as *harām* in spite of the prevailing Berti view that the Koranic prohibition on alcohol does not apply to it. But the *fugarā* never preach against millet beer, and they never try to dissuade people from drinking it. It is not unusual that a *fakī*'s wife brews beer in her household as any other wife does, not only for her and her children's consumption but also so that there will be beer in the household for guests. Although the *fakī* would not drink it, he often brings a pot to his guests. This tolerant attitude to the sinful ways of others derives from the fact that the pious do not feel themselves in any way implicated by the acts of others. This is also one of the reasons for their generally tolerant attitude towards customary rituals.

This tolerance, however, breaks down in the case of ritual aimed at restoring the natural order because everybody, including the pious, becomes inevitably implicated. If a pious person commits one of the acts which are believed by others to stop the rain, like leaving a village in which twins have been born, or leaving a hoe overnight in the field, he will be accused of having spoiled the country and he will be pressed to provide the sacrificial animal so that the proper retributive ritual can be performed. Whether he likes it or not, the persistence of beliefs that certain events spoil the country affects his or her freedom to perform actions which are proscribed in the Koran or *ḥadīth*. The pious get inevitably implicated by others' beliefs which they consider to be in conflict with the Islamic religion, and the only action open to them is to fight them as unfounded superstitions.

Paradoxically, in spite of being branded by many as non-Islamic superstitions, rituals aimed at restoring the country after it has been 'spoilt' have a vitality which many customary rituals lack. This is the result of the fact that they are not aimed at securing the desirable future state of specific individuals, but at securing the normal course of natural events. If they were not performed in the case of an abnormal birth, or after other events which are believed to have an adverse effect on the country, no rain would arrive, which of course affects all members of the community. People who have done something that is believed to affect the rainfall are reminded of the consequences of their act by the standard saying 'you spoiled the country for us' (*kharabta lēna al-wata*). The pressure to perform the appropriate ritual when it is called for is thus much stronger than the pressure to perform other customary rituals, as the following case illustrates. An unmarried girl became pregnant. Her parents kept it secret and, when she miscarried, they saw it as a blessing: no illegitimate child would be born and they would be spared the shame. However, what actually happened was widely gossiped about and many people in the village were afraid of the consequences if the proper ritual were not performed. Eventually, the father was forced to admit what had happened and to sacrifice a goat and sprinkle its blood around the village.

The persistence of customary rituals in contemporary Berti culture cannot thus be seen as resulting solely from the fact that they fulfil an important cognitive function and communicate to the Berti important information about the world. They also do not persist simply as a result of the tolerance of Islam to the ideas about the multiplicity of mystical power in the world, or of the exclusion of women from the main Islamic rituals. Although these factors undoubtedly play their role, they do not provide an exhaustive explanation. The customary rituals also have important pragmatic functions in that they are important signs of Berti identity. This is an equally strong motive behind their persistence. Whereas one motivation may be all important for some Berti, the other one is all important for others. Ultimately it is the dynamics of the social distribution of knowledge among the various categories of the Berti – the illiterate villagers, the *fugarā* and those with school education – which keeps the customary rituals in existence alongside the Islamic ones, and at the same time generates the view that only some customary rituals are compatible with Islam whereas others are not. Most importantly, the knowledge which the different categories of the Berti possess is a resource that is used to exact social pressure which, on the one hand, gives form and shape to particular social actions and, on the other hand, generates a varying degree of compliance with local custom in each particular case. Ultimately, it is the combination of the rituals' cognitive and pragmatic functions and the strength of the social pressure which particular categories of people can exert on others, which accounts for the vitality of all customary rituals, in spite of the fact that different rituals may be differently evaluated from the point of view of the dominant Islamic ideology.

Glossary

abu binei – a man whose first child is a girl
abu wilēd – a man whose first child is a boy
'agīd al-hilla – a man in charge of organising the communal activities of a village.
agūga – the name-giving ceremony
ajr – a reward from God for a good deed
amāna – safety
'angarēb – a frame bed on which men sleep
ansār – helpers
'ārid – a kind of *shētān* (devil)
'awāid (sg. *'āda*) – customary rituals
'azūma – a wedding celebration
banu – *Eragrostis* sp.
bārid – cold
bayād (lit. whiteness) – a voluntary payment to a diviner, healer or midwife
belīla – boiled millet
bēt 'āda (lit. house of the customary ritual) – a house built for a newly married
    couple
bēt nār (lit. house of the fire) – a woman's hut which forms the core of a
    household
bīr – a well
dakar – male
dam wilāda – the blood of birth, including blood shed during circumcision
dashīsha – crushed millet mixed with water
dāya – a midwife
denī – a sloppy woman or a careless or inefficient housewife
dīn – religion
du'a – a prayer to induce God into granting a specific favour
dukhla (from *dakhal* – to enter) – the ritual bringing of the first millet from the
    field into the village
'ēn – the evil eye
fadīha – shame
fakī (pl. *fugarā*) – a local religious leader
fakī al-hilla – a religious leader in charge of the religious rituals in the village
fātha – the opening sura of the Koran; the first stage of a wedding

gafal – *Balsamodendron africanum*
garad – the crushed fruit of *Acacia scorpioides* used for tanning leather
gibla – the direction one faces during prayer
gubba – the tomb of a saint
habbōba – grandmother; measles, or a mystical being which afflicts children with measles
ḥadīth – the collection of the reported sayings of the Prophet, his companions and other pious scholars of early Islam
haj (fem. *hajja*) – a pilgrim to Mecca
hajlīd – *Balanites aegyptica*
halāl – ritually clean and permitted
harām – ritually forbidden
harāz – *Acacia albida*
harr – hot
hasīr – a woman's bed
hijāb (pl. *hijbāt*) – an amulet
hilla – a village
iblīs – a kind of *shētān* (devil)
'īd al-dahīya – the festival commemorating Ibrahim's offer to sacrifice his son
'īd al-fatur – the festival held on the first day after Ramadan
'īd al-maulid – the festival to commemorate the Prophet's birthday
imām – a prayer leader
intāi – female
'irs – the second stage of a wedding, when the bridegroom starts to cohabit with the bride
izāna – the call to prayer
jelīd – unlucky
jinn (pl. *junūn*) – spirit
jīr ŋaŋa – the anointing of a baby on the day following the name-giving ceremony
jīza – the second stage of a wedding, when the bridegroom starts to cohabit with the bride
jurāb (pl. *jurbān*) – a bag made of cow hide, used for transporting grain
jurn – a low platform for storing the ears of millet before threshing
kabbūs – small balls made of millet flour mixed with water
kajāna – fermented dough from which beer is filtered
kanūz – superstition
karāma – an offering to God; a sacrifice
kawal – the fermented leaves of the cassia plant used for spicing relish
khalā – wilderness; the world outside the human settlement
khalwa – a Koranic school; privacy or seclusion
kharīf – the rainy season
khuruj – a pair of large water bags carried on a donkey's back
kisra – thin wafer-like pancakes made of millet flour
kitr – *Acacia melifera*
lalōba – fruit of the *hajlīd* (*Balanites aegyptica*)
lōh – a wooden slate for writing on
makhēt – *Boscia senegalensis*
makrūh – ritually disapproved, although not explicitly forbidden

marhabēb – *Cympobogon nervatus* (?)

masāib – misfortune

masīd – a village mosque

medīda – a special dish for a woman who has given birth

mētam – the three days of mourning after a funeral

mihāi – religious and magical formulae written on a wooden slate and washed with water, used for curing illness and other benevolent, as well as malevolent, purposes

mukmāt – a small wicker basket for flour

murhāka – a grinding stone

murr – bitter; often used in the sense of *harām* and *nijis*

mushuk – the flour left after millet beer has been filtered

nabag – *Ziziphus mauritiana*

nabātī (fem. *nābatīya*) – a ghost

nijis – polluted; ritually unclean

nīsha – a sweet non-alcoholic beverage

omda – a chief in charge of an *omodiya*

omodiya – the main administrative division of the tribal territory

qāḍī – an Islamic judge

rahma – mercy

rahūla (from *rahal* – to move) – the final stage of a wedding when the bride moves to the couple's new house

rakūba – a flat-roofed shelter

Ramadan – the month of fasting

ramul (from *ramla* – sand) – sand divination

rēka – a large basket used mainly for carrying grain and flour

rūh – spirit; life force

rushāsh – the period of the first rains at the beginning of the rainy season

sabbar (from *sabara* – to last) – a person whose firstborn child is alive and who has not been divorced or widowed

sadaga – alms

sagit or *sagit al-kitāb* – book divination

samih – nice; lucky, auspicious

sanam – superstition

sarganiya – a wicker bin for storing grain

sēf – the dry season

shahāda – the profession of the Islamic creed

sharī'a – Islamic law

shēbi – a greyish plant used in the *dukhla* ritual

shēkh – a headman

shēla – a large wicker basket for flour

shēn – bad, ugly; inauspicious

shētān (pl. *shayātīn*) – devil

sīd abyad (lit. owner of the white) – a man whose first child is a girl

sidāda – a wicker door to the hut or the fence around the homestead

sīd adlam (lit. owner of the dark) – a man whose first child is a boy

sidāg – the payment to the bride's guardian which legalises the marriage contract

sīd azrag (lit. owner of the black) – a man whose first child is a boy

sihir – sorcery

subhaniya – the counting of rosary beads
subu' – dances accompanying weddings and circumcisions
sunna – Islamic traditions: Islamic community
sunna Berti – Berti traditions
sutra (from *satar* – to cover or shroud parts of the body which are not to be seen) – modesty
tabag – a flat winnowing basket
tahār (from *tahhar* – to clean) – circumcision
tahāra – ritual cleansing; ablution before prayer
tāhir – ritually cleansed
tanjīm (from *nijim* – star) – a divination to establish a person's star
tērāb mina'ash – the ritual sowing of a field whose owner has died
tumām – *Panicum turgidum*
ugāl – a hobble used to prevent a camel from standing up
umbatri – a loose-leaf book containing a collection of handwritten texts on divination, the writing of amulets, the interpretation of dreams, etc.
um binei – a woman whose first child is a girl
um wilēd – a woman whose first child is a boy
'urf – local custom
'ushar – *Calotropis procera*
'ushūr – a tithe of grain given to the *shēkh*
usta – a specialist like a saddler, a blacksmith, a circumciser, etc.
wakīl – a marriage guardian
wazīr – deputy, attendant, first minister
yōm al-hisāb – (lit. the day of counting) – the day on which the first part of bridewealth is transferred to the bride's guardian
zaka – religious dues
zikr – the counting of rosary beads

References

Abu-Lughod, L. 1986. *Veiled sentiments: honor and poetry in a Bedouin society*. Berkeley and Los Angeles: University of California Press.

Abun-Nasr, J. M. 1965. *The Tijaniyya: a Sufi order in the modern world*. London: Oxford University Press.

Abu Zahra, N. 1982. *Sidi Ameur – a Tunisian village*. London: Ithaca Press.

Aglen, E. F. 1936. Kordofan superstitions. *Sudan Notes and Records* 19: 343–5.

Ahmed, A. S. 1976. *Millenium and charisma among Pathans: a critical essay in social anthropology*. London: Routledge and Kegan Paul.

Ahmed, A. S. 1984. Religious presence and symbolism in Pukhtun society. In *Islam in tribal societies: from the Atlas to the Indus* (eds.) A. S. Ahmed and D. M. Hart. London: Routledge & Kegan Paul.

Ahmed, A. S. 1986. *Pakistan society: Islam, ethnicity and leadership in South Asia*. Delhi: Oxford University Press.

Ahmed, A. S. 1988. *Discovering Islam: making sense of Muslim history and society*. London: Routledge.

Al-Awa, M. 1973. The place of custom (*'urf*) in Islamic legal theory. *Islamic Quarterly* 17: 175–82

Allen, M. R. 1967. *Male cults and secret initiations in Melanesia*. Melbourne: Melbourne University Press.

Al-Shahi, A. 1987. The persistence of sectarian politics in Northern Sudan: the case of the Shaygiyya tribe. In *The diversity of the Muslim community: anthropological essays in memory of Peter Lienhardt* (ed.) A. Al-Shahi. London: Ithaca Press.

Altorki, S. 1980. Milk-kinship in Arab society: an unexplored problem in the ethnography of marriage. *Ethnology* 19: 233–44.

Ardener, E. 1972. Belief and the problem of women. In *The interpretation of ritual: essays in honour of A. I. Richards* (ed.) J. S. LaFontaine. London: Tavistock Publications.

Ardener, E. 1975. The 'Problem' revisited. In *Perceiving women* (ed.) S. Ardener. London: J. M. Dent & Sons.

Ardener, S. 1975. Introduction. In *Perceiving women* (ed.) S. Ardener. London: J. M. Dent & Sons.

Arkell, A. J. 1946. Darfur antiquities III. *Sudan Notes and Records* 27: 185–202.

Augé, M. 1982. *The anthropological circle: symbol, function, history.* Cambridge: Cambridge University Press.

Balfour-Paul, H. G. 1955. *History and antiquities of Darfur.* Khartoum.

Barclay, H. B. 1964. *Buurri al Lamaab: a suburban village in the Sudan.* Ithaca, N. Y.: Cornell University Press.

Bateson, G. 1958. *Naven.* 2nd edn. Stanford: Stanford University Press.

Beaton, A. C. 1948. The Fur. *Sudan Notes and Records* 29: 1–39.

Beck, L. 1980. The religious lives of Muslim women. In *Women in contemporary Muslim societies* (ed.) J. I. Smith. Lewisburg: Bucknell University Press.

Benedict, R. 1934. *Patterns of culture.* New York: Houghton Mifflin.

Bloch, M. 1986. *From blessing to violence: history and ideology in the circumcision ritual of the Merina of Madagascar.* Cambridge: Cambridge University Press.

Bourdieu, P. 1977. *Outline of a theory of practice.* Cambridge: Cambridge University Press.

Browne, W. G. 1806. *Travels in Egypt, Syria and Africa.* 2nd edn London.

Brunton, R. 1980. Misconstrued order in Melanesian religion. *Man* (N.S.) 15: 112–28.

Bunker, H. A. and B. D. Lewis. 1965. A psychoanalytic notation on the root GN, KN, CN. In *Psychoanalysis and culture* (eds.) G. B. Wilber and W. Muensterberger. New York: International Universities Press.

Chelhod, J. 1973. A contribution to the problem of the pre-eminence of the right, based upon Arabic evidence. In *Right and left: essays on dual symbolic classification* (ed.) R. Needham. Chicago: The University of Chicago Press.

Cohen, R. 1971. *Dominance and defiance: a study of marital instability in an Islamic society.* Anthropological Studies No.6. Washington, D.C.: American Anthropological Association.

Constantinides, P. 1977. Ill at ease and sick at heart: symbolic behaviour in a Sudanese healing cult. In *Symbols and sentiments* (ed.) I. M. Lewis. London: Academic Press.

Crapanzano. V. 1973. *The Hamadsha: a study in Moroccan ethnopsychiatry.* Berkeley and Los Angeles: University of California Press.

Cronin, C. 1977. Illusion and reality in Sicily. In *Sexual stratification* (ed.) A. Schlegel. New York: Columbia University Press.

Crowfoot, J. W. 1918. Customs of the Rubatab. *Sudan Notes and Records* 1: 119–34.

Daly, M. W. (ed.) 1985. *Al Madhubiyya and Al Mikashfiyya: two Sufi tariqas in the Sudan.* Graduate College Publications No. 13. Khartoum: University of Khartoum.

Davis, J. 1984. The sexual division of labour in the Mediterranean. In *Religion, power and protest in the local community: the north shore of the Mediterranean* (ed.) E. Wolf. Berlin: Mouton.

Denny, F. M. 1985. Islamic ritual: perspectives and theories. In *Approaches to Islam in religious studies* (ed.) R. C. Martin. Tucson: The University of Arizona Press.

Douglas, M. 1975. *Implicit meanings: essays in anthropology.* London: Routledge and Kegan Paul

Dundes, A. 1980. *Interpreting folklore.* Bloomington: Indiana University Press.

Dwyer, D. H. 1978a. *Images and self-images: male and female in Morocco*. New York: Columbia University Press.

Dwyer, D. H. 1978b. Women, Sufism and decision-making in Moroccan Islam. In *Women in the Muslim world* (eds.) L. Beck and N. Keddie. Cambridge, Mass.: Harvard University Press.

Eickelman, D. F. 1976. *Moroccan Islam: tradition and society in a pilgrimage center*. Austin: University of Texas Press.

Eickelman, D. F. 1981a. The study of Islam in local contexts. *Contributions to Asian Studies* 17: 1–16.

Eickelman, D. F. 1981b. *The Middle East: an anthropological approach*. Englewood Cliffs, N. J.: Prentice-Hall, Inc.

Eickelman, D. F. 1985. *Knowledge and power in Morocco*. Princeton: Princeton University Press.

El Guindy, F. 1966. Ritual and the river in Dahmit. In *Contemporary Egyptian Nubia*, 2 (ed.) R. A. Fernea. New Haven, Conn.: Human Relations Area Files, Inc.

El Tayib, A. 1955. Changing customs of the Riverain Sudan I. *Sudan Notes and Records* 36: 146–58.

El Tayib, A. 1965. The changing customs of the Riverain Sudan III. *Sudan Notes and Records* 45: 12–28.

El-Zein, A. H. M. 1974. *The sacred meadows: a structural analysis of religious symbolism in an East African town*. Evanston: Northwestern University Press.

El-Zein, A. H. M. 1977. Beyond ideology and theology: the search for the anthropology of Islam. *Annual Review of Anthropology* 6: 227–54.

Evans-Pritchard, E. E. 1937. *Witchcraft, oracles and magic among the Azande*. Oxford: Clarendon Press.

Fabian, J. 1983. *Time and the other: how anthropology makes its object*. New York: Columbia University Press.

Ferchiou, S. 1972. Survivances mystique et cultes de possession dans le maraboutism tunisien. *L'Homme* 12, No. 3: 47–69.

Fernandez, J. 1965. Symbolic consensus in a Fang reformative cult. *American Anthropologist* 67: 902–29.

Fernea, R. A. and E. W. Fernea 1972. Variation in religious observance among Islamic women. In *Scholars, saints and Sufis: Muslim religious institutions in the Middle East since 1500* (ed.) N. R. Keddie. Berkeley and Los Angeles: University of California Press.

Fisher, H. J. 1973. Conversion reconsidered: some historical aspects of religious conversion in Black Africa. *Africa* 43: 27–40.

Freeman, J. D. 1968. Thunder, blood and the nicknaming of God's creatures. *Psychoanalytic Quarterly* 37: 353–99.

Friedl, E. 1975. *Women and men: an anthropologist's view*. New York: Holt, Rinehart and Winston.

Friedl, E. 1980. Islam and tribal women in a village in Iran. In *Unspoken worlds: women's religious lives in non-western cultures* (eds.) N. A. Falk and R. M. Gross. San Francisco: Harper and Row Publishers.

Geertz, C. 1968. *Islam observed*. Chicago: University of Chicago Press.

Geertz, C. 1971. Deep play: notes on the Balinese cockfight. In *Myth, symbol and culture* (ed.) C. Geertz. New York: W. W. Norton.

Gellner, E. 1968. A pendulum swing theory of Islam. *Ann. Maroc. Sociol.* 1, 5–14.

Gellner, E. 1969. *Saints of the Atlas*. Chicago: University of Chicago Press.

Gellner, E. 1981. *Muslim society*. Cambridge: Cambridge University Press.

Gibb, H. A. R. 1969. *Mohammedanism: a historical survey*. London: Oxford University Press.

Gibb, H. A. R. and H. Bowen 1957. *Islamic society and the West*. London: Oxford University Press.

Gilsenan, M. 1973. *Saint and Sufi in modern Egypt*. Oxford: Clarendon Press.

Gilsenan, M. 1982. *Recognizing Islam: an anthropologist's introduction*. London: Croom Helm.

Goody, J. (ed.) 1968a. *Literacy in traditional societies*. Cambridge: Cambridge University Press.

Goody, J. 1968b. Restricted literacy in Northern Ghana. In *Literacy in traditional societies* (ed.) J. Goody. Cambridge: Cambridge University Press.

Goody, J. 1973. Literacy and the non-literate in Ghana. In *The future of literacy* (ed.) R. Dish. London: Prentice Hall International.

Goody, J. 1977. *The domestication of the savage mind*. Cambridge: Cambridge University Press.

Graham, W. A. 1983. Islam in the mirror of ritual. In *Islam's understanding of itself* (eds.) R. G. Hovannisian and S. Vryonis, Jr. Malibu, Calif.: Udena Publications.

Gudeman, S. 1986. *Economics as culture: models and metaphors of livelihood*. London: Routledge and Kegan Paul.

Hills-Young, E. 1940. Charms and customs associated with child-birth. *Sudan Notes and Records* 23: 331–6.

Holt, P. M. 1963. Funj origins: a critique and new evidence. *Journal of African History* 4: 39–55.

Holt, P. M. 1973. *Studies in the history of the Near East*. London: Routledge.

Holy, L. 1974. *Neighbours and kinsmen: a study of the Berti people of Darfur*. London: C. Hurst.

Holy, L. 1983. Symbolic and non-symbolic aspects of Berti space. *Man* (N.S.) 18: 269–88.

Holy, L. 1987. Decline of reciprocal farm labour among the Berti. In *Communal labour in the Sudan* (ed.) L. O. Manger. Bergen Studies in Social Anthropology No. 41. Bergen: Department of Social Anthropology, University of Bergen.

Holy, L. 1988. Cultivation as a long-term strategy of survival: the Berti of Darfur. In *The ecology of survival: case studies from northeast African history* (eds.) D. H. Johnson and D. M. Anderson. London: Lester Crook Academic Publishing.

Holy, L. 1990. Strategies for old age among the Berti of the Sudan. In *Anthropology and the Riddle of the Sphinx: paradoxes of change in the life course* (ed.) P. Spencer. ASA Monographs 28. London: Routledge.

Holy, L. and M. Stuchlik. 1983. *Actions, norms and representations: foundations of anthropological inquiry*. Cambridge: Cambridge University Press.

Horton, R. 1970. The African traditional thought and western science. In *Rationality* (ed.) B. Wilson. Oxford: Basil Blackwell.

Hurreiz, S. H. 1986. The legend of the wise stranger: an index of cultural unity of the Central Bilad al-Sudan. In *Sudan Sahel Studies II* (ed.) M. Tomikawa. Tokyo: Institute for the Study of Languages and Cultures of Asia and Africa.

Jackson, H. C. 1926. A trek in Abu Hamed District, *Sudan Notes and Records* 9, No. 2: 1–35.

Jackson, M. 1982. *Allegories of the wilderness: ethics and ambiguity in Kuranko narratives.* Bloomington: Indiana University Press.

James, W. 1988. *The listening ebony: moral knowledge, religion and power among the Uduk of Sudan.* Oxford: Clarendon Press.

Karim, Wazir-Jahan 1981. *Ma' Betisek concepts of living things.* London: Athlone Press.

Keesing, R. M. 1982. *Kwaio religion: the living and the dead in a Solomon Island society.* New York: Columbia University Press.

La Fontaine, J. S. 1972. Ritualisation of women's life crises in Bugisu. In *The interpretation of ritual: essays in honour of A. I. Richards* (ed.) J. S. LaFontaine. London: Tavistock Publications.

Lakoff, G. and M. Johnson. 1980. *Metaphors we live by.* Chicago: The University of Chicago Press.

Lamphere, L. 1974. Strategies, cooperation and conflict among women in domestic groups. In *Woman, culture and society* (eds.) M. Z. Rosaldo and L. Lamphere. Stanford: Standford University Press.

Lane, E. W. 1978 (1836). *An account of the manners and customs of the modern Egyptians.* London: East-West Publications.

Lange, D. 1972. L'Intérieur de l'Afrique Occidentale d'après Giovanni Lorenzo Anania (XIVe siècle). *Cahiers d'histoire mondiale* 14: 299–351.

Lévi-Strauss, C. 1966. *The savage mind.* London: Weidenfeld and Nicholson (quoted from the 1972 edition).

Lévi-Strauss, C. 1967. The story of Asdiwal. In *The structural study of myth and totemism* (ed.) E. Leach. ASA Monographs 5. London: Tavistock.

Lévi-Strauss, C. 1970. *The raw and the cooked: Introduction to a science of mythology I.* London: Jonathan Cape.

Lewis, G. 1980. *Day of shining red: an essay on understanding ritual.* Cambridge: Cambridge University Press.

Lewis, I. M. 1966. *Islam in tropical Africa.* London: Oxford University Press for the International African Institute.

Lewis, I. M. 1971. *Ecstatic religion.* London: Penguin.

Lewis, I. M. 1986. *Religion in context: cults and charisma.* Cambridge: Cambridge University Press.

Macmichael, H. A. 1922. *A history of the Arabs in the Sudan.* 2 vols. Cambridge: Cambridge University Press.

Maddi, S. R. 1968. The pursuit of consistency and variety. In *Theories of cognitive consistency: a sourcebook* (eds.) R. P. Abelson, E. Aronson, W. J. McGuire, T. M. Newcomb, M. J. Rosenberg and P. H. Tannenbaum. Chicago: Rand McNally.

Malinowski, B. 1923. The problem of meaning in primitive languages. In *The meaning of meaning* (eds.) C. K. Ogden and I. A. Richards. London: Harcourt Brace & Co.

Malinowski, B. 1948. *Magic, science and religion, and other essays.* Boston: Beacon Press.

Marx, E. 1973. Circumcision feasts among the Negev Bedouins. *International Journal of Middle East Studies* 4: 411–27.

Middleton, J. 1982. Lugbara death. In *Death and the regeneration of life* (eds.) M. Bloch and J. Parry. Cambridge: Cambridge University Press.

Morsy, S. 1978. Sex differences and folk illness in an Egyptian village. In *Women in the Muslim world* (eds.) L. Beck and N. Keddie. Cambridge, Mass.: Harvard University Press.

Mortimer, E. 1982. *Faith and power: the politics of Islam.*

Nachtigal, G. 1971. *Sahara and Sudan. Volume Four: Wadai and Darfur.* Trans. A. G. B. and H. J. Fisher. London: C. Hurst & Co.

Nasr, S. H. 1972. *Ideals and realities of Islam.* Boston: Beacon Press.

Needham, R. (ed.) 1973. *Right and left: essays in dual symbolic classification.* Chicago: The University of Chicago Press.

Needham, R. (ed.) 1979. *Symbolic classification.* Santa Monica: Goodyear.

O'Fahey, R. S. 1979. Islam, state and society in Dār Fūr. In *Conversion to Islam* (ed.) N. Levtzion. New York: Holmes & Meier Publishers, Inc.

O'Fahey, R. S. 1980. *State and society in Dār Fūr.* London: C. Hurst.

O'Fahey, R. S. and J. L. Spaulding. 1974. *Kingdoms of the Sudan.* London: Methuen & Co. Ltd.

Osman el-Tom, A. 1982. Berti Quranic schools. *Sudan Notes and Records* 63: 1–19.

Osman el-Tom, A. 1983. *Religious men and literacy in Berti society.* Ph.D. thesis. University of St Andrews.

Osman el-Tom, A. 1985. Drinking the Koran: the meaning of Koranic verses in Berti erasure. *Africa* 55: 414–31.

Osman el-Tom, A. 1987. Berti Qur'anic amulets. *Journal of Religion in Africa* 17: 224–44.

Parkin, D. 1982. Introduction to *Semantic anthropology* (ed.) D. Parkin. ASA Monographs 22. London: Academic Press.

Paulme, D. 1963. Introduction to *Women of Tropical Africa* (ed.) D. Paulme. Berkeley: University of California Press.

Petráček, K. 1975. Die sprachliche Stellung der Berti (Siga) -Sprache in Dar Fur (Sudan). *Asian and African Studies* (Bratislava) 11: 107–18.

Petráček, K. 1978. Berti and the Central Saharan Group. In *Aspects of learning in the Sudan* (ed.) R. Thelwall. Occasional Papers in Linguistics and Language Learning 5: 155–80.

Poewe, K. O. 1981. *Matrilineal ideology: male-female dynamics in Luapula, Zambia.* London: Academic Press.

Rahman, F. 1985. Approaches to Islam in religious studies. In *Approaches to Islam in religious studies* (ed.) R. C. Martin. Tucson: University of Arizona Press.

Redfield, R. 1956. *Peasant society and culture.* Chicago: University of Chicago Press.

Robinson, M. S. 1968. 'The house of mighty hero' or 'The house of enough paddy?': some implications of a Sinhalese myth. In *Dialectic in practical religion* (ed.) E. R. Leach. Cambridge Papers in Social Anthropology 5. Cambridge: Cambridge University Press.

Rogers, S. C. 1975. Female forms of power and the myth of male dominance: a model of female/male interaction in peasant society. *American Ethnologist* 2: 727–56.

Rosaldo, M. Z. 1974. Woman, culture and society: a theoretical overview. In *Woman, culture and society* (eds.) M. Z. Rosaldo and L. Lamphere. Stanford: Stanford University Press.

Sanday, P. R. 1974. Female status in the public domain. In *Woman, culture and society* (eds.) M. Z. Rosaldo and L. Lamphere. Stanford: Stanford University Press.

Slatin Pasha, R. C. 1896. *Fire and sword in the Sudan: a personal narrative of fighting and serving the dervishes. 1879–1895.* London: Edward Arnold.

Smith, M. G. 1960. *Government in Zazzau.* London: Oxford University Press.

Spiro, M. E. 1982. Collective representations and mental representations in religious symbol systems. In *On symbols in cultural anthropology: essays in honor of Harry Hoijer* (ed.) J. Maquet. Malibu, Calif.: Udena.

Stewart, C. C. 1985. Introduction: Popular Islam in twentieth-century Africa. *Africa* 55: 363–8.

Stirrat, R. L. 1984. Sacred models. *Man* 19: 199–215.

Strange, H. 1984. Traditional ceremony in an Islamic milieu: melenggang perut among Malaysian women. In *Muslim women* (ed.) F. Hussein. London: Croom Helm.

Strathern, M. 1972. *Women in between: female roles in a male world: Mount Hagen, New Guinea.* London: Seminar Press.

Tambiah, S. R. 1973. The form and meaning of magical acts: a point of view. In *Modes of thought.* (eds.) R. Horton and R. Finnegan. London: Faber & Faber.

Tambiah, S. R. 1979. A performative approach to ritual. *Proceedings of the British Academy* 65: 113–66.

Tapper, N. 1983. Gender and religion in a Turkish town: a comparison of two types of formal women's gatherings. In *Women's religious experience: cross-cultural perspectives* (ed.) P. Holden. London: Croom Helm.

Tapper, N. and R. 1987. The birth of the prophet: ritual and gender in Turkish Islam. *Man* (N.S.) 22: 69–92.

Tapper, R. 1979. *Pasture and politics: economics, conflict and ritual among Shahsevan nomads of northwestern Iran.* London: Academic Press.

Tapper, R. 1984. Holier than thou: Islam in three tribal societies. In *Islam in tribal societies: from the Atlas to the Indus* (eds.) A.S. Ahmed and D. M. Hart. London: Routledge & Kegan Paul.

Todorov, T. 1977. *Theories of the symbol.* Trans. by C. Porter. Oxford: Basil Blackwell.

Trimingham, J. S. 1949. *Islam in the Sudan.* London: Oxford University Press.

Trimingham, J. S. 1968. *The influence of Islam upon Africa.* London: Longman.

Trimingham, J. S. 1980. *The influence of Islam upon Africa.* 2nd edn. London: Longman.

Tubiana, M. -J. 1963. *Survivances préislamique en pays Zaghawa.* Paris: Institut d'Ethnologie.

Turner, B. 1985. Towards an economic model of virtuoso religion. In *Islamic dilemmas: reformers, nationalists and industrialization* (ed.) E. Gellner. Berlin, New York, Amsterdam: Mouton Publishers.

Turner, V. 1967. *The forest of symbols: aspects of Ndembu ritual.* Ithaca: Cornell University Press.

Ullrich, H. E. 1977. Caste differences between Brahmin and non-Brahmin women in a South Indian village. In *Sexual stratification* (ed.) A. Schlegel. New York: Columbia.

Voll, J. 1972. Mahdis, walis and new men in the Sudan. In *Scholars, saints and Sufis: Muslim religious institutions in the Middle East since 1500* (ed.) N. R. Keddie. Berkeley and Los Angeles: University of California Press.

Waardenburg, J. D. J. 1978. Official and popular religion in Islam. *Social Compass* 25: 315–41.

Waardenburg, J. D. J. 1979. Official and popular religion as a problem in Islamic studies. In *Official and popular as a theme in the study of religion* (eds.) P. H. Vrijhof and J. Waardenburg. The Hague: Mouton.

Warburg, G. R. 1985. Islam and state in Numayri's Sudan. *Africa* 55: 400–13.

Weiner, A. B. 1976. *Women of value, men of renown: new perspectives in Trobriand exchange*. Austin: University of Texas Press.

Werbner, R. P. 1984. World renewal: masking in a New Guinea festival. *Man* (N.S.) 19: 267–90.

Westermarck, E. 1926. *Ritual and belief in Morocco*. 2 vols. London: Macmillan & Co.

Westermarck, E. 1933. *Pagan survivals in Mohammedan civilisation*. London: Macmillan & Co.

Whyte, S. R. 1981. Men, women and misfortune in Bunyole. *Man* (N.S.) 16: 350–66.

Wikan, U. 1982. *Behind the veil in Arabia: women in Oman*. Baltimore: The Johns Hopkins University Press.

Willis, R. G. 1967. The head and the loins: Lévi-Strauss and beyond. *Man* (N.S.) 2: 519–34.

Worsley, P. 1970. *The trumpet shall sound*. 2nd edn. London: Paladin.

Index

Cambridge Studies in
Social and Cultural Anthropology

Editors: JACK GOODY, STEPHEN GUDEMAN, MICHAEL HERZFELD, JONATHAN PARRY